T0330306

Game Practice and the Environment

THE FONDAZIONE ENI ENRICO MATTEI (FEEM) SERIES ON
ECONOMICS AND THE ENVIRONMENT

Series Editor: Carlo Carraro, *University of Venice, Venice and Research Director,
Fondazione Eni Enrico Mattei (FEEM), Milan and Venice, Italy*

The Fondazione Eni Enrico Mattei (FEEM) was established in 1989 as a non-
profit, non-partisan research institution. It carries out high-profile research in the
fields of economic development, energy and the environment, thanks to an
international network of researchers who contribute to disseminate knowledge
through seminars, congresses and publications. The main objective of the
Fondazione is to foster interactions among academic, industrial and public policy
spheres in an effort to find solutions to environmental problems. Over the years it
has thus become a major European institution for research on sustainable
development and the privileged interlocutor of a number of leading national and
international policy institutions.

   The Fondazione Eni Enrico Mattei (FEEM) Series on Economics and the
Environment publishes leading-edge research findings providing an authoritative
and up-to-date source of information in all aspects of sustainable development.
FEEM research outputs are the results of a sound and acknowledged
cooperation between its internal staff and a worldwide network of outstanding
researchers and practitioners. A Scientific Advisory Board of distinguished
academics ensures the quality of the publications.

   This series serves as an outlet for the main results of FEEM's research
programmes in the areas of economics, energy and the environment.

   Titles in the series include:

Game Practice and the Environment

Edited by

Carlo Carraro

Professor of Econometrics and Environmental Economics, University of Venice, Italy, Research Director, Fondazione Eni Enrico Mattei (FEEM), Milan and Venice, Italy

Vito Fragnelli

Professor of Game Theory, University of Eastern Piedmont, Italy

THE FONDAZIONE ENI ENRICO MATTEI (FEEM) SERIES ON ECONOMICS AND THE ENVIRONMENT

Edward Elgar
Cheltenham, UK • Northampton, MA, USA

Published by
Edward Elgar Publishing Limited
Glensanda House
Montpellier Parade
Cheltenham
Glos GL50 1UA
UK

Edward Elgar Publishing, Inc.
136 West Street
Suite 202
Northampton
Massachusetts 01060
USA

A catalogue record for this book
is available from the British Library

Library of Congress Cataloguing in Publication Data

Game Practice and the environment / edited by Carlo Carraro, Vito Fragnelli.
     p. cm. – (The Fondazione Eni Enrico Mattei (FEEM) series on economics, energy, and the environment
    Includes bibliographical references and index.
    1. Environmental policy–Economic aspects–Mathematical models.
2. Climatic changes–International cooperation–Mathematical models.
3. Pollution–Economic aspects–Mathematical models. 4. Environmental protection–Finance–Mathematical models. 5. Natural resources–Management–Mathematical models. 6 Game theory. I. Carraro, Carlo. II. Fragnelli, Vito, 1956– III. Series.

HC79.E5G326 2004
363.7'001'5193–dc22

2004041175

ISBN 1 84376 685 X

Printed and bound in Great Britain by MPG Books Ltd, Bodmin, Cornwall

Contents

Contributors

Gian Italo Bischi, Istituto di Scienze Economiche, University of Urbino, Italy – *bischi@econ.uniurb.it*

Francesco Bosello, Fondazione Eni Enrico Mattei, Venice and ICTP, Trieste, Italy – *francesco.bosello@feem.it*

Rodica Brânzei, Faculty of Computer Science, Alexandru Ioan Cuza University, Iaşi, Romania – *branzeir@infoiasi.ro*

Barbara Buchner, Fondazione Eni Enrico Mattei, Venice, Italy – *buchner.barbara@feem.it*

Carlo Carraro, University of Venice and Fondazione Eni Enrico Mattei, Milan and Venice, Italy – *ccarraro@unive.it*

Juan Carlos Císcar, European Commission-DG JRC, Institute for Prospective Technological Studies (IPTS), Seville, Spain – *juan-carlos.ciscar@jrc.es*

Sergio Currarini, Dipartimento di Scienze Economiche, Università di Venezia, Venice, Italy – *s.currarini@unive.it*

Sjur Didrik Flåm, Department of Economics, University of Bergen, Bergen, Norway – *sjur.flaam@econ.uib.no*

Vito Fragnelli, Dipartimento di Scienze e Tecnologie Avanzate, Università del Piemonte Orientale, Alessandria, Italy, – *vito.fragnelli@mfn.unipmn.it*

Odd Godal, Department of Economics, University of Bergen, Bergen, Norway – *odd.godal@econ.uib.no*

Hans Keiding, Institute of Economics, University of Copenhagen, Copenhagen, Denmark – *Hans.Keiding@econ.ku.dk*

Fabio Lamantia, OAAP Department, University of Calabria, Italy – *lamantia@unical.it*

Carmen Marchiori, Fondazione Eni Enrico Mattei, Venice, Italy and LSE, UK – *marchiori@feem.it*

Maria Erminia Marina, Dipartimento di Economia e Metodi Quantitativi Università di Genova, Genoa, Italy – *marina@economia.unige.it*

Marco Marini, Istituto di Scienze Economiche, Università degli Studi di Urbino, Urbino, Italy and IIM, LSE, UK – *marinim@econ.uniurb.it*

Stefano Moretti, Department of Mathematics, University of Genoa, Genoa, Italy – *moretti@dima.unige.it*

Davide Raggi, Department of Economics, University of Padova, Italy and Duke University, Durham, USA – *daviragg@stat.unipd.it*

Lucia Sbragia, Istituto di Scienze Economiche, University of Urbino, Italy – *lucias@supereva.it*

Antonio Soria, European Commission-DG JRC, Institute for Prospective Technological Studies (IPTS), Seville, Spain – *Antonio.Soria@jrc.es*

Stef Hendrikus Tijs, Center and Department of Econometrics and Operations Research, Tilburg University, Tilburg, The Netherlands – *S.H.Tijs@uvt.nl*

Henry Tulkens, CORE, Universite Catholique de Louvain, Louvain la Neuve, Belgium – *tulkens@core.ucl.ac.be*

Introduction

Carlo Carraro and Vito Fragnelli

Game theory is one of the most useful mathematical tools that economists and mathematicians have been using to deal with complex economic and policy problems. At the same time, environmental issues are at the heart of many domestic and international policy processes, where interactions among different stakeholders play a crucial role. It is therefore natural to adopt game theory as one of the analytical instruments that can enhance our understanding of the interrelations between the economy and the environment, and that can also provide practical suggestions for policy interventions.

The existing literature on game theory and the environment is vast (Cf. Carraro, 2002, 2003; Finus, 2001; Hanley and Folmer, 1998; and many others). Therefore, when designing this book, and the conference where the chapters of this book were presented and discussed, the main questions were: What are the original features of the book? How does it differ from the many books already published on the application of game theory to environmental matters?

Of course, each single chapter contains some innovative results that will be highlighted below. However, the design of the book also contains some specific features that are worth mentioning. First, the book is the outcome of interdisciplinary work involving economists and mathematicians. Some of the chapters have been written by mathematicians who possess sophisticated mathematical tools and look for an interesting environmental economic problem to apply them to. Other chapters have been written by economists who seek adequate tools to deal with relevant policy issues. All chapters are the outcome of the interactions between these two groups of researchers, who helped each other through personal and on-line discussions and through the reviewing process.

A second distinguishing feature of this book is the 'practice' of game theory. The goal was indeed to induce the authors to look for practical solutions to environmental problems and to use game theory to identify these concrete solutions. Despite the fact that this second goal has not always been achieved by the chapters in this book, it is clear, when reading the various chapters, that there is a common denominator defined by the objective just described.

The book is divided into three parts. The first is devoted to climate policy. This is one of the major environmental problems and certainly one where game theory has been largely used, notably to assess the prospects of future climate negotiations. This is also the main objective of the four chapters in Part I of the book. They all use game theory to identify the incentives to sign an international climate treaty as a function of countries' characteristics, political institutions, policy strategies and future commitments. For example, Currarini and Tulkens recognise that international agreements on climate change control require approval by domestic political institutions. Therefore, they employ a voting game-theoretic model to characterise the stability of such agreements when each country's participation is conditioned upon a domestic ratification vote. To describe the pre-treaty or no treaty international situation, they propose a concept of (non-cooperative) political equilibrium and prove its existence. They then move to the diplomatic level, and employ a coalition formation game to show that there exist cooperative joint policies, yielding a treaty, that are ratified by all countries and that can be considered *stable* at the international level. The problem addressed in this chapter has been widely neglected by the existing literature and this chapter actually provides a major innovation in the economic analysis of climate change negotiations and international environmental agreements.

The second chapter, by Bosello, Buchner, Carraro and Raggi, addresses another important but neglected issue, namely how equity can influence the participation decision of countries that negotiate on climate change control. A widespread conjecture suggests that a more equitable distribution of the burden of reducing emissions would enhance the incentives for more countries – particularly big emitters – to accept an emission reduction scheme defined within an international climate agreement. This chapter shows that this conjecture is only partly supported by the empirical evidence that can be derived from the recent outcomes of climate negotiations. Even though an equitable sharing of the costs of controlling GHG emissions can provide better incentives to sign and ratify a climate agreement than the burden sharing implicit in the Kyoto agreement, a stable global agreement cannot be achieved. A possible strategy to achieve a global agreement without free-riding incentives is a policy mix in which global emission trading is coupled with a transfer mechanism designed to offset incentives to free-ride.

The third chapter, by Carraro and Marchiori, is also aimed at assessing the validity of a practical policy proposal. In particular, this chapter analyses issue linkage as a way to increase cooperation on environmental problems where the incentives to free-ride are strong. The goal is to determine under what conditions players prefer to link negotiations on two different economic issues rather than to negotiate on the two issues separately. Suppose that players are asked to vote on issue linkage before starting negotiations. Under what conditions would they vote in favour of issue linkage? The answer to this question is not trivial. Issue linkage may indeed increase the number of cooperators on the provision of a public environmental good (a typical issue characterised by strong incentives to free-ride). However, at the same time, issue linkage may reduce the number of cooperating players on the other economic issue which is linked to the provision of a public good. Players therefore face a trade-off. This chapter analyses this trade-off within a game-theoretic framework and shows under what conditions issue linkage is players' equilibrium strategy.

The fourth chapter of Part I, by Císcar and Soria, has a more methodological flavour. Most studies assessing the Kyoto Protocol on climate change have implemented a (simultaneous) single-stage game with an *open-loop* information structure, where countries decide at once and at the same time their mitigation efforts for all future periods. Alternatively a (sequential) multi-stage game can allow a player to react to past moves of the other players. The information structure of this second game is called *feedback*. The goal of this chapter is to compare the outcomes under the open-loop and feedback frameworks. For that purpose a numerical two-region (Annex B and non-Annex B countries) integrated assessment model of the economic and climatic systems is coupled with a non-cooperative five-stage game. When the game is solved with utility payoffs, the open-loop and feedback Nash equilibria provide very similar outcomes. With consumption payoffs, the outcomes are different. Therefore, this chapter suggests that the information structure of the game may matter and must be carefully analysed.

The second part of the book is devoted to another important environmental and economic issue. How can stakeholders, whether domestically or internationally, share the costs of undertaking emission abatement or more generally the cost of environment-friendly activities? In this part, cost sharing methods are applied to different environmental problems and practical answers to the above question are proposed.

In the first chapter of Part II, by Tijs and Brânzei, a group of agents aims to work together in a joint project that can have different forms. Each feasible form corresponds to a subset of a given set of basic units. The cost of the chosen project is the sum of the costs of the basic units involved in the project. The benefit of each of the agents is dependent on the form of the chosen project. A related cooperative game may be helpful in solving the question of how to share the costs. Under certain conditions this game turns out to be a convex game. For structured joint projects also a flexible procedure using cost sharing rules from the taxation literature applied to simple cost sharing problems is proposed. It is worth noticing that many well-known cases in the cost sharing literature fit in the model proposed in this chapter and that some earlier results are special cases of the results which are obtained in this chapter.

Chapter 6, by Moretti, focuses on sharing the cost of waste collection. Due to economies of scale imposed by the need for specialist staff and facilities, inter-municipal cooperation can be very beneficial in achieving groupings large enough to develop – at an affordable cost – a waste collection system suitable to the high standards demanded by EU legislation. Moreover, municipalities want a cost allocation mechanism that is efficient, equitable and provides appropriate incentives to cooperate. The aim of this chapter is to offer a model for ex-ante quantitative evaluation of specialist staff and facilities (and their costs) required for supplying waste collection in new emerging contexts of inter-municipal cooperation. A validation of the model on a real situation is also presented.

Chapter 7, by Fragnelli and Marina, proposes a framework to share environmental insurance costs. There are risks, in particular environmental risks, that are too large and heavy for a single insurance company, but they can be insured by n companies. This chapter uses a game-theoretic approach to analyse how the n insurance companies should split the risk and the premium in order to be better off. Under suitable hypotheses, there exists an optimal decomposition of the risk, from which a cooperative game can be defined and its properties and some particular solutions analysed.

In the final chapter of Part II, by Keiding, the environmental costs to be shared are those related to consumption activities. For the assignment of environmental effects to activities, Keiding proposes to use the method of cost allocation, applied to a multiple of different environmental impacts considered as different 'costs'. This leads to a consideration of vector cost allocation and its relation to ordinary one-dimensional cost allocation methods; in particular, he considers the stability of cost sharing rules under composition of cost functions, a property which is important in the application at hand. In addition, the author exploits the well-established methodology of DEA (Data Envelopment Analysis) in order to aggregate vectors of environmental effects into a single index of relative environmental impact of a consumption activity. An application of the last part of the approach is given, based on Danish national accounts data and using emission data as a proxy for environmental effect.

Part III deals with environmental management and pollution control. The first chapter, by Bischi, Lamantia and Sbragia, proposes a dynamic model to describe the commercial exploitation, by a population of strategically interacting agents, of a common property renewable resource. The population of players is assumed to be divided into two groups: coopera-tors, who decide their harvesting policy by maximising the overall profit of their group, and defectors, who just maximise their own profit. An evolu-tionary mechanism is introduced to describe how the share of defectors and cooperators within the population changes over time. The chapter provides a qualitative study of a two-dimensional non-linear dynamical system that describes the time evolution of the resource stock and the population share between cooperators and defectors. The long run evolution of this dynam-ical system is analysed by analytical and numerical methods, and the role of some economic and ecological parameters is investigated.

Chapter 10, by Flåm and Godal, analyses emission trading in an oligop-olistic market. Oligopolistic firms use factor inputs that generate emissions of greenhouse gases. The producers are entitled to emission permits, and they exchange parts of these. Each firm, when planning its net purchase of permits, anticipates the market clearing price. This chapter models the clearing mechanism as a core solution of a transferable-utility production game. Agents may reckon that they affect prices of products and permits. The existence and characterisation of the equilibrium is discussed.

The final chapter, by Currarini and Marini, presents a new cooperative equilibrium for strategic form games, denoted Conjectural Cooperative Equilibrium (CCE). This concept is based on the expectation that joint deviations from any strategy profile are followed by an optimal and non-cooperative reaction of non-deviators. The authors show that a CCE exists for all symmetric supermodular games. Furthermore, they discuss the exis-tence of a CCE in specific submodular games derived from the environmen-tal literature.

As a whole, the eleven chapters of this book improve the toolbox we have to deal with environmental issues and, at the same time, provide some inter-esting applications and practical solutions to some relevant environmental policy problems. The work to achieve this result has been long and difficult. All chapters have been reviewed twice and revised accordingly. All chapters have been presented at a conference in Alessandria and there discussed and compared. The organisation of this entire process has been possible thanks to the financial and organisational support of the Fondazione Eni Enrico Mattei, of the University of Eastern Piedmont and of 'Ambiente, Territorio e Formazione'. The role of Alberto Cassone, Vice Dean of the University of Eastern Piedmont, and of Fabio Gastaldi, Dean of the Faculty of Sciences, has also been very important in facilitating the organ-isation of the Alessandria meeting. Special thanks also to Lucia Ceriani, Monica Eberle, Anna Iandolino and Giovanni Monella for their help in the organisation of the meeting. All reviewers did an excellent job to enhance the quality of the chapters. We are very grateful to them, as well as to all those who provided comments on earlier versions of the chapters of this book.

REFERENCES

Carraro, C. (2002), *Governing the Global Environment*, Cheltenham: Edward Elgar.
Carraro, C. (2003), *The Endogenous Formation of Economic Coalitions*, Cheltenham: Edward Elgar.
Finus, M. (2001), *Game Theory and International Environmental Cooperation*, Cheltenham: Edward Elgar.
Hanley, N. and Folmer, H. (1998), *Game Theory and the Environment*, Cheltenham: Edward Elgar.

PART I

Climate negotiations and policy

1. Stable international agreements on transfrontier pollution with ratification constraints[1]

Sergio Currarini[2] and Henry Tulkens[3]

1. INTRODUCTION

International agreements on environmental standards usually require the approval of domestic political institutions. Once an agreement is found at the international level, its prescriptions must be translated into domestic laws through a ratification process. The fact that negotiating countries are in all respects sovereign and independent decision makers, makes ratification a substantial element (possibly a constraint) in the decisional process. The difficulty of attaining the full commitment of many countries in actual cooperation problems (as, for instance, at the Rio and Kyoto Conferences on Climate Change) may be partially explained as the effect of such domestic political constraints on the decisions of countries' political leaders.

The *stability* of an international agreement has been identified in the literature with the properties of various equilibrium concepts in game-theoretic models of cooperation. Part of this literature has looked at the possibility of 'full' cooperation, that is, cooperation among all involved countries. Some of these works have studied the *core* of cooperative games representing the decisional process at the international level (see Chander and Tulkens, 1992, 1995 and 1997; Maler 1989; and Kaitala et al., 1995). Core agreements are 'stable' solutions to the negotiation problem in that no coalition of countries is able to induce a preferred outcome by its own means. Other contributions have studied the possibility of the formation of smaller coalitions: see, for example, Carraro and Siniscalco (1993); Barrett (1994); and Hoel and Schneider (1997). Both approaches lack an institutional specification of the collective decision processes involved at the domestic levels.

In particular, countries' representatives are able to choose among all technologically feasible domestic policies in the attempt to maximize aggregate domestic welfare. Domestic politics and decisional procedures do not play any role and, in particular, do not impose any constraint on the set of feasible policies.[4]

This chapter studies the effect of the domestic institutions of ratification on the stability of international environmental agreements in an economy of the type studied by Chander and Tulkens (1997), in which domestic production activities have, as a by-product, the emission of some transboundary pollutant.

We assume that in the absence of international cooperation, each domestic parliament independently determines *by voting* the level of domestic environmental regulation. We formally describe this pre-treaty (or no-treaty) state of the economy by means of the concept of International Non-cooperative Political Equilibrium (INPE). We prove existence and uniqueness of the INPE for our economy.

We then study international cooperation taking as a status quo the INPE of the economy. The key element of our analysis is that an international agreement, defined as an emission abatement plan and some rule to share the associated costs among the involved countries, becomes effective in a country only if it is ratified by its parliament. Therefore, the only feasible agreements are those which are ratified by all signatories. We show that for each configuration of coalitions (of countries) in the international economy (that is, for each 'coalition structure'), there exists a unique collection of agreements – one for each coalition of cooperating countries – which are simultaneously ratified.

We then turn to the analysis of the incentives of national delegates to sign agreements at the international level. We assume that national delegates act on behalf of a supporting majority, maximizing the aggregate payoff of its members. The crucial assumption at this stage is that, in the design of an international agreement, delegates anticipate the outcome of the ratification vote, and only consider agreements that would be eventually ratified by their national parliaments. Since each set of cooperating countries in a given coalition structure has only one agreement that would be ratified, delegates are able to order coalition structures by using the aggregate payoffs of their domestic supporting coalitions at the relevant ratified agreements.

These considerations motivate the use of a game of coalition formation, in which each delegate announces a coalition to which he wishes to belong, anticipating that this coalition will implement the unique ratified agreement (we use a specification of this game first introduced by Hart and Kurz, 1983). We look for coalitions structures that are *stable* to objections by a subset of national delegates, identifying such stable structure with the set of Strong Nash Equilibria of the coalition formation game.

We find that the grand coalition is always a Strong Nash Equilibrium outcome, and the associated ratified international agreement shares abatement costs proportionally to the national incomes at the pre-treaty stage. Although other inefficient structures may emerge in equilibrium, we show that some degree of cooperation always occurs when domestic politicians maximize the aggregate welfare of their whole population. If politicians only maximize the welfare of their voters (that is, of their supporting majority), the complete absence of cooperation may occur as a Strong Nash Equilibrium, but never as a Strict Strong Nash Equilibrium.

The chapter is organized as follows. In Section 2 we introduce the international economy. In Section 3 we formulate the voting game that describes the domestic decisional process, in the absence of international cooperation. In Section 4 we prove existence and uniqueness of the international equilibrium resulting from these independent domestic policies. In Section 5 we study international cooperation: after an informal presentation of the decisional structure, which is of a diplomatic nature at this stage, we present the game that bears upon the formation of coalitions among countries and prove our main result on politically stable international environmental agreements. Section 6 concludes the chapter by summarizing its main points, comparing them with some of the alternative approaches mentioned above, and pointing towards generalization of our results for a larger class of preferences.

2. THE INTERNATIONAL ECONOMY

We consider an international economy E with a set K of countries, indexed by $k = 1,..., K$, a single private good and ambient pollution, which is the outcome of the discharges emitted by the countries as a by-product of their private good production.

2.1 Components of E

The elements of the economy are as follows.

- *Agents.* The set of individual economic agents (citizens) is denoted by $I = \{1,...,i,...,n\}$. The agents are partitioned into K countries; B_k denotes the set of agents living in country k, with $\#B_k = n_k$.
- *Commodities.* There are three types of commodities in the economy: a private good x; pollutant discharges p_k occurring in country k, for all k in K, with $p = (p_1, p_2,..., p_K)$ denoting the vector of emissions occurring in all countries, and ambient pollution z.

- *Ecological Transfer Function.* Countries' discharges determine linearly and additively the amount of ambient pollution, according to the relation

$$z = -\sum_{k=1}^{K} p_k.$$

We will sometimes use the notation $z(p)$.

- *Production Technology.* Each country k produces a positive amount of the private good, denoted by the value of the production function[5] $g_k(p_k)$. We denote by $g_k'(p_k)$ and $g_k''(p_k)$ the first and second derivative of $g_k(p_k)$.

We assume the following:

Assumption 1. $g_k(p_k) \geq 0$, $g_k'(p_k) \geq 0$, $g_k''(p_k) \leq 0$ *for all* $p_k \geq 0$.

Assumption 2.   *There exists some p_k^0 such that $g_k'(p_k) = 0$ if and only if $p_k \geq p_k^0$. Moreover, $g_k'(0) = \infty$.*
     The level p_k^0 measures the maximal amount of emissions that are economically valuable: above this level, additional increases in emissions do not increase production. The level p_k^0 can be interpreted as a technological constraint due to unspecified inputs other than pollution.

- *Preferences.* Each agent i has a utility function $u_i(z, x_i)$ satisfying:

Assumption 3. $u_i(z, x_i) = v(z)x_i$;

Assumption 4. $v(z)$ *is twice differentiable, with $v'(z) > 0$, $\infty > v'(z) > 0$ and $v''(z)\} \leq 0$ for all $z \geq 0$, where $v'(z)$ and $v''(z)$ are the first and second derivatives of v.*

By Assumption 3 any difference in the way agents value the environmental quality is only due to differences in the consumption level of the private good. In other words, we assume that there exists a fundamental valuation of the ambient quality which is common to all agents in the economy E, and is represented by the functional form $v(z)$.

- *Individual incomes.* For each country k, agent i in B_k is allocated a share θ_i^k (with $0 \leq \theta_i^k \leq 1$ and $\sum_{i \in B_k} \theta_i^k = 1$) of the private good $g_k(p_k)$ produced in his country. The value $\theta_i^k g_k(p_k)$ is the private income of agent i living in country k. We will denote by θ^k the vector $(\theta_1^k, \theta_2^k,..., \theta_{n_k}^k)$. The vector θ^k represents the only source of heterogeneity within any given country, where all agents have the same preference ordering, and in which agents with the same private consumption share the same utility level. We also remark that the amount $\theta_i^k g_k(p_k)$ does not identify the consumption x_i of agent i, but rather his endowment of private good. As we will see, private consumption will be co-determined by taxation and, possibly, by transfers.

Assumption 5.　$\theta_i^k > 0$ *for all* $i \in B_k$, $k = 1, 2,..., K$.

Definition 1:　*A **feasible state** of the international economy E is a vector* $(z, p, x) \in \mathcal{R} \times \mathcal{R}_+^k \times \mathcal{R}^n$ *such that*

$$\sum_{k=1}^{K} g_k(p_k) \geq \sum_{i \in I} x_i;$$

$$z = -\sum_{k=1}^{K} p_k.$$

For any feasible state (z, p, x) the pair (p, x) is called an allocation.

Definition 2.　*A **Pareto optimum** of the economy E is a feasible state* (z, p, x) *such that there exists no other feasible state* (z', p', x') *such that* $u_i(z', x_i') \geq u_i(z, x_i)$ *for all* i *in* I *and* $u_h(z', x_h') > u_h(z, x_h)$ *for some* h *in* I.

We now define an equilibrium concept for the economy E that will prove useful in the following. We will refer to the abatement cost function $C_k(p_k)$ defined for all k by the expression $[g_k(p_k^0) - g_k(p_k)]$.

Definition 3.　*A **ratio equilibrium** of the economy E is a triple* (p, x, r) *in which* $r = (r_1, r_2,..., r_n)$ *is a cost sharing ratio, with* $r_i = (r_i^1,..., r_i^K)$, *such that for each k* $\sum_{i \in I} r_i^k = 1$ *and such that for all* $i \in B_k$ *and all* k:

$$x_i = \theta_i^k g_k(p_k^0) - \sum_{k=1}^{K} r_i^k C_k(p_k);$$

$$u_i\left(-\sum_{k=1}^{K} p_k, x_i\right) \geq u_i\left(-\sum_{k=1}^{K} p_k', x_i'\right), \forall(p', x_i') : x_i' \leq \theta_i^k g_k(p_k^0) - \sum_{k=1}^{K} r_i^k C_k(p_k').$$

An equilibrium ratio r is a cost sharing vector with the property of inducing the same demand for emissions by all the agents in the economy. A property of ratio equilibria is that they always induce a Pareto Optimum of the economy. The converse is obviously not true, since some Pareto Optimal states distribute private good consumption in a way which is not compatible with the equilibrium constraint of the above definition. Additive of the ecological transfer function implies that at every ratio equilibrium (p, x, r) we have $r_i^k = r_i^j$ for all agents i and for all pairs of countries j, k.

The next Lemma, recording a uniqueness property of the set of Pareto optima of the economy E, is basically a restatement of Proposition 1 in Chander and Tulkens (1997). Since the economy considered in this chapter differs from the one considered there, in that the functional form of utility functions is not linearly separable in the private good, their uniqueness result needs be re-established for this case (see Appendix for the proof).

Lemma 1.   *Let (z, p, x) and (z', p', x') be two Pareto Optima of E. Then $p = p'$.*

Proof.   Appendix.

2.2   Sub-economies $E_k(p'_{-k})$

In what follows, it will be useful to consider some variations on the economy E.

For all k, we denote by $E_k(p'_{-k})$ the sub-economy obtained by restricting the economy E to the set of agents B_k and for a given vector of emissions $p_{-k} = (p_1, p_{k-1}, p_{k+1}, ..., p_K)$ of countries other than k. A feasible state of the sub-economy $E_k(p'_{-k})$ is a vector such that :

$$g_k(p_k) \geq \sum_{i \in B_k} x_i;$$

$$p_{-k} = p'_{-k};$$

$$z = -\sum_{j \neq k} p_j - p_k.$$

For any such feasible state, the pair (p_k, x_k) is called an allocation for $E_k(p'_{-k})$.

The definition of a ratio equilibrium directly applies to the sub-economy $E_k(p'_{-k})$.

Lemma 2.   *The sub-economy $E_k(p'_{-k})$ admits a unique ratio equilibrium (p_k^*, x_k^*, r_k^*), inducing a Pareto optimum of the economy $E_k(p'_{-k})$, with $r_i^{k*} = \theta_i^k$ for all i.*

Proof. Appendix.

Some consistency relations between the sets of ratio equilibria of E and of the economies $E_k(p'_{-k})$, $k = 1,..., K$, will be established and used later on.

3. DOMESTIC DECISION MAKING

3.1 The Private Sector

If we assume that within each country k the private good is produced by the private sector, the level of emissions p^0_k may be thought of as the outcome of the absence of any environmental regulation, be it domestic or international, in country k. In this case, the amount $g_k(p^0_k)$ of private good is produced and consumed.

3.2 The Public Sector

Countries are organized democratically. A legislative body decides by voting the level of domestic environmental regulation by fixing a maximal amount of emissions.

3.2.1 The voting game G_k

We formally represent the voting procedure within country k by means of the voting game $G_k(B_k, W^d_k, p_{-k})$, in which B_k is the set of players (members of parliament), p_{-k} denotes the vector of emissions outside country k and W^d_k is the set of winning coalitions, that is, the coalitions that are decisive on domestic issues for the population of country k. In the case of simple majority rule, the set W^d_k contains all the coalitions that contain a majority of the population in k. The fact that the game is defined for a given vector p_{-k} of external emissions reflects the assumption that the players' payoffs are defined on the states of the whole international economy E. For short we henceforth write $G_k(p_{-k})$ for $G_k(B_k, W^d_k, p_{-k})$.

We make the following assumptions on voting rules:

Assumption 6. *(non-dictatorship): for all $i \in B_k$, for all $k = 1, 2,..., K$:* $B_k \setminus \{i\} \in W^d_k$.

Assumption 7. *(monotonicity): for all i in B_k, for all $k = 1, 2,..., K$: $S \in W^d_k$ and $S \subset T$ imply $T \in W^d_k$.*

We remark that the above two properties are the minimal requirement for our results. They do not rule out the case in which winning coalitions count less than the majority of voters. The properness property (requiring that the complement of a winning coalition cannot be winning), although not needed for the formal derivation of our results, would rule out such undesirable cases.

A strategy for a winning coalition $S_k \in W_k^d$ is a level of domestic emissions p_k. Given p_k, the distributive vector θ^k imputes a well-defined level of consumption to each agent in country k. Coalitions not in W_k^d have an empty strategy set. We assume that agents belonging to a winning coalition can operate any transfers of private good among them,[6] so that coalition S can induce any feasible state (z, p, x_k) of the sub-economy $E_k(p_{-k})$ such that:

$$\sum_{i \in S} x_i \leq \sum_{i \in S} \theta_i^k g_k(p_k);$$
$$x_h = \theta_h^k g_k(p_k), \ \forall h \in B_k \backslash S.$$

We say that coalition $S_k \in W_k^d$ *improves* upon the allocation (p_k, x_k) in $G_k(p_{-k})$ if it can induce a state of the economy that all members prefer to (p_k, x_k), with strict preference for at least one member.

Definition 4. *The **core** of the voting game $G_k(p_{-k})$ is the set of allocations (p_k, x_k) that no coalition can improve upon.*

3.2.2 Political equilibrium in country k

The core of any voting game $G_k(p_{-k})$ has the property of being a stable collective decision in the parliamentary debate. We therefore define a political equilibrium in country k as any state of the sub-economy $E_k(p_{-k})$ induced by a core allocation in the game $G_k(p_{-k})$.

Definition 5. *The feasible state (z, p, x_k) of the sub-economy $E_k(p_{-k})$ is a **political equilibrium** for $E_k(p_{-k})$ if and only if (p_k, x_k) belongs to the core of the associated voting game $G_k(p_{-k})$.*

The next Proposition fully characterizes the political equilibria of country k for any given vector of external emissions (p_{-k}).

Proposition 1. *The state (z, p, x_k) of the sub-economy $E_k(p_{-k})$, in which p_k is the unique Pareto optimal emission level and $x_i = \theta_i^k g_k(p_k)$ for all $i \in B_k$, is the unique political equilibrium for the sub-economy $E_k(p_{-k})$.*

Proof. Appendix.

Remark: *In a political equilibrium no transfers of private good take place, and each agent consumes exactly the amount of private good determined by the efficient emission level of the restricted economy and by his distributive parameter.*

4. INTERNATIONAL NON-COOPERATIVE POLITICAL EQUILIBRIUM

Once we have determined the political equilibrium within each country as a function of the vector of external emissions, it is possible to characterize which states of the economy are expected to occur in the absence of international coordination of policies. Any such state must be such that all countries are simultaneously at a domestic political equilibrium.

Definition 6. *An **International Non-cooperative Political Equilibrium** (INPE) is a state of the economy $(\bar{z}, \bar{p}, \bar{x})$ such that for all k the state $(\bar{z}, \bar{p}, \bar{x}_k)$ is a political equilibrium of the economy $E_k(\bar{p}_{-k})$.*

The INPE may be considered as representing a no-treaty or pre-treaty equilibrium, in the sense that it describes the outcome of national policies in absence of coordination. We here remark that because of the uniqueness of Pareto Optimal emission policies within each country, the INPE prescribes the same emissions vector that would obtain in a model of central planners, each maximizing the aggregate payoff of his domestic agents (this is the case, for instance, of the model studied in Chander and Tulkens (1997)). However, the domestic political constraints implicit in the definition of an INPE fully determine the domestic distribution of private consumption, which is not determined in Chander and Tulkens (1977).

Proposition 2. *There exists a unique INPE for the economy E.*

Proof. Appendix.

By comparing the first-order conditions characterizing the INPE and the Pareto Optimal state of the economy E (these are necessary and sufficient conditions by Assumptions 1–4, see also the proofs of Lemmas 1 and 2) we deduce that the INPE is generically not efficient. Indeed, these conditions can be written for any efficient state (z^*, p^*, x^*) as

$$\frac{v'(z^*)}{v(z^*)}\sum_{j=1}^{K}g_j(p_j^*) = g_k'(p_k^*), \quad \forall k = 1, 2, ..., K,$$

and for the unique INPE as

$$\frac{v'(\bar{z})}{v(\bar{z})} g_k(\bar{p}_k) = g'_k(\bar{p}_k), \quad \forall k = 1, 2, ..., K.$$

Since under the present assumptions production levels are always positive in any efficient state, inefficiently high aggregate emission levels are associated with the INPE. These types of properties are explored in detail in the next section.

5.   INTERNATIONAL COOPERATION

5.1   An Informal Discussion

The INPE can be considered as the predictable outcome in the economy E if countries do not communicate and coordinate their domestic policies. However, the inefficiency of the INPE provides countries with incentives to promote some sort of international cooperation. Such coordinated actions are carried out by means of international agreements, that is, cooperative plans in which countries commit themselves to specific emission abatement plans as well as to cost sharing schemes.

Definition 7. *An **International Agreement (IA)** among the countries of the set K is a pair* $(\Delta p, \alpha)$ *consisting of a vector of emission changes* $(\Delta p = \Delta p_1, \Delta p_2, ..., \Delta p_K)$ *with respect to the INPE levels, with (i)* $\Delta p_k \in [-\bar{p}_k, p_k^0 - \bar{p}_{-k}]$ *for all k, and (ii) of a total cost sharing rule* $\alpha = (\alpha_1, \alpha_2, ..., \alpha_K)$ *such that* $\alpha_k \in [0, 1]$ *for all k and* $\sum_{k=1}^{K} \alpha_k = 1$.

An IA thus prescribes changes in emissions with respect to those prevailing at the INPE, as well as a sharing rule among countries for the aggregate cost involved. In terms of foregone consumption of the private good, this cost is given by

$$C(\Delta p) = \sum_{k=1}^{K} g_k(\bar{p}_k) - g_k(\bar{p}_k + \Delta p_k)$$

while the induced ambient quality is:

$$z(\Delta p) = -\sum_{k=1}^{K} (\bar{p}_k + \Delta p_k).$$

Institutionally, for an IA to come into existence, it must be the result of some collective decision process that comprises at least two levels: (i) the signature (or diplomatic) level, consisting of the adoption of the agreement's content by (delegates of) the countries involved; and (ii) the ratification (or political) level, consisting of the acceptance of that content within each of the countries involved.

In our analysis below, the ratification level is assumed to take place through voting on proposed agreements in each country. Domestic winning coalitions can object to a proposed IA by either rejecting it, in which case the economy remains at the no-treaty (INPE) state, or by proposing some alternative emissions vector. The mathematical model we use to describe the ratification stage is a cooperative *voting game* played by the committee of parliamentary members. The solution concept that identifies the ratified agreements is the *core*.

As far as the signature level is concerned, we assume that each country is represented by a delegate, and we consider that for a proposed agreement to be adopted by the delegates it must be ratified in all countries. Moreover, in order to be adopted, an agreement must be coalitionally rational in the following sense: no set of delegates finds it preferable to engage in a different agreement that they could get ratified in their respective countries. The two levels are intimately related through the fact that the ratification level sets limitations to the proposals that can be considered by the delegates, both as final outcome of cooperation and as conceivable deviations from it. We represent the diplomatic signature level as a *coalition formation game*, in which delegates propose collations, and payoffs are given by the unique core allocations of the ratification voting games.

We show that the grand coalition is a Strong Nash Equilibrium of the coalition formation game, implying emission abatement plans ratified by all countries, and inducing a Pareto optimum of the (world) economy E. Moreover, although (inefficient) outcomes with several coexisting partial agreements are not ruled out in equilibrium, some degree of cooperation always emerges when political delegates maximize the aggregate welfare of their citizens.

5.2 Politics: The Ratification Voting Game

For any IA involving all countries, we denote by $G_k(B_k, W_k^r, \alpha)$ the domestic ratification voting game in country k bearing on an international agreement that imputes to that country the cost share α_k. For a winning coalition $S_k, \in W_k^r$, a strategy is any vector of abatements Δp and possibly transfers among its members, with total imputed cost $\sum_{i \in S_k} \theta_i^k C(\Delta p)$.

Note that we are including as a feasible strategy for a domestic winning coalition $S_k \in W_k^r$ the strategy $\Delta p' = 0$ inducing the INPE state of the economy. If this strategy is adopted, the cooperation process is rejected at the ratification stage.

Individual payoffs yield the following expression for coalition S_k's worth:

$$\sum_{i \in S_k} \theta_i^k g_k(\bar{p}_k) - \theta_i^k \alpha_k g_k C(\Delta p).$$

Definition 8. *We say that the IA $(\Delta p^*, \alpha^*)$ is **ratified by country k** if for some vector of transfers $\tau^{*k} = (\tau_1^{*k}, \tau_2^{*k}, ..., \tau_{n_k}^{*k})$ such that $\sum_{i \in S_k} \tau_i^{*k} = 0$ the allocation induced in the sub-economy $E_k(\bar{p}_{-k} + \Delta p_{-k}^*)$ by the triple $(\Delta p^*, \alpha^*, \tau_k^*)$ is in the core of the game $G_k(B_k, W_k^r, \alpha^*)$. An IA is simply **ratified** if it is ratified by all countries.*

The unique ratified IA is characterized in the next proposition.

Proposition 3. *The IA $(\Delta p^*, \alpha^*)$ such that:*

1. $(\bar{p} + \Delta p^*)$ *is the efficient emissions vector of the economy E;*

2. $\alpha_k^* \dfrac{g_k(\bar{p}_k)}{\sum\limits_{j=1}^{K} g_j(\bar{p}_j)}$ *for all k,*

is the unique ratified international agreement. Moreover, within each country k the associated transfers scheme $\tau^{*k} = (\tau_1^{*k}, \tau_2^{*k}, ..., \tau_{n_k}^{*k})$ is such that $\tau_i^{*k} = 0$ for all $i \in B_k$.

Proof. Appendix.

Proposition 3 shows that the unique ratified international agreement prescribes the efficient emission levels and shares total costs proportionally to the relative income levels at the pre-treaty INPE.

The above definition and characterization can be applied to partial agreements within a subcoalition T of countries. Following the definition and letting α_T^* denote a cost sharing vector for countries in T, we say that the IA $(\Delta p_T^*, \alpha_T^*)$ is *ratified* by the coalition of countries T given the emissions vector Δp_{-T} if for all k in T there exists some vector of transfers τ^{*k} such that the allocation induced by the vector $(\Delta p_T^*, \Delta p_{-T}, \alpha_T^*, \tau^{*k})$ is in the core of the game $G_k(B_k, W_k^r, \alpha_T^*, \Delta p_{-T})$.

Proposition 3 easily extends as follows.

Proposition 4.   *The partial agreement.* $(\Delta p_T^*, \alpha_T^*)$ *such that:*

1. $(\bar{p}_T + \Delta p_T^*)$ *is the efficient emissions vector of the economy* $E_T(\bar{p}_{-T} + \Delta p_{-T}^*)$ E;

2. $\alpha_k^* = \dfrac{g_k(\bar{p}_k)}{\displaystyle\sum_{j \in T} g_j(\bar{p}_j)}$ *for all k in T,*

is the unique ratified partial agreement for the set of countries T given Δp_{-T}.
Moreover, in each country k in T the associated transfers scheme τ_k^* *is such that* τ_i^{*k} *for all i in* B_k.

5.3   Diplomacy: The Coalition Formation Game

We now move to the international cooperation process itself. We wish to consider a model of cooperation in which national delegates only consider agreements which would eventually be ratified by their parliaments. As the previous section has shown, this restriction leaves national delegates with the sole choice of which coalition they wish to form, since once this choice is made, the ratified agreement is uniquely determined. This remark motivates us to model delegates' diplomatic behaviour by means of a coalition formation game, in which delegates consider different 'partners' at the international stage, anticipating the effect of their choices on the payoff of the domestic winning coalition they represent.

   The game we consider was first introduced by Hart and Kurz (1983) as the Γ coalition formation game. The set of players is the set $\{1, 2,..., K\}$ of all national delegates, with $S_k^* \in W_k^d$ denoting the winning coalition represented by the *k-th* delegate (the coalition in power in country k).

   Players act simultaneously. Each player k announces a coalition T_k to which he wishes to belong. A strategy for player k is denoted by σ_k.

5.3.1   From strategies to coalition structures
Once a profile of strategies $\sigma = (\sigma_1, \sigma_2,..., \sigma_K)$ is announced, players must be able to predict which coalitions will form in the system. Since the coalitions announced by the players may not lead to a partition of the set K (or, in other words, players' wishes may not be compatible), a rule mapping strategy profiles into partitions of K is needed.

   We will adopt the 'gamma' rule, proposed by Hart and Kurz, predicting that coalition T effectively forms only if all of its members have announced precisely T.[7] Formally, the profile σ induces the cooperation structure $\pi(\sigma) = \{T_\sigma^k : k \in \{1, 2,..., K\}\}$ where

$$T_\sigma^k = \begin{cases} T_k \text{ if } T_j = T_k \ \forall j \in T_k \\ k \text{ otherwise.} \end{cases}$$

Under this rule, defections from a coalition induce the remaining players to split up as singletons.[8] In particular, any joint deviation $\bar{\sigma}_T = (T, T,..., T)$ by a coalition of players T from, for example, the strategy profile σ in which all players announce the grand coalition $\{1, 2,..., K\}$ induces a coalition structure

$$\pi(\bar{\sigma}_T, \sigma_{-T}) = \{T, \{\{k\} : K \notin T\}\}$$

in which the unique smaller coalition T forms.

5.3.2 Payoffs

We now define an imputation rule, specifying the players' payoffs for each possible coalition structure. This, together with the coalition formation rule, will yield a well-defined game.

Since we are only interested in ratified agreements, we associate with each coalition structure $\pi = \{T_1, T_2,..., T_m\}$ a series of partial agreements, one for each element of π, with the property of being all simultaneously ratified. This leads to:

Definition 9. *The vector of partial agreements* $((\Delta\bar{\bar{p}}_1, \bar{\bar{\alpha}}_1), (\Delta\bar{\bar{p}}_2, \bar{\bar{\alpha}}_2),..., (\Delta\bar{\bar{p}}_m, \bar{\bar{\alpha}}_m))$ *is a* **Partial Agreements Equilibrium (PAE)** *for the coalition structure* $\pi = \{T_1, T_2,..., T_m\}$ *if* $(\Delta\bar{\bar{p}}_h, \bar{\bar{\alpha}}_h)$ *is a ratified partial agreement for* T_h *given* $\Delta\bar{\bar{p}}_{-T_h}$, *for all* $h = 1,..., m$.

A PAE consists of a set partial agreements that are simultaneously ratified by all cooperating countries in the cooperation structure π.

Lemma 3. *For each coalition structure* π *there exists a unique PAE w.r.t.* π.

Proof. Appendix.

The utility levels induced on the economy E by the PAE for the members of the cooperation structure π are used to define the payoffs in the game Γ. In particular, the payoff of delegate k when the profile of strategies σ is played is given by

$$u_k(\sigma) = v\left(-\sum_{j=1}^{K}(\bar{p}_j + \Delta\bar{\bar{p}}_j)\right)\sum_{i \in S_k^*} x_i(\Delta\bar{\bar{p}}, \bar{\bar{\alpha}}_k),$$

where $(\Delta\bar{\bar{p}}, \bar{\bar{\alpha}}_k)$ is the PAE with respect to $\pi(\sigma)$. The fact that in the above equation the sum of private consumptions is taken over players in S_k^* formally represents the assumption that each delegate behaves on behalf of the domestic winning coalition he represents.

5.3.3 Strong Nash Equilibria of the Game Γ

When seen as outcomes of a coalition formation game, equilibrium coalition structures identify stable agreements. In particular, Strong Nash Equilibria of the game Γ are strategy profiles with the property of being immune from both individual and coalitional deviations.

Definition 10. *A **Strong Nash Equilibrium** of the coalition formation game Γ is a profile of strategies σ^* such that there exists no coalition of players T with a vector of strategies σ_T such that for all $k \in T$:*

$$u_k(\sigma_T, \sigma^*_{-T}) \geq u_k(\sigma^*)$$

and for at least one j in T

$$u_j(\sigma_T, \sigma^*_{-T}) > u_j(\sigma^*).$$

Equilibrium coalition structures identify politically stable agreements. We will now assert that the grand coalition always obtains as a Strong Nash Equilibrium outcome of the game Γ.

Theorem 1. *The strategy profile σ^* in which all players declare the grand coalition $\{1, 2,..., K\}$ is a Strong Nash Equilibrium of the game Γ.*

This directly implies that the unique IA ratified by all countries is also immune from deviations by means of national leaders. In this sense, this agreement can be legitimately expected to be proposed (and ratified) at national levels.

We prove the theorem in the Appendix, under an additional Assumption on total cost of cooperation, closely related to Assumption 1″, defined on preferences, used in Chander and Tulkens (1997).

Assumption 8 *Let coalition T be such that $\#T \geq 2$ and let $\pi(T)$ be any partition of T. Let $\pi = \{\pi(T), \{\{k\}: k \notin T\}\}$ denote the cooperation structure in which all countries not in T appear as singletons. Then the aggregate abatement cost of at least one element $T_j \in \pi(T)$ at the Partial Agreement Equilibrium $(\Delta \bar{\bar{p}}, \bar{\bar{\alpha}})$ w.r.t. π is weakly greater than at the INPE. Formally,*

$$\sum_{k \in T_j} [g_k(\bar{p}_k) - g_k(\bar{p}_k + \Delta p_k)] \geq 0.$$

Assumption 8 imposes a constraint on the way in which welfare improvements are attained through cooperation. It requires that if some sets of countries cooperate, then at least one of them does not obtain a higher level of private consumption than at the non-cooperative equilibrium. In other words, the benefits of international cooperation must be, at least for one set of cooperating countries, not in terms of higher consumption levels but rather in terms of a higher environmental quality. This assumption is always satisfied if countries have the same production technology and/or constant returns to scale.

One final issue to be addressed is whether coalition structures other than the grand coalition may occur as equilibria of the game Γ – equilibria that would necessarily be inefficient in view of the uniqueness property of the strategy adopted by any coalition of delegates. Let us consider in particular the most extreme case of inefficiency, namely the complete absence of cooperation, here represented by the coalition structure $\bar{\pi}$ consisting of all countries as singletons: can it be an equilibrium outcome of the game Γ?

It is instructive to deal first with the case in which domestic delegates maximize the aggregate welfare of their citizens (in terms of the game Γ, the case in which $S_k^* = B_k$ for all $k = 1, 2,..., K$). Let σ^* be the profile of strategies in which all players announce the grand coalition, and $\bar{\sigma}^*$ be any strategy profile inducing the coalition structure $\bar{\pi}$. The uniqueness of the Pareto optimum of the economy E (proved in Lemma 1), together with the characterization result of Proposition 3, imply that:

$$\sum_{k=1}^{K} u_k(\sigma^*) = \sum_{i \in I} u_i(z^*, x_i^*) > \sum_{i \in I} u_i(\bar{z}, \bar{x}_i) = \sum_{k=1}^{K} u_k(\bar{\sigma}). \tag{1.1}$$

Note also that since the international agreement $(\Delta p^*, \alpha^*)$, induced by the profile σ^*, satisfies the conditions for a ratio equilibrium of the economy $\bar{E}$ (obtained from E by considering the INPE as initial endowment), the induced allocation is individually rational for all agents in the economy, in the sense that it is weakly preferred to the INPE allocation. This leads to the following inequalities:

$$u_i(z^*, x_i^*) \geq u_i(\bar{z}, \bar{x}_i), \quad \forall i \in I \tag{1.2}$$

implying that

$$u_k(\sigma^*) \geq u_k(\bar{\sigma}), \quad \forall k = 1, 2,..., K. \tag{1.3}$$

Conditions (1.1) and (1.2) imply that for some agent $i^* \in I$:

$$u_{i^*}(z^*, x_{i^*}^*) > u_{i^*}(\bar{z}, \bar{x}_{i^*}). \tag{1.4}$$

Since we are assuming that $i^* \in B_k$, for some country k, we conclude that for some k:

$$u_k(\sigma^*) > u_k(\bar{\sigma}). \tag{1.5}$$

Conditions (1.3) and (1.5) directly imply the following proposition.

Proposition 5. *Let* $S_k^* = B_k$ *for all* $k = 1, 2, ..., K$. *Then, the coalition structure* $\bar{\pi}$ *in which no cooperation occurs is never a Strong Nash Equilibrium of the game* Γ.

Thus, if political delegates maximize their countries' aggregate welfare, an international equilibrium must always contain some degree of cooperation. By contrast, if lack of cooperation prevails, it can only be imputed to the fact that political delegates do not represent the totality of their population but only a majority of it. To see how this may undermine the result of Proposition 5, consider again condition (1.1). If $S_k^* \subset B_k$ for some k, we obtain

$$\sum_{k=1}^{K} u_k(\sigma^*) \neq \sum_{i \in I} u_i(z^*, x_i^*)$$

so that condition (1.1) can only be stated in the following form:

$$\sum_{i \in I} u_i(z^*, x_i^*) > \sum_{i \in I} u_i(\bar{z}, \bar{x}_i). \tag{1.6}$$

Again, we can use (1.6) to conclude that some agent $i^* \in I$ exists for which condition (1.4) is satisfied. However, it may now be the case that (1.4) only holds for one agent $i^* \in B_k \backslash S_k^*$. If this is the case, no incumbent winning coalition strictly prefers the efficient outcome (z^*, x^*) to the INPE allocation, and the proof of Proposition 5 does not extend.

Notice that when complete non-cooperation arises in equilibrium, it is because all members of incumbent winning coalitions are as well off as at the efficient outcome (z^*, x^*), while the 'minority' agents are prevented from exploiting the surplus of cooperation. In this sense it can be argued that inefficiency is here strictly due to the political nature of delegates' strategies.

These arguments show that no cooperation may be a stable outcome, in the particular sense of Strong Nash Equilibria. However, condition (1.2) also implies that the set of all delegates must either prefer full cooperation to the complete absence of cooperation, or be indifferent between these two outcomes. If we define the notion of Strict Strong Nash Equilibrium by relaxing the requirement of strict improvement of at least one player in Definition 10 above,[9] the following directly follows:

Proposition 6.   *The coalition structure $\bar{\pi}$ in which no cooperation occurs is never a Strict Strong Nash Equilibrium of the game Γ.*

6.   CONCLUSIONS

In this chapter we have looked at international agreements that satisfy two stability requirements: they are a stable solution of the international negotiation process and they are domestically stable in the sense that they are ratified by all parliaments. We identify a unique IA among the whole set of countries, with the following properties:

1. It prescribes the efficient emissions levels for the international economy (Lemma 2);
2. It shares abatement costs among countries proportionally to the relative incomes at the INPE (Proposition 2);
3. Domestically, no transfers occur, and each agent consumes the amount of private good determined by his distributive parameter and by his country's cost share (Proposition 2).

Our main theorem establishes that if this agreement is chosen, then the grand coalition is a stable outcome of a suitably defined coalition formation game. Moreover, although (inefficient) cooperation structures with several coexisting coalitions are not ruled out in equilibrium, some degree of cooperation always emerges when political delegates represent the totality of their population.

The specific cost sharing rule implied by the stable IA in the present chapter should be related with the core-stable allocation identified by Chander and Tulkens (1997) for a similar economy with quasi-linear preferences. In both cases, the way in which costs are imputed in equilibrium satisfies the property of the 'ratio equilibrium', introduced for an economy with public goods by Kaneko (1977). More precisely, both papers propose the ratio equilibrium of the economy $\bar{E}$ obtained from the economy E by considering the INPE as initial endowment. The induced allocation has the nice feature of being *computable*, requiring only, in the present chapter, the information about aggregate income levels at the no-treaty state of the economy. While in Chander and Tulkens (1997) this allocation is shown only *to belong to the core* of the international economy (among possibly other ones), in the present chapter it is shown to characterize the unique stable agreement among the whole set of countries. This difference is due to the introduction of voting as domestic decision process, replacing the traditional aggregate utility maximization within each coalition. Since objections are 'easier' for winning coalitions than for unanimous coalitions, all allocations other than the ratio equilibrium are objected to in the present chapter, while some of them may still be stable in Chander and Tulkens (1997). In contrast, while no inefficient outcome was stable in the core-theoretic analysis (mainly due to the possibility of benevolent delegates operating a desired transfers scheme), here inefficient cooperation structures may emerge because of the impossibility of operating such transfers of private goods as would be needed to attain Pareto improvements.

A final word must be said on the robustness of our result to larger classes of preferences. The special class adopted in this chapter simplifies the analysis in three respects. First, it is responsible for the uniqueness of the various solution concepts adopted in the paper. Second, equilibrium ratios of the sub-economies coincide with the distributional vectors θ, making the present environment equivalent to one of linear income taxation and allowing for a non-empty set of political equilibria. Third, the transferable utility property of preferences allowed us to determine the payoffs of national delegates as the aggregate utility of the supporting winning coalition. Our main results would still carry over to a more general class of preferences, requiring monotonicity of preferences in the private good and normality of the public good 'ambient quality'. Our characterization of the stable agreement, on the contrary, is strictly related to the specific form of preferences we have adopted. Although politically stable IA would still satisfy the ratio equilibrium property, cost shares would not be directly related to national incomes at the INPE.

APPENDIX

Proof of Lemma 1

Assumptions 1–4 ensure that efficient states of the economy E are all associated with points in the interior of the sets $[0, p_k^0]$, for all $k \in \{1, 2,..., K\}$. In fact, $p_k = 0$ is never an efficient emission level, since $v'(0, p_{-k})$ is bounded and $g_k'(0) = +\infty$. Similarly, p_k^0 is never an efficient emission level, since $g_k'(p_k^0) = 0$ and $v'(z(p_k^0, p_{-k}) > 0$.

Efficient emission vectors maximize the aggregate welfare of the economy E, given by the expression

$$v(z) \sum_{j=1}^{K} g_j(p_j). \tag{1.7}$$

By Assumptions 1–4, (1.7) is a concave function of p_k, for all k. Therefore, Samuelson's conditions are necessary and sufficient for an efficient emission vector. These conditions imply that for all efficient emission vectors p and p', for all $k \in \{1, 2,..., K\}$:

$$\frac{v'(z)}{v(z)} \sum_{j=1}^{K} g_j(p_j) = g_k'(p_k);$$

$$\frac{v'(z')}{v(z')} \sum_{j=1}^{K} g_j(p_j') = g_k'(p_k'). \tag{1.8}$$

Suppose now that $p \neq p'$ and, without loss of generality, $p_k > p_k'$. By concavity of technology, $g_k'(p_k) \leq g_k'(p_k')$. Since, by conditions (1.8), $g_k'(p_k) = g_j'(p_j)$ for all $j, k \in \{1, 2, ..., K\}$ and $g_k'(p_k) = g_j'(p_j)$ for all $j, k \in \{1, 2, ..., K\}$, this would imply that $p_j \geq p_j'$ for all $j, \in \{1, 2, ..., K\}$, and thus $z' > z$. It follows from strict monotonicity of g_j for all $j, \in \{1, 2, ..., K\}$ that

$$\sum_{j=1}^{K} g_j(p_j) > \sum_{j=1}^{K} g_j(p_j') \tag{1.9}$$

and by concavity of v w.r.t. z that

$$\frac{v'(z)}{v(z)} \geq \frac{v'(z')}{v(z')}. \tag{1.10}$$

Conditions (1.8), (1.9) and (1.10) contradict the requirement that $g_j'(p_j) \leq g_j'(p_j')$. It follows that $p_k = p_k'$ for all $j, \in \{1, 2, ..., K\}$.∎

Proof of Lemma 2

A ratio equilibrium is a triple (p_k, x_k, r_k) such that every agent $i \in B_k$ demands the same vector p_k facing the distributive vector r_i. Agent $i \in B_k$ demanding the emission p_k and facing the ratio r_i consumes the amount

$$x_i = \theta_i^k g(p_k^0) - r_i \lfloor g_k(p_k^0) - g_k(p_k) \rfloor.$$

Therefore, agent i faces the following problem

$$\max_{pk} v(p_k, p_{-k}) \lfloor \theta_i^k g_k(p_k^0) - r_i (g_k(p_k^0) - g_r(p_k)) \rfloor. \tag{1.11}$$

The maximand is a concave function of p_k by Assumptions 1–4. Moreover, by the arguments used in the previous lemma to show that efficient emissions vectors are interior, we know that $p_k = 0$ is never a solution of (1.11). First order conditions yield

$$-v'(z(p_k, \bar{p}_{-k})) \lfloor \theta_i^k g_k(p_k^0) - r_i (g_k(p_k^0) - g_k(p_k)) \rfloor + v(z(p_k, \bar{p}_{-k})) r_i g_k'(p_k) = 0, \tag{1.12}$$

from which

$$r_i = \frac{v'(z(p_k, \bar{p}_{-k})) \theta_i^k g_k(p_k^0)}{v'(z(p_k, \bar{p}_{-k})) \lfloor (g_k(p_k^0) - g_k(p_k)) \rfloor + v(z(p_k, \bar{p}_{-k})) g_k'(p_k)}. \tag{1.13}$$

By imposing the condition $\sum_{i \in B_k} r_i = 1$, we get

$$\sum_{i \in B_k} \frac{v'(z(p_k, \bar{p}_{-k})) \theta_i^k g_k(p_k^0)}{v'(z(p_k, \bar{p}_{-k})) \lfloor (g_k(p_k^0) - g_k(p_k)) \rfloor + v(z(p_k, \bar{p}_{-k})) g_k'(p_k)} = 1, \tag{1.14}$$

from which, using the fact that $\sum_{i \in B_k} \theta_i^k = 1$, we get

$$\frac{v'(z(p_k, \bar{p}_{-k}))g_k(p_k^0)}{v'(z(p_k, \bar{p}_{-k}))\left[(g_k(p_k^0) - g_k(p_k)\right] + v(z(p_k, \bar{p}_{-k}))g_k'(p_k)} = 1, \qquad (1.15)$$

yielding, together with (1.13), $r_i = \theta_i^k$.

The fact that p_k is the efficient vector of the economy $E_k(\bar{p}_{-k})$ comes from the fact that ratio equilibria trivially satisfy the Samuelson's conditions for that sub-economy.∎

Proof of Proposition 1

We know by Lemma 2 that the distributive parameter θ^k is the unique vector of equilibrium ratios of the sub-economy $E_k(\bar{p}_{-k})$. We also know by Theorems 1 and 2 in Hirokawa (1992) that the core of the voting game $G_k(\bar{p}_{-k})$ coincides with the set of ratio equilibrium allocations of the sub-economy $E_k(\bar{p}_{-k})$. It follows that the unique political equilibrium is the state of the economy associated with the ratio equilibrium allocation of $E_k(\bar{p}_{-k})$.∎

Proof of Proposition 2

Existence. We denote by $f_j(p_{-j})$ the Pareto efficient level of emissions in country j given the levels p_{-j}. Let also $f(p)$ be the k-th product of the functions $f_j(p_{-j})$ for $j = 1$, $2,..., K$. A fixed point p^* of the map $f(p)$ is such that $p^* = f(p^*)$. By definition of an INPE and by Proposition 1, if p^* is a fixed point of f then the pair $\lfloor p^*, (\theta_i^k g_k(p_k^*))_{i \in I} \rfloor$ is an INPE. By Kakutani fixed point theorem, f admits a fixed point if it is upper hemicontinuous, convex valued and defined on a non-empty, compact and convex set. As the product maintains these properties, it is enough to check these conditions on each projection map $f_j(p_{-j})$. Since the domain of $f_j(p_{-j})$ is the closed, convex and non-empty set $\prod_{j \neq k} \lfloor 0, p_k^0 \rfloor$ and since f is a function by Lemma 1, we just need to show upper hemi continuity of f, that is, of the efficient value p_k of the economy $E_k(\bar{p}_{-k})$ as a function of $\bar{p}_{-k}$. This directly follows from continuity of v and of g_k.

Uniqueness: Assume that there exist two INPEs, $(p, x) \neq (p', x')$. Let z and z' be the induced amounts of ambient pollution. By the characterization of INPE, for all $j, k \in \{1, 2,..., K\}$:

$$\frac{v'(z)}{v(z)} \sum_{j=1}^{K} g_j(p_j) = g_k'(p_k);$$

$$\frac{v'(z')}{v(z')} \sum_{j=1}^{K} g_j(p_j') = g_k'(p_k').$$

By the assumptions that $g_k' \geq 0$, $g_k'' \leq 0$, $v' \geq 0$, and $v'' \leq 0$, the following implications hold:

$$p_k' \geq p_k \Rightarrow g_k'(p_k') \leq g_k'(p_k) \Rightarrow \frac{v'(z')}{v(z')} \leq \frac{v'(z)}{v(z)} \Rightarrow z' \geq z.$$

Then, for some $j \neq k$, it must be that $p'_j \leq p_j$, implying, by the same series of implications, that $z' \leq z$. The two inequalities together yield that $z' = z$. Then, in any INPE, the aggregate ambient pollution is the same. Suppose now that $p'_k \geq p_k$ for some k. Then, by concavity,

$$g'_k(p'_k) \leq g'_k(p_k) \tag{1.16a}$$

and, by strict monotonicity,

$$g_k(p_k) > g_k(p'_k). \tag{1.16b}$$

These two facts, together with the fact that $z' = z$ and the two first order conditions in (1.16a)–(1.16b), imply a contradiction.∎

Proof of Proposition 3

Let $\bar{E}$ be the economy derived by E considering the INPE as initial endowment. In terms of Ito and Kaneko (1981), $\bar{E}$ is defined by considering the level of emissions at the INPE as *allowance level*, and individual incomes at the levels defined by the INPE production and by the distributive vector θ. A ratio equilibrium for this economy is a triple (p, x, r) such that every agent i demands vector p facing the distributive vector r_i. We first show that the triple (p^*, x^*, r^*), inducing the efficient vector of the economy E, and such that for all $i \in B_k$, $k = 1, 2, ..., K$, and for all pairs, $l, m \in \{1, 2, ..., K\}$,

$$r_i^{l*} = r_i^{m*} = \theta_i^k \frac{g_k(\bar{p}_k)}{\displaystyle\sum_{j=1}^{K} g_j(\bar{p}_j)} = r_i^*$$

and

$$x_i^* = \theta_i^k g(\bar{p}_k) - r_i^* \sum_{j=1}^{K} \left[g_j(\bar{p}_j) - g_j(p_j^*) \right]$$

is the unique ratio equilibrium of $\bar{E}$. Agent i faces the following problem

$$\max_p v(z(p)) \left[\theta_i^k g_k(\bar{p}_k) - \sum_{j=1}^{K} r_i^j (g_j(\bar{p}_j) - g_j(p_j)) \right].$$

First order conditions yield, for all $m \in \{1, 2, ..., K\}$,

$$v'(z(p)) \left[\theta_i^k g_k(\bar{p}_k) - \sum_{j=1}^{K} r_i^j (g_j(\bar{p}_j) - g_k(p_j)) \right] - v(z(p)) [r_i^m g'_m(p_m)] = 0.$$

For any pair $l, m \in \{1, 2, ..., K\}$ we therefore write:

$$r_i^l = \frac{v'(z(p)) \theta_i^k g_k(\bar{p}_k)}{v'(z(p)) \displaystyle\sum_{j=1}^{K} r_i^j (g_j(\bar{p}_j) - g_j(p_j)) + v(z(p)) [g'_l(p_l)]};$$

$$r_i^m = \frac{v'(z(p)) \theta_i^k g_k(\bar{p}_k)}{v'(z(p)) \displaystyle\sum_{j=1}^{K} r_i^j (g_j(\bar{p}_j) - g_j(p_j)) + v(z(p)) [g'_m(p_m)]}.$$

Since Pareto Optimality requires that $g'_m(p_m) = g'_l(p_l)$, it follows that in equilibrium $r^l_i = r^m_i$. By imposing the condition $\sum_{i\in I} r^m_i = 1$ we get

$$\sum_{k=1}^{k} g_k(\bar{p}_k) \frac{v'(z(p))}{v'(z(p))\sum_{j=1}^{K} r_i\{g_j(\bar{p}_j) - g_j(p_j)\} + v(z(p))[g'_m(p_m)]} = 1$$

from which:

$$r^m_i = \frac{\theta^k_i g_k(\bar{p}_k)}{\sum_{k=1}^{K} g_k(\bar{p}_k)}.$$

It can be easily checked by means of the relevant first order conditions that the vector p^* is indeed the efficient emission vector of the economy E.

We can again apply the results of Lemmas 5 and 6 to conclude that α^* is the only vector inducing the same vector of emissions changes as a ratio equilibrium of every sub-economy $E_k(\alpha^*_k)$. The result then follows from Theorems 1 and 2 in Hirokawa (1992).∎

Proof of Lemma 3

Existence of the PAE can then be proved by direct application of the formal argument used in the proof of existence of an INPE. In this respect, note that in the case of the PAE, each group of countries belonging to the same element of π jointly choose their vector of emissions, while in the case of the INPE each country is choosing a single level of emission. Since by Lemma 4 every element of π is choosing the unique efficient level of emissions in any PAE, the existence proof for the INPE, relying on Kakutani's fixed point theorem, can be applied, provided upper hemi continuity is preserved. In this respect, the same argument used in the proof of Proposition 2 extends. Similarly, the argument for uniqueness used in Proposition 2 carries over to this case.∎

Theorem. *The strategy profile σ^* in which all players declare the grand coalition $\{1, 2,..., K\}$ is a Strong Nash Equilibrium of the game Γ.*

We will first prove three preparatory lemmas. The first extends to the present setting the characterization results of Proposition 1 in Chander and Tulkens (1997). Let T be some subset of countries, and let $\pi(T)$ be any partition of T. Let $\pi = \{\pi(T), \{\{k\}: k \notin T\}\}$ denote the cooperation structure in which all countries not in T appear as singletons. Let $(\Delta\bar{\bar{p}}, \bar{\bar{\alpha}}) = [(\Delta\bar{\bar{p}}_T, \bar{\bar{\alpha}}_T), (\Delta\bar{\bar{p}}_j)_{j\notin T}]$ be the PAE with respect to π.

Lemma 4

(a) $(\bar{\bar{p}}_{T_j} + \Delta\bar{\bar{p}}_{T_j})$ is the efficient emissions vector of the economy $E_{T_j}(\bar{p}_{-T_j} + \Delta\bar{\bar{p}}_{-T_j})$ for all $T_j \in \pi(T)$, and $(\bar{p}_j + \Delta\bar{\bar{p}}_j)$ is the efficient emissions vector of the economy $E_j(\bar{p}_{-j} + \Delta\bar{\bar{p}}_{-j})$ for all $j \notin T$;
(b) the total emissions induced by the vector $\Delta\bar{\bar{p}}$ are smaller than or equal to the INPE emissions;

(c) the emissions level of each country $j \notin T$ at $\Delta\bar{\bar{p}}$ is greater than or equal to its INPE level. Moreover, the aggregate emissions of the countries in T is not greater than at the INPE.

Proof of Lemma 4

(a)   Directly implied by Lemma 4.

(b)   Let $\bar{\bar{p}} = (\bar{p} + \Delta\bar{p})$. First order optimality conditions imply that for all $j \notin T$

$$\frac{v'(\bar{z})}{v(\bar{z})} g_j(\bar{p}_j) = g'_j(\bar{p}_j) \tag{1.17}$$

and

$$\frac{v'(\bar{\bar{z}})}{v(\bar{\bar{z}})} g_j(\bar{\bar{p}}_j) = g'_j(\bar{\bar{p}}_j). \tag{1.18}$$

Suppose now that $\bar{z} > \bar{\bar{z}}$; by strict concavity of v in z we have

$$\frac{v'(\bar{z})}{v(\bar{z})} \leq \frac{v'(\bar{\bar{z}})}{v(\bar{\bar{z}})}.$$

Using (1.17)–(1.18) we get

$$\frac{g'_j(\bar{p}_j)}{g_j(\bar{p}_j)} \leq \frac{g'_j(\bar{\bar{p}}_j)}{g_j(\bar{\bar{p}}_j)}$$

Since the term $g'_j(p_j)/g_j(p_j)$ is decreasing in p_j by concavity of g_j we get that $\bar{z} > \bar{\bar{z}} \Rightarrow \bar{p}_j \geq \bar{\bar{p}}_j$ for every $j \notin T$. Consider now the partition $\pi(T)$. By point (a) it follows that for all $k \in T_m$ and all $T_m \in \pi(T)$:

$$\frac{v'(\bar{z})}{v(\bar{z})} g_j(\bar{p}_j) = g'_j(\bar{p}_j)$$

and

$$\frac{v'(\bar{\bar{z}})}{v(\bar{\bar{z}})} \sum_{k \in T_m} g_j(\bar{\bar{p}}_j) = g'_j(\bar{\bar{p}}_j).$$

If $\bar{z} > \bar{\bar{z}}$ then, by similar arguments to the one used above we get

$$\frac{g'_k(\bar{p}_k)}{g_k(\bar{p}_k)} \leq \frac{g'_k(\bar{\bar{p}}_k)}{\sum_{j \in T_m} g_j(\bar{\bar{p}}_j)}.$$

Rewriting the term $\sum_{j \in T_m} g_k(\bar{\bar{p}}_k)$ as $\sum_{j \in T_m \backslash k} g_j(\bar{\bar{p}}_j) + g_j(\bar{\bar{p}}_j)$ and using the fact that $\sum_{j \in T_m \backslash k}$ $g_j(\bar{\bar{p}}_j) \geq 0$ we obtain the following inequality

$$\frac{g'_k(\bar{p}_k)}{g_k(\bar{p}_k)} \leq \frac{g'_k(\bar{\bar{p}}_k)}{g'_k(\bar{\bar{p}}_k)}$$

which implies that $(\bar{p}_k \geq \bar{\bar{p}}_k)$ for all $k \in T_m$.

The two results together imply that $\bar{z} \leq \bar{\bar{z}}$, which contradicts the assumption. Then it must be that $\bar{z} \leq \bar{\bar{z}}$.

(c)   Suppose that $\bar{\bar{p}}_j < \bar{p}_j$ for some country $j \notin T$. Concavity of g_j implies $g'_j(\bar{\bar{p}}_j) \geq g'_j(\bar{p}_j)$ or, by points (a) and (b),

$$\frac{v'(\overline{\overline{z}})}{v(\overline{\overline{z}})} g_j(\overline{\overline{p}}_j) \geq \frac{v'(\overline{z})}{v(\overline{z})} g_j(\overline{p}_j).$$

Since we know from point (b) that $\overline{z} \leq \overline{\overline{z}}$, and by the fact that the term $v'(z)/v(z)$ is decreasing in z, we obtain that $g_j(\overline{p}_j) \leq g_j(\overline{\overline{p}}_j)$, which, by the fact that g_j is monotonically increasing, implies a contradiction. This fact, together with point (b), implies that aggregate emissions of countries in T are smaller at the PAE than at the INPE. ∎

The next two lemmas establish consistency properties of the set of ratio equilibria. For a given real number $\alpha_k \in (0, 1]$ let $E_k(\alpha_k)$ denote the economy with set of agents B_k and all other fundamentals as in E, and in which the cost function is given by $\alpha_k C_j(p_j)$ for all $j = 1, 2,..., K$.

Lemma 5 (Van den Nouweland, Tijs and Wooders, 2002). If (p^*, x^*, r^*) is a ratio equilibrium of the economy E and $\alpha_k^* = \sum_{i \in B_k} r_i^*$, then $\left(p^*, x_k^*, \left(\dfrac{r_i^*}{\alpha_k^*}\right)_{i \in B_k}\right)$ is a ratio equilibrium of $E_k(\alpha_k^*)$.

Lemma 6. Let $(\alpha_1^*,..., \alpha_K^*)$ be such that $\sum_{k=1}^{K} \alpha_k^* = 1$. If there exists (p^*, τ^*) such that (p^*, x_k^*, τ_k^*) is a ratio equilibrium of $E_k(\alpha_k^*)$ for all k, then there is a ratio equilibrium (p^*, x^*, r^*) of the economy E such that $\alpha_k^* = \sum_{i \in B_k} r_i^*$ and $\tau_k^* = \left(\dfrac{r_i^*}{\alpha_k^*}\right)_{i \in B_k}$.

Proof of Lemma 6

Since (p^*, x^*, τ_k^*) is a ratio equilibrium of $E_k(\alpha_k^*)$ for all k, we can write that for all $i \in B_k$, for all k and for all p:

$$u_i(p^*, x_i^*) \geq u_i(p, \theta_i g_k(p_k^0)\tau_k^{*i}\alpha_k^* \sum_{j=1}^{K} C_j(p_j))$$

Since $\sum_{i \in B_k} \tau_i^* = 1$ for all k and $\sum_{k=1}^{K} \alpha_k^* = 1$, it follows that

$$\sum_{k=1}^{K} \sum_{i \in B_k} \tau_i^* \alpha_k^* = \alpha_1^* \sum_{i \in B_k} \tau_i^* + \alpha_2^* \sum_{i \in B_k} \tau_i^* + ... + \alpha_K^* \sum_{i \in B_k} \tau_i^* = 1$$

so that $(p^*, x^*, \alpha^*, \tau^*)$ is a ratio equilibrium of the economy E. The facts that

$\alpha_k^* = \sum_{i \in B_k} r_i^*$ and $\tau_k^* \left(\dfrac{r_i^*}{\alpha_k^*}\right)_{i \in B_k}$ follow directly from definitions. In particular, for the

economy E we have that $\alpha_k^* = \sum_{i \in B_k} \theta_i^k$ for all k is the unique vector compatible with a ratio equilibrium in each sub-economy $E_k(\alpha_k^*)$. ∎

Proof of Theorem 1

We are now ready to prove the theorem. We proceed by contradiction. Suppose that some coalition of players T improves upon the strategy profile σ^* by means of the alternative profile σ_T. Denote by $(\Delta p^*, \alpha^*)$ the ratified IA for the grand coalition, and by $(\Delta \bar{\bar{p}}, \bar{\bar{\alpha}})$ the PAE w.r.t. coalition structure $\pi = \{\pi(T), \{\{k\}: k \notin T\}\}$ induced by the deviation of T and whose elements are the partition $\pi(T)$ of the set T and all the players outside T as singletons. We will use the notation z^* and $\bar{\bar{z}}$ to indicate the induced environmental qualities. Using the definition of payoffs, the fact that T improves upon σ^* implies that $\forall i \in S_k^*$ and $\forall k \in T$:

$$v(\bar{\bar{z}})x_i(\Delta \bar{\bar{p}}, \bar{\bar{\alpha}}_T) > v(z^*)x_i(\Delta p^*, \alpha^*). \tag{1.19}$$

By Lemma 4 we know that $\Delta \bar{\bar{p}}_k \geq 0$ for all $k \notin T$. Denoting by 0_{-T} the vector of zero changes in emissions of countries not in T, this, together with monotonicity of v, implies

$$v(z(\Delta \bar{\bar{p}}_T, 0_{-T})) \geq v(z(\Delta \bar{\bar{p}})). \tag{1.20}$$

Inequalities (1.19) and (1.20) imply that

$$v(z(\Delta \bar{\bar{p}}_T, 0_{-T}))x_i(\Delta \bar{\bar{p}}, \bar{\bar{\alpha}}_T) > v(z^*)x_i(\Delta p^*, \alpha^*). \tag{1.21}$$

We show that (1.21) implies a contradiction. The argument goes by showing that $\forall i \in S_k^*$ and $\forall k \in T$:

$$x_i(\Delta \bar{\bar{p}}, \bar{\bar{\alpha}}_T) > x_i(\Delta \bar{\bar{p}}_T, 0_{-T}, \alpha^*). \tag{1.22}$$

Suppose not, so that for some $i \in S_k^*$ and some $k \in T$

$$x_i(\Delta \bar{\bar{p}}, \bar{\bar{\alpha}}_T) \leq x_i(\Delta \bar{\bar{p}}_T, 0_{-T}, \alpha^*). \tag{1.23}$$

By the equilibrium properties of the cost share vector α_k^*, we obtain (see Lemmas 5 and 6 and Proposition 3):

$$v(z^*)x_i(\Delta p^*, \alpha^*) \geq v(z(\Delta \bar{\bar{p}}_T, 0_{-T}))x_i(\Delta \bar{\bar{p}}_T, 0_{-T}, \alpha_k^*). \tag{1.24}$$

Using (1.23) and (1.24) we obtain a contradiction of (1.23).

We then use the definitions of $x_i(\Delta \bar{\bar{p}}, \bar{\bar{\alpha}}_T)$ and of $x_i(\Delta \bar{\bar{p}}_T, 0_{-T}, \alpha^*)$ and sum up (1.22) over $i \in S_k^*$ and $k \in T_m$ for some $T_m \in \pi(T)$ to obtain:

$$\sum_{i \in S_k^*} \sum_{k \in T_m} \bar{x}_i - \theta_i^k \bar{\bar{\alpha}}_k \sum_{j \in T_m} (g_j(\bar{p}_j) + g_j(\bar{p}_j + \Delta \bar{\bar{p}}_j)) > \sum_{i \in S_k^*} \sum_{k \in T_m} \bar{x}_i - \theta_i^k \alpha_k^*$$

$$\sum_{j \in T_m} (g_j(\bar{p}_j) + g_j(\bar{p}_j + \Delta \bar{\bar{p}}_j)),$$

or, more simply,

$$\sum_{i \in S_k^*} \sum_{k \in T_m} \theta_i^k(\alpha_k^* - \bar{\bar{\alpha}}_k) \sum_{j \in T_m} (g_j(\bar{p}_j) + g_j(\bar{p}_j + \Delta \bar{\bar{p}}_j)) > 0.$$

Using now Assumption 8 and the definitions of α_k^* and $\bar{\bar{\alpha}}_k$ we obtain

$$\sum_{i \in S_k^*} \sum_{k \in T_m} \theta_i^k \left[\frac{g_k(\bar{p}_k)}{\sum_{j=1}^K g_j(\bar{p}_j)} - \frac{g_k(\bar{p}_k)}{\sum_{j \in T_m} g_j(\bar{p}_j)} \right] > 0.$$

Note that in the above summation, all terms in brackets are weakly negative, since

$\sum_{j=1}^K g_j(\bar{p}_j) \geq \sum_{j \in T_m} g_j(\bar{p}_j)$. This implies a contradiction and concludes the proof.∎

NOTES

1. This chapter was first presented as a paper at the IIPF meeting in Linz, August 2001, and at the BARCELONA-CORE-LEA Workshop on Economic Design held in Barcelona, November 2001. A previous version of this chapter, substantially different as to the proposed concept of international cooperation, was circulated as CORE Discussion Paper no. 9793 as well as CLIMNEG Working Paper no. 3 under the title 'Core-theoretic and political stability of international agreements on transfrontier pollution' and was presented at the EAERE Tilburg meeting of June 1997, at the EEA Toulouse meeting of September 1997 and at the third CORE-FEEM Workshop on Coalition Formation in Venice, January 1998. The authors are grateful to Professor Wiesmeth for his detailed examination of that early version and to Professor Jean François Mertens for insightful queries on this version.
2. Corresponding author. Department of Economics, University of Venice. Email: s.currarini@unive.it. Financial support through the TMR Grant no. ERB-4001CT950920 is acknowledged.
3. CORE, Université Catholique de Louvain, 34 Voie du Roman Pays, 1348 Louvain la Neuve, Belgium. Email: tulkens@core.ucl.ac.be. The research of this author is part of the 'CLIMNEG' program conducted at CORE under contract with the Belgian State, Prime Minister's Office (SSTC). CORE, Université Catholique de Louvain.
4. A notable exception is the paper by Haller and Holden (1997) on the effect of different ratification rules on countries' international bargaining power.
5. We abstract here from all inputs of production other than polluting discharges.
6. This framework is essentially the one used by Nakayama (1977), in which winning coalitions can choose the desired level of public goods and have to finance it proportionally to their relative incomes.
7. This game has been studied under the name 'Simultaneous Coalition Unanimity Game', see Yi (1997). Hart and Kurz also consider the more permissive 'delta' rule, allowing all players that have announced the same coalition to stay together.
8. In particular, defections from the grand coalition lead to the formation of a unique, smaller coalition. A similar and closely related assumption underlies the concept of *gamma core* studied in Chander and Tulkens (1997). We shall discuss the relation of the present chapter to their work in our conclusion.
9. We are here extending the notion of Strict Nash Equilibrium to coalitional deviations, considered in the Strong Nash Equilibrium concept. Intuitively, the strictness refinement requires that players can only do worse by changing their strategies from the equilibrium.

REFERENCES

Barrett, S. (1994), 'Self-enforcing international environmental agreements', *Oxford Economic Papers*, **46**, 878–94.

Carraro, C. and D. Siniscalco (1993), 'Strategies for the protection of the environment', *Journal of Public Economics*, **52**, 309–28.

Chander, P. and H. Tulkens (1992), 'Theoretical foundations of negotiations and cost sharing in transfrontier pollution models', *European Economic Review*, **36**, 388–98.

Chander, P. and H. Tulkens (1995), 'A core-theoretic solution for the design of cooperative agreements on transfrontier pollution', *International Tax and Public Finance*, **2(2)**, 279–94.

Chander, P. and H. Tulkens (1997), 'The core of an economy with multilateral externalities', *International Journal of Game Theory*, **26**, 379–401.

Haller, H. and S. Holden (1997), 'Ratification requirement and bargaining power', *International Economic Review*, **38(4)**, 825–52.

Hart, S. and M. Kurz (1983), 'Endogenous formation of coalitions', *Econometrica*, **51**, 1047–64.

Hirokawa, M. (1992), 'The equivalence of the cost share equilibria and the core of a voting game in a public goods economy', *Social Choice and Welfare*, **9**, 63–72.

Hoel, M. and K. Schneider (1997), 'Incentives to participate in an international environmental agreement', *Environmental and Resource Economics*, **9(2)**, 153–70.

Ito, Y. and M. Kaneko (1981), 'Ratio equilibrium in an economy with externalities', *Zeitschrift für Nationalökonomie*, **41(3–4)**, 279–94.

Kaitala, V., K. G. Maler, and H. Tulkens (1995), 'The acid rain game as a resource allocation process, with applications to negotiations between Finland, Russia and Estonia', *Scandinavian Journal of Economics*, **97(2)**, 325–43.

Kaneko, M. (1977), 'The ratio equilibrium and a voting game in a public goods economy', *Journal of Economic Theory*, **16**, 123–36.

Maler, K.G. (1989), 'The acid rain game', chapter 12 in H. Folmer and E. van Ierland (eds), *Valuations Methods and Policy Making in Environmental Economics*, Amsterdam: Elsevier, pp. 231–52.

Nakayama, M. (1977), 'Proportional income taxes and cores in a public goods economy', *Journal of Economic Theory*, **17**, 295–300.

Peleg, B. (1984), *Game-Theoretic Analysis of Voting in Committees*, Cambridge: Cambridge University Press.

Van den Nouweland, A., S. Tijs and M. Wooders (2002), 'Axiomatizations of ratio equilibria in public good economies', *Social Choice and Welfare*, **19(3)**, 627–36.

Yi, S. (1997) 'Stable coalition structures with externalities', *Games and Economic Behavior*, **20**, 201–37.

2. Can equity enhance efficiency? Some lessons from climate negotiations

Francesco Bosello, Barbara Buchner, Carlo Carraro and Davide Raggi

1. INTRODUCTION

In the last decades, the importance of international and global environmental problems, such as acid rain, the depletion of the ozone layer and the greenhouse effect, has increased continually. In the absence of a supranational authority which enforces environmental policies and regulations, emission reductions can only be achieved via voluntary initiatives and international cooperation. Given the global nature of the above environmental problems, an effective international agreement which implements these emission reductions has to involve as many countries as possible, or at least a number of countries which account for a large share of total emissions. This is particularly true for global warming whose effects and the mitigation policies subsequently required are pushed to an unprecedented spatial and time scale.

Unfortunately, broad participation is difficult to achieve (Carraro and Siniscalco, 1993). Given that emission control is costly and a 'clean' atmosphere is a public good, countries hardly have incentives to sign an agreement on greenhouse gases (GHG) emission control (the well known free-riding problem). Moreover, structural differences among countries (polluters most often do not suffer the highest damages) imply the difficulty of sharing the burden of emission reductions in a way that makes it convenient for most countries to sign the agreement (in some countries, abatement costs may not be smaller than the benefits from avoided damages).

These considerations lead to the conclusion that a global agreement on climate change policy (that is, an agreement signed by all world countries) is generally unrealistic and that emission reduction policies should focus on two interrelated objectives (IPCC 2001, Working Group 3, chapter 10): (i) on the one hand, a cost-effective reduction of emissions; (ii) on the other hand, ways of providing incentives for more countries to sign the agreement.

A recent strand of literature analyses the incentives underlying the emergence of international environmental cooperation and the formation of climate coalitions within the general framework of non-cooperative games. This literature highlights that 'self-enforcing agreements', that is, agreements based on profitable and stable coalitions, may emerge at the equilibrium (see, for example, Carraro and Siniscalco, 1993 and Barrett, 1994). However, in most studies, the size of stable coalitions remains limited for any functional specification of countries' welfare functions (Hoel, 1992; Barrett, 1994; Carraro and Siniscalco, 1993; Heal, 1994). Hence, the need to develop strategies which enhance the incentives to sign a climate agreement by making it profitable for most relevant countries and by offsetting their incentives to free-ride.

One of the ideas currently proposed in the debate on climate change policy is that more equitable agreements could be a way of increasing consensus and thus of having more signatories to the climate treaty. This idea is at the heart of many of the conclusions, based on the present state of knowledge on the economics of climate change, contained in the recent 2001 IPCC *Summary for Policymakers* from Working Group 3. However intuitive, there is no substantial analysis that a more equitable distribution of the burden of reducing GHG emissions would induce more countries to sign and ratify the Kyoto Protocol or another climate agreement. The goal of this chapter is exactly to address this issue and to assess whether increased equity enhances the likelihood that more countries – and above all the relevant countries – agree to sign and ratify a climate agreement.

Notice that, were the above conjecture true, we could conclude that equity enhances efficiency, because a larger number of relevant signatories (possibly the big emitters) obviously implies a larger amount of emission abatement.

The first step of our analysis is a careful examination of the self-enforcing properties of the Kyoto agreement. To achieve this goal, we use a revealed preference approach, that is, we start from the actual outcome of the Kyoto negotiations to identify countries' weights in the function defining the optimal cooperative solution. This enables us to assess whether the Kyoto agreement is stable (that is, no country has an incentive to free-ride, by not ratifying and/or implementing the Protocol).[1] Section 3 analyses the profitability and stability of the Kyoto agreement in two extreme situations. The first is when all emission reductions are undertaken domestically without using the so-called Kyoto flexibility mechanisms. The second is when emission reductions can also be undertaken using an emission trading scheme which involves all signatory countries without constraints (no ceilings). It has indeed been argued (see, for example, Eyckmans, 2001) that the possibility of emission trading, by increasing the cost-effectiveness of the agreement, also increases its stability (that is, incentives to free-ride are lower and more countries sign). Therefore, we will also assess this conjecture in the case of the Kyoto agreement.

In section 4, we carry out the same type of profitability and stability analysis by introducing equity. Three 'equitable' burden-sharing criteria – which are different from the one implicit in the emission abatement targets agreed to in Kyoto – are considered. These are: (i) the equalisation of average abatement costs; (ii) the equalisation of per capita abatement costs; and (iii) the equalisation of abatement costs on the GDP ratio.[2] For each of these criteria, the profitable and stable coalitions (within all possible coalition structures) are computed in order to verify whether more equity enhances the incentives for self-enforcing agreements to emerge.

The results achieved in Section 4 are not encouraging. Indeed, most coalition structures are neither stable, nor strongly profitable. Therefore, in Section 5 we develop a further alternative. Specifically, we complement the three 'equitable' burden sharing criteria with ex-post transfer policies designed to offset countries' incentives to free-ride. Can these transfer policies help in achieving a global agreement or something close to it? Which equity criterion enhances the effectiveness of these transfer mechanisms?

The surprising answer to these questions will be discussed in the concluding section of this chapter, which will also outline directions for further research.

2. PROFITABILITY AND STABILITY OF CLIMATE AGREEMENTS

Two profitability criteria and two stability criteria will be used to assess the self-enforcing properties of climate agreements. The definitions of profitability and stability have been derived directly from Carraro and Siniscalco (1993) (see also Eyckmans, 2001 and Yang, 2000 for recent applications to climate policy). We say that an agreement is *weakly profitable* if the sum of the individual payoffs of the signatories is larger than the sum of their payoffs when no agreement is signed. In this case, the agreement produces a surplus (overall benefits are larger than costs), but this surplus may not profit all signatories, that is, some countries may gain, others may lose. By contrast, an agreement is *strongly profitable* if the payoff of all signatories is larger when the agreement is signed and implemented than when no agreement is signed. Hence, each single participant obtains a net benefit from the agreement.

We say that an agreement is *internally stable* if there is no incentive to free-ride, that is, the payoff of each signatory is larger than the payoff he/she would obtain by defecting from the group of signatories (those who remain are supposed to keep cooperating even after the defection). Finally, an agreement is *stable* if there is no incentive to free-ride and no incentive to join the group of signatories, that is, the payoff to those countries that are not signatories is larger than the one they would achieve by signing the agreement.

Notice that these four criteria are increasingly demanding. Stability implies internal stability which implies strong profitability which implies weak profitability (see Botteon and Carraro, 1997a). In particular, profitability is a necessary condition for stability. Also notice that a stable agreement is nothing more than a Nash equilibrium agreement (D'Aspremont et al., 1983 and Carraro and Marchiori, 2003). See the Appendix for a formal presentation of the above definitions and results.

Following recent suggestions coming from the theoretical literature (Carraro, 1998), we do not only consider the possibility that countries agree on a single climate treaty, but we also allow countries to negotiate on different tables and to form different regional agreements (similarly to what happens in trade negotiations). Therefore, both single and multiple coalition structures will be analysed. In the case of multiple coalitions, the definition of stability is slightly more complex because agreements should also be intra-coalitionally stable (Yi, 1997). In other words, there should be no incentives to leave one coalition to join a different one.

Therefore, in this chapter, we assess the profitability and stability of all possible coalition structures that can emerge on the basis of the three equity criteria mentioned above. As a consequence, we evaluate both the incentives to sign a Kyoto-type agreement (that is, whether Annex I countries are willing to sign and ratify a climate agreement when the burden sharing is changed) and the incentives to sign any other climate agreements (for each given burden-sharing rule).

3. INCENTIVES TO SIGN AND RATIFY THE KYOTO PROTOCOL

The goal of this section is to analyse the profitability and stability of the Kyoto agreement, both when all emission reductions are undertaken domestically without using the so-called Kyoto flexibility mechanisms, and when emission reductions can also be undertaken using an unconstrained emission trading scheme which involves all signatory countries.

The analysis is carried out using the original version of the RICE model (Nordhaus and Yang, 1996). The RICE model is a single sector optimal growth model that has been extended to incorporate the interactions between economic activities and climate. One such model has been developed for each macro region into which the world is divided (USA, Japan, Europe, China, Former Soviet Union, and Rest of the World). Within each region a central planner chooses the optimal paths of fixed investment and emission abatement that maximise the present value of per capita consumption. Output (net of climate change) is used for investment and consumption and is produced according to a constant returns Cobb–Douglas technology, which combines the inputs from capital and labour with the level of technology. Population (taken to be equal to full employment) and technology levels grow over time in an exogenous fashion, whereas capital accumulation is governed by the optimal rate of investment. There is a wedge between output gross and net of climate change effects, the size of which is dependent upon the amount of abatement (rate of emission reduction) as well as the change in global temperature. The model is completed by three equations representing emissions (which are related to output and abatement), carbon cycle (which relates concentrations to emissions), and climate module (which relates the change in temperature relative to 1990 levels to carbon concentrations) respectively.

As said, the chapter focuses on long-term incentives to sign a climate agreement. Therefore, we need to define the outcome of climate negotiations beyond the first commitment period. In this chapter, we adopt the so-called 'Kyoto forever' hypothesis (see, for example, Manne and Richels, 1999 among others), namely we assume that the abatement targets agreed upon in Kyoto are binding until the end of this century. In other words, all Annex I countries are assumed to meet the Kyoto constraints from 2010 onward.[3] This is already a standard practice adopted in most economic analyses of climate policy (although there exist studies where different assumptions are made; see, for example, the study by Ciscar and Soria in Chapter 4). We use the 'Kyoto forever' hypothesis not because it represents a realistic scenario, but as a benchmark with respect to which policy alternatives can be compared.[4] Nonetheless, the adoption of this scenario helps also to understand some underlying motivations of the Kyoto agreement:

- Although being a scenario with an overall weak objective (700 ppmv), all the emission reduction requirements are focused on the industrialised countries – the Annex I countries – since the other regions are allowed to follow their business as usual paths until 2100. In this sense, there is a kind of equity built into the Kyoto forever scenario.
- Being very penalising for Annex I if only domestic policies and measures are allowed, the scenario becomes advantageous as soon as emissions trading is allowed. The reason is that in this case, by leaving

the other countries outside the coalition, the Annex I countries can buy emissions at a low cost. Highlighting the low permit price for Annex I countries, the scenario thus provides an explanation of why the Non-Annex I countries are excluded from emission reduction commitments.[5]

Given the RICE representation of the economic system in different world regions and the related impacts on climate, we solved the joint maximisation process through which countries determine cooperative emission levels (and as a consequence emission reduction targets). Our business as usual corresponds to the non-cooperative case in which countries set emission levels (and other decision variables) by maximising their own welfare function given the policy decisions taken by the other countries.

To identify the implicit weights in the joint maximisation process which lead to the cooperative outcome, we used an 'inverse optimisation approach' (see, for example, Carraro, 1988, 1989, 1997), that is, we iteratively computed the weights in the joint welfare function until each region's optimal investment and abatement levels are such as to yield the emission targets agreed in Kyoto. In this way, the solution of the maximisation process can replicate (a) the emission abatement levels for each Annex I country and (b) the share of the abatement costs borne by Annex I and by Non-Annex I countries.

The weights implicit in the 'Kyoto forever agreement' are shown in Table 2.1. Notice that the largest bargaining powers are associated with China and the Rest of the World. The reason for this result is that in the 'Kyoto forever' scenario binding emission targets are imposed only on industrialised countries, whereas China and the Rest of the World are not committed to reduce their emissions. FSU (the Former Soviet Union), which is often considered as a 'winner' of Kyoto negotiations because of 'hot air', has a low bargaining power, because our analysis adopts a long-term perspective in which short-term 'hot air' has little weight. These results also confirm that some forms of equity are already embodied in the 'Kyoto forever' scenario.

Given the weights of Table 2.1, we can move on to the second step of our analysis, namely the analysis of the self-enforcing features of the 'Kyoto forever agreement'. In order to assess the profitability and stability of this 'agreement', we had to compare the payoffs which Annex I countries achieve when they cooperate, to the payoffs when no cooperation takes place and/or when a different agreement is signed (this second comparison is crucial in assessing the free-riding incentives and therefore the stability of the 'Kyoto forever agreement'. See the Appendix).

To achieve this goal, we computed the costs and benefits of all possible

Table 2.1   Weights revealed by the 'Kyoto forever agreement'

Country	Weights
USA	0.10655
Japan	0.03707
EU	0.03848
China	0.51732
FSU	0.02289
Rest of World	0.27769

climate agreements (that is, coalition structures. See Carraro and Marchiori, 2003). These costs and benefits can be obtained by solving the game between the six regions of RICE using a numerical iterative algorithm. In the non-cooperative case (our business-as-usual), the equilibrium concept used to solve the game is the usual Nash equilibrium. By contrast, when a coalition forms, it is assumed that countries which sign the agreement maximise their joint welfare and play Nash against the free-riding countries. The resulting equilibrium is equivalent to the PANE-equilibrium proposed in Chander and Tulkens (1995, 1997).[6]

The results of our optimisation experiments, where 203 different coalition structures have been examined, can be summarised as follows:

1.   The 'Kyoto forever agreement' is neither weakly nor strongly profitable. The reason is that the total surplus provided by the agreement from now to 2100 is slightly negative. Moreover, all Annex I regions would lose from signing the agreement (see Table 2.2). This result is not surprising as cooperation may not be beneficial in the presence of free-riders (see, for example, Carraro and Siniscalco, 1993; Chander and Tulkens, 1997; Carraro and Marchiori, 2003).[7] When emission trading is allowed for, given the cost-effectiveness properties of unconstrained emission trading, losses are lower; this result confirms the theoretical analysis in Chander et al. (1999) but the 'Kyoto forever agreement' still remains neither weakly nor strongly profitable (see Table 2.2 again).[8] The reason is that the emission levels attained by Non-Annex I countries in the long run are very large.[9] Hence, signatory countries pay the cost of emission abatement without getting any benefits. Notice that, in the presence of emission trading, the winner would be Japan, whereas the USA, the EU and the FSU would keep losing from signing the agreement. The reason is that Japan greatly benefits from Annex I emission trading because it is the country with the highest marginal abatement costs.

Table 2.2.   Winners and losers under the 'Kyoto forever agreement'

	Relative net gains (%)			
	USA	Japan	Europe	FSU
'Kyoto forever' with domestic abatement only	−0.021	−0.015	−0.009	−0.020
'Kyoto forever' with emission trading	−0.020	+0.008	−0.004	−0.003

Note: Benefits from avoided damages minus abatement costs in the case of 'Kyoto forever' vs. the case of no-cooperation.

Table 2.3   Incentives to free-ride on the 'Kyoto forever agreement'.

	Relative net gains (%)			
	USA	Japan	Europe	FSU
'Kyoto forever' with domestic abatement only	−0.021	−0.015	−0.010	−0.032
'Kyoto forever' with emission trading	−0.018	+0.007	−0.005	−0.020

Note: Benefits from avoided damages minus abatement costs in the case of 'Kyoto forever' vs. the case of individual free-riding.

2.   In addition, the 'Kyoto forever agreement' is neither stable, nor internally stable. Hence, at least one country has an incentive to free-ride on the other Annex I countries' abatement efforts. Both when emission reductions are only domestic and when emission trading is allowed, Russia and the USA have the largest incentive to free-ride (see Table 2.3). In the absence of a market for emission permits, those two countries are closely followed by Japan. However, being the country that benefits most from emissions trading, Japan is also the one without any incentives to free-ride after the implementation of the trading scheme.

3.   The burden-sharing distribution implicit in the 'Kyoto forever agreement' and represented by the weights of Table 2.1 can lead to some weakly profitable agreements (see Table 2.4) even though the 'Kyoto forever agreement' itself is not weakly profitable, as seen above. However, no coalition structure (that is, no agreement) is either strongly profitable, or stable. The situation improves in the presence of emission trading. Indeed, the share of both weakly and strongly

Table 2.4   Share of profitable and stable coalitions with the 'Kyoto forever' burden sharing (%)

	Weakly profitable	Strongly profitable	Internally stable	Stable
'Kyoto forever' with domestic abatement only	0.5	0	0	0
'Kyoto forever' with emission trading	43.3	5.9	5.9	1 over 203

profitable and internally stable coalitions increases when emission trading is allowed. Moreover, one coalition structure (over the 203 possible coalition structures) becomes both internally and externally stable. The improved profitability and stability in the presence of emission trading confirms the results contained in Eyckmans (2001).

4.   The possibility of forming multiple coalitions, rather than negotiating on a single agreement, is of no help. Indeed, no coalition structure with multiple coalitions is stable using the 'Kyoto forever' burden-sharing rule. The only stable coalition structure, a Nash equilibrium of the game in which countries decide whether or not to join the coalition under the 'Kyoto forever' burden-sharing rule, is formed by a coalition of four countries and by two free-riders. However, the four countries are not the Annex I countries, but Japan, China, FSU and the Rest of the World. The reason for this result lies in the incentives for cooperation provided by emission trading which favour those countries with the largest differences in marginal abatement costs: in our case, Japan on the one hand, and China, FSU, and the Rest of the World on the other. The incentive for developing countries to participate in the agreement is further increased by the high damages they would suffer from the impacts of climate changes.

If one believes in the features of the RICE model, the above results cast some doubt on the equity properties of the burden-sharing criterion which is implicit in the 'Kyoto forever' scenario. Indeed, it may be argued that a more equitable distribution of the burden of controlling GHG emissions would induce all or almost all countries to sign and ratify a climate agreement. The validity of this conjecture will be explored in the next section.

4. EQUITY CRITERIA AND THE STRUCTURE OF EQUILIBRIUM AGREEMENTS

In this section, the analysis of the profitability and stability of alternative coalition structures is carried out by using three burden-sharing criteria which are different from the one implicit in the emission abatement targets of the 'Kyoto forever' scenario. The goal is to check whether more equity induces more countries to sign a climate agreement, thus enhancing efficiency.

The background of the equity debate in mitigating the risks of global climate change can be found in the 1992 UN Framework Convention on Climate Change. Article 3 states that the parties have to engage in the protection of the climate system with 'common but differentiated responsibilities'. This phrase characterises the real beginning of the search for equity proposals, both in the international and intergenerational range. Since the debate about the adequacy of scope and timing of emission reduction commitments is still ongoing, it becomes more and more obvious that the definition of 'fairness' or 'equity' in the context of climate change control is not a straightforward task. Different preconditions and characteristics of the countries, strong and diverse self-interests, incentives to free-ride as well as the special features of climate change, render the approval and acceptance of equity criteria difficult. There exist a number of proposals regarding what could constitute equity in GHG mitigation. Corresponding to the wide variety of equity principles, a range of possible burden-sharing rules emerged.[10]

Equity proposals can usually be classified by distinguishing whether the applied equity criterion has been chosen according to the initial allocation of emissions ('allocation-based equity criteria'), according to the final outcome of the implementation of the policy instruments ('outcome-based equity criteria') or according to the process by which the criterion has been chosen ('process-based equity criteria').[11]

Tables 2.5 to 2.7 below summarise the main features of these three different groups of equity proposals and describe the way in which they are usually implemented. The tables are based on suggestions provided in the literature, among others by Cazorla and Toman (2000), Tol (2001), Rose and Stevens (1993), Rose et al. (1998) and Schmidt and Koschel (1998).

Notice that 'allocation-based equity criteria' are implemented with reference to the abatement cost function. They are the dominating concepts used and examined in the literature (cf. Eyckmans and Cornillie, 2000; Schmidt and Koschel, 1998), because they can be easily applied even without specifying the welfare function for each country. Nevertheless, a number of other possible equity formulations emerged, mainly related to a redistribution of total welfare. For example, Tol (2001) analyses the impacts of three equity concepts based on welfare distribution. The first relates to Kant with a 'Rawlsian touch' ('Do not do to others what you do not want to be done to you', whereby the 'others' are the least well-off regions, thus 'act as if the impact on the worst-off country is your own'). The second can be seen as a principle based on Varian's no-envy criterion (for all regions, at all times, the sum of costs of emissions reductions and the costs of climate change should be equal; income distribution should be at the same level as it would have been without climate policy). The third maximises a global welfare function which explicitly includes an inequality aversion.

The reasons why most empirical studies focus on cost-related equity concepts are their simple implementation and the possibility of comparing the

Table 2.5 Allocation-based equity criteria

Equity principle	Definition	Implied burden-sharing rule
Egalitarian	All people have an equal right to pollute and to be protected from pollution.	Equal emissions reductions (abatement costs) per capita (in proportion to population or historic responsibilities). Implementation criterion: *Equal per capita abatement costs*
Ability to pay	Abatement costs should vary directly with economic circumstances and national well-being.	Equal emissions reductions (abatement costs) per unit GDP Implementation criterion: *Equal abatement costs per unit of GDP*
Sovereignty[1]	All nations have an equal right to pollute and to be protected from pollution.	Grandfathering (equal emissions reductions or abatement costs in proportion to emissions). Implementation criterion: *Equal average abatement costs*

Notes: 1. Closely related to the equity principle of sovereignty is the 'Polluter Pays Principle' which also says that the abatement burden has to be allocated corresponding to emissions (which may include historical emissions). As in the case of sovereignty, equal emissions reductions (abatement costs) in proportion to emission levels are required. Since this principle almost coincides with the principle of sovereignty, only rarely is a distinction made between them in the literature (see, for example, Cazorla and Toman, 2000). Due to the similarities we also decided not to take it into account explicitly but to deal with it implicitly through the sovereignty equity concept.

Source: Adapted from Cazorla and Toman (2000), Tol (2001), Rose and Stevens (1993), Rose et al. (1998) and Schmidt and Koschel (1998).

Table 2.6   Outcome-based equity criteria

Equity principle	Definition	Implied burden-sharing rule
Horizontal	All nations have the right to be treated equally both concerning emission rights and burden-sharing responsibilities.	Welfare changes across nations such that welfare costs or net abatement costs as a proportion of GDP or of population are the same in each country. Implementation criterion: *Equal welfare costs per unit of GDP or per capita*
Vertical	Welfare gains should vary inversely with national economic well-being; welfare losses should vary directly with GDP. The greater the ability to pay, the greater the economic burden.	Emissions reductions such that net abatement costs grow with GDP. Implementation criterion: *Equal abatement costs per unit of GDP*
Compensation (Pareto rule)	'Winners' should compensate 'losers' so that both are better off after mitigation.	Distribute abatement costs so that no nation suffers a net loss of welfare. Implementation criterion: *Strong profitability*

Source: Adapted from Cazorla and Toman (2000), Tol (2001), Rose and Stevens (1993), Rose et al. (1998) and Schmidt and Koschel (1998).

results across studies. Indeed, criteria based on welfare distribution depend on the specification of the welfare function. Existing specifications largely differ across models. In some models, the welfare function is not even defined. By contrast, the specification of abatement costs, and in particular of marginal abatement costs, is subject to much lower variability across models.

For these same reasons, in this chapter we also focus on cost-related equity concepts. However, we do not limit our analysis to ex-ante 'allocation-based equity criteria' (Egalitarian, Ability-to-pay and Sovereignty), but we rather require that these criteria also hold ex post. In other words, we compute profitable and stable coalition structures under the constraint that either one of the following equity criteria holds:

1.   Equal average abatement costs
2.   Equal per capita abatement costs
3.   Equal abatement costs per unit of GDP

Table 2.7   Process-based equity criteria

Equity principle	Definition	Implied burden-sharing rule
Rawls' max-min	The welfare of the worst-off nation should be maximised, thus maximise the net benefit to the poorest nations.	Distribute largest proportion of net welfare change to poorest nations; majority of emissions reductions (abatement costs) imposed on wealthier nations.
Market justice	The market is 'fair', thus make greater use of markets.	Distribute emissions reductions to highest bidder; lowest net abatement costs by using flexible mechanisms (ET).
Consensus	The international negotiation process is fair, thus seek a political solution promoting stability.	Distribute abatement costs (power weighted) so the majority of nations are satisfied.
Sovereign bargaining	Principles of fairness emerge endogenously as a result of multistage negotiations.	Distribute abatement costs according to equity principles that result from international bargaining and negotiation over time.
Kantian allocation rule[1]	Each country chooses an abatement level at least as large as the uniform abatement level it would like all countries to undertake.	Differentiate emissions reductions by country's preferred world abatement, possibly in tiers or groups.

Note: [1] According to Rose et al. (1998) this rule can be considered roughly equal to the principle of sovereignty plus elements of the principle of consensus.

Source: Adapted from Cazorla and Toman (2000), Tol (2001), Rose and Stevens (1993), Rose et al. (1998) and Schmidt and Koschel (1998).

Therefore, the equity criteria adopted in this chapter are 'outcome based'. As in the previous section, for each equity criterion, all 203 possible coalition structures have been computed and countries' payoffs compared in order to assess the profitability and stability of each coalition structure. The total amount of abatement in the alternative cases, that is, in the climate agreements based on the three equity rules, is the same as under the 'Kyoto forever' hypothesis.[12]

The results of our optimisation experiments are presented in Tables 2.8, 2.9, 2.10 and 2.11. They can be summarised as follows:

1. All three outcome-based equity criteria increase the probability that a climate agreement yields a surplus. Indeed, the share of weakly profitable coalition structures is much larger with the three new equity criteria than with the burden-sharing rule implicit in the 'Kyoto forever agreement' (see Table 2.8). Nevertheless, the possibility of regional agreements does not improve the results: no multiple coalition structure is weakly profitable.
2. The situation is less positive when the more restrictive criterion of strong profitability is used. Indeed, even the three equity criteria proposed above fail to guarantee a large number of strongly profitable coalition structures. Nonetheless, two of the proposed equity criteria imply that the share of strongly profitable coalition structures is larger than with the burden-sharing rule implicit in the 'Kyoto forever' scenario (see Table 2.9). When the goal is strong profitability, multiple coalitions again do not provide an incentive structure better than the one provided by single coalitions.
3. In addition, no coalition structure with multiple coalitions is internally stable (see Table 2.10). Hence, the only coalition structures which could be stable are the ones in which a single coalition forms. However, the share of single coalitions which are both strongly profitable and internally stable further decreases for all burden-sharing criteria (see Table 2.10 again). Again, only two equity criteria (equal per capita abatement costs and equal abatement costs per unit of GDP) show better results than the burden-sharing rule implicit in the 'Kyoto forever agreement'.
4. As a consequence, only very few coalition structures are likely to be stable, that is, without any incentives to leave or to enter the coalition. As shown by Table 2.11, only one coalition is both profitable and stable, namely it emerges as an equilibrium of the game in which countries non-cooperatively decide whether or not to join the coalition. This equilibrium coalition structure is formed by a coalition of three countries and by three free-riders. It can be obtained only if ex-ante all countries agree that abatement efforts must be such as equalise abatement costs per capita. This coalition is formed by Japan, the FSU and the Rest of the World.

Summing up, *the adoption of more equitable burden-sharing rules enhances the profitability of a climate agreement but not its stability, that is, equity improves the distribution of costs and benefits but does not seem to be effective in offsetting the incentives to free-ride.*

Two possible ways of addressing the problem are available. First, policy strategies could be designed to further redistribute the surplus provided by the cooperative behaviour within a coalition. This would increase the

Table 2.8   *Weak profitability: share of weakly profitable coalitions for each burden-sharing criterion (%)*

	Single coalitions	Multiple coalitions	Total percentage of coalitions
'Kyoto forever' implicit burden sharing	1.7	0	0.5
Equal average abatement costs	29.3	0	8.4
Equal per capita abatement costs	32.8	0	9.4
Equal abatement costs per unit of GDP	32.8	0	9.4

Table 2.9   *Strong profitability: share of strongly profitable coalitions for each burden-sharing criterion (%)*

	Single coalitions	Multiple coalitions	Total percentage of coalitions
'Kyoto forever' implicit burden sharing	0	0	0
Equal average abatement costs	0	0	0
Equal per capita abatement costs	6.9	0	2.0
Equal abatement costs per unit of GDP	1.7	0	0.5

Table 2.10   *Internal stability: share of internally stable coalitions for each burden-sharing criterion (%)*

	Single coalitions	Multiple coalitions	Total percentage of coalitions
'Kyoto forever' implicit burden sharing	0	0	0
Equal average abatement costs	0	0	0
Equal per capita abatement costs	3.4	0	1.0
Equal abatement costs per unit of GDP	1.7	0	0.5

Table 2.11   *Stability: number of stable coalitions for each burden-sharing criterion*

	Single coalitions	Multiple coalitions	Total number of coalitions
'Kyoto forever' implicit burden sharing	0	0	0
Equal average abatement costs	0	0	0
Equal per capita abatement costs	1	0	1
Equal abatement costs per unit of GDP	0	0	0

number of strongly profitable coalitions and hence the probabilities of identifying a stable coalition structure. Transfer schemes designed to make a climate agreement profitable to all countries have been proposed, for example in Chander and Tulkens (1997) and applied to climate models in Weyant (1999) or Eyckmans (2001).[13] A more detailed analysis of how equity criteria can be used to achieve strong profitability (*fairness* in their wording) is contained in Hourcade and Gilotte (2001).

Second, policy strategies could be designed to redistribute the surplus achieved by internally stable coalitions with the goal of inducing other countries to enter the coalition. This idea is proposed and analysed in Carraro and Siniscalco (1993) where it is shown that, with *symmetric* countries, transfer mechanisms can be used to broaden the coalition only if all countries in the initial, internally stable coalition are committed to cooperation once the transfer scheme is adopted. However, in Botteon and Carraro (1997a) a counter-example is provided in which *asymmetric* countries could use the surplus of cooperation achieved by a stable coalition to move to a grand coalition through appropriate transfers and without any form of commitment.

In the next section, we will explore this second possibility. The first – transfers to increase the number of strongly profitable coalitions – has previously been analysed in other papers (above all in Yang, 2000 and in Eyckmans and Tulkens, 1999, where a version of the RICE model is also used).

5. EQUITY, TRANSFERS AND GLOBAL AGREEMENTS

The conditions required for transfers to achieve the goal of expanding a coalition are presented in the Appendix. Here we would like to stress that, at equilibrium:

- Transfers are self-financed, that is, countries are allowed to transfer only the surplus yielded by their cooperation. Hence, we analyse how weakly and strongly profitable coalitions can be broadened through a transfer mechanism.
- The transfer mechanism is Pareto optimal, that is, all countries gain from using transfers to broaden the coalition.

Given this latter restriction, the broadened coalition is also weakly or strongly profitable. However, self-financing implies that there may not be enough resources to offset the free-riding incentives of all countries which are not in the initial, internally stable coalition. Finally, notice that even countries in the initial stable coalition may have an incentive to free-ride when other countries join. Hence, the transfer mechanism must also be such as to offset these latter incentives to free-ride.

Table 2.12 presents our results. The first column shows the initial, internally stable coalitions for each of the three burden-sharing criteria analysed in the previous section. The second column shows the largest internally stable coalition that can be achieved through a transfer mechanism starting from the corresponding initial, internally stable coalition.

Table 2.12   Internally stable coalitions before and after the use of transfers

	Internally stable coalitions without and with transfers	
	Internally stable coalitions before transfers	Internally stable coalitions after transfers
Equalisation of average abatement costs	0	0
Equalisation of abatement costs/ GDP	USA + China	USA + China + Rest of the World
Equalisation of per capita abatement costs	EU + China + Rest of the World	USA + EU + China + Rest of the World
	Japan + FSU + Rest of the World	USA + Japan + EU + FSU + Rest of the World

Our results can be summarised as follows:

1. No transfer mechanism and no ex-ante burden-sharing criterion (of the three that we considered) yields an incentive structure or enough resources to achieve the grand coalition, that is, a global agreement on climate change. At least one region free-rides on the agreement.
2. The burden-sharing criteria that are most effective in guaranteeing the achievement of a large coalition with no free-riding incentive are the equalisation of per capita abatement costs and the equalisation of abatement costs per unit of GDP. For example, with the former, a coalition formed by Japan, the FSU and the Rest of the World can offset the free-riding incentives of the EU and the USA. With the latter, a coalition formed by China and the USA can induce the Rest of the World to sign the climate agreement. Notice that the USA needs a compensating transfer to enter a coalition which forms according to the criterion

of equal per capita abatement costs, whereas they belong to the initially stable coalitions if the burden-sharing criterion is equal abatement costs per unit of GDP. This is quite intuitive: the USA has high per capita emissions, but relatively small emissions per unit of GDP.

Nonetheless, a stable global agreement cannot be achieved. Hence, we wonder whether the introduction of emission trading, regardless of the ex-ante burden-sharing criterion, can provide enough resources which, once transferred to free-riding countries, can induce them to sign the climate agreement.[14] The answer to this question is provided by the following two propositions, which summarise our numerical results:

Proposition 1: *Regardless of the ex-ante burden-sharing criterion (equity), and regardless of the initial, internally stable coalition, the equalisation of marginal abatement costs, coupled with an appropriately designed ex-post transfer mechanism, can lead to a grand coalition, that is, a global climate agreement signed by all countries or regions, which is stable.*

In other words, through emission trading and transfers, *all* internally stable coalitions can be broadened to achieve a stable grand coalition. By using a twofold transfer mechanism, one designed to transform a weakly profitable coalition into a strongly profitable one (that is, as in Gilotte, 2001), and a second one designed to make it internally stable, we achieve an even stronger conclusion:

Proposition 2: *The result of Proposition 1 holds for all initial weakly profitable coalitions.*[15]

The list of all weakly and strongly profitable coalitions is provided in Table 2.13. Starting from any of these coalition structures, and applying an unconstrained trading scheme jointly with appropriate transfer mechanisms, it is possible to achieve a stable grand coalition.

There is a major weakness in the above conclusions, which derives from the specification of the RICE model. Most of the resources to fund the transfer mechanism which helps to achieve the grand coalition do not come from the USA or the EU, but from Japan, China and the Rest of the World. The example shown in Table 2.14 can help us to show why this is.

Let us assume that the EU and the Rest of the World form the initially stable coalition. A different initially stable coalition would lead to similar conclusions. Step 1 analyses the profitability and stability of the coalition formed by the EU and the Rest of the World using the definitions provided in Section 2. It is easy to see that the coalition is weakly profitable. The

Table 2.13   Weakly and strongly profitable coalitions

Coalitions that can be broadened into the grand coalition by means of transfers	
JPN + EU + CHN + FSU + ROW	Weakly profitable
EU + CHN + FSU + ROW	Weakly profitable
EU + FSU + ROW	Weakly profitable
EU + ROW	Weakly profitable
EU + CHN + ROW	Weakly profitable
EU + CHN	Weakly profitable
EU + CHN + FSU	Weakly profitable
JPN + EU + FSU + ROW	Weakly profitable
JPN + EU + ROW	Weakly profitable
JPN + EU + CHN + ROW	Weakly profitable
JPN + EU + CHN	Weakly profitable
JPN + EU + CHN + FSU	Weakly profitable
USA + EU + CHN + FSU + ROW	Weakly profitable
USA + CHN + FSU + ROW	Weakly profitable
USA + FSU + ROW	Weakly profitable
USA + ROW	Weakly profitable
USA + CHN + ROW	Weakly profitable
USA + CHN	Weakly profitable
USA + CHN + FSU	Weakly profitable
USA + EU + FSU + ROW	Weakly profitable
USA + EU + ROW	Weakly profitable
USA + EU + CHN + ROW	Weakly profitable
USA + JPN + CHN + FSU + ROW	Weakly profitable
USA + JPN + FSU + ROW	Weakly profitable
USA + JPN + ROW	Weakly profitable
USA + JPN + CHN + ROW	Weakly profitable
USA + JPN + CHN	Weakly profitable
USA + JPN + CHN + FSU	Weakly profitable
USA + JPN + EU + FSU + ROW	Weakly profitable
USA + JPN + EU + ROW	Weakly profitable
USA + JPN + EU + CHN + ROW	Weakly profitable
CHN + FSU	Strongly profitable
FSU + ROW	Strongly profitable
CHN + ROW	Strongly profitable
JPN + CHN + ROW	Strongly profitable
JPN + CHN	Strongly profitable
JPN + ROW	Strongly profitable
CHN + FSU + ROW	Strongly profitable
JPN + CHN + FSU	Strongly profitable
JPN + FSU + ROW	Strongly profitable
JPN + CHN + FSU + ROW	Strongly profitable

Table 2.14 *Incentive structure and transfer mechanisms to achieve a global agreement when the EU and the ROW form the initial internally stable coalition (in welfare units)*

Step 1	USA	Japan	EU	China	FSU	Rest of the World
Profitability $P_i(s) - P_i(\theta)$			-0.124			5.488
Internal stability $Q_i(s \cup i) - P_i(s)$			0.126			-5.488
External stability $P_f(s \cup i) - Q_f(s)$	-0.223	0.152		0.504	0.17	

Step 2	USA	Japan	EU	China	FSU	Rest of the World
Profitability $P_f(s) - P_f(\theta)$		0.155	-0.117	0.322	0.195	5.793
Internal stability $Q_f(s \cup i) - P_f(s)$		-0.146	0.139	-0.3	-0.188	-5.523
External stability $P_f(s \cup i) - Q_f(s)$	-0.227					

Step 3	USA	Japan	EU	China	FSU	Rest of the World
Profitability $P_f(s) - P_f(\theta)$	-0.21	0.174	-0.075	0.186	0.19	5.742
Internal stability $Q_f(s \cup i) - P_f(s)$	0.227	-0.158	0.113	-0.149	-0.18	-5.36

surplus can thus be used to make it both strongly profitable and internally stable. However, it would not be externally stable. Japan, China and the FSU would like to join. If the three countries enter the coalition, one of the previous participating countries (the EU) will wish to exit the coalition. Hence, transfers can be used to stabilise the coalition formed by Japan, the EU, China, the FSU and the Rest of the World (Step 2). Further transfers are necessary to induce the USA to enter the coalition (Step 3). This is certainly feasible, because the benefit achieved by the Rest of the World in the grand coalition is large and can easily be used to compensate the free-riding incentive of the EU and the USA (0.227 and 0.113 respectively). However, what is odd is that the EU and the USA should receive transfers rather than transferring resources. Of course, we could design a transfer mechanism where resources flow from developed to developing countries. However, we would like to stress that, given the structure of RICE, most gains from a climate agreement go to the FSU, China and the Rest of the World – because they suffer more than the other regions from climate change impacts – which implies that these countries have an incentive to induce the others to participate in the global agreement.

The realism of this result is obviously open to debate. However, we do not believe that this result undermines the general conclusions achieved above; it simply calls for additional analyses of the incentive structure of climate agreements undertaken using models different from RICE.

6.   CONCLUSIONS

Previous sections have analysed the incentive structure of different types of climate agreements using the RICE model as the device for representing the interactions between economic and climate variables. First, we focused on the 'Kyoto forever agreement', which we analysed for profitability and stability. The conclusion is that almost all Annex I countries lose by signing the agreement and that more than one of these countries has an incentive to free-ride, that is, the net benefit of letting other countries reduce emissions is larger than the net benefit of reducing emissions. Of course, net benefits take into account the averted damage from climate change at least as far as this is represented in RICE.

Second, we analysed the conjecture that a more equitable ex-post distribution of the burden of reducing emissions could enhance the incentives for more countries – particularly big emitters – to accept an emission reduction scheme defined within an international climate agreement. Our optimisation experiments only partly support this conjecture. Even though equitable burden-sharing rules provide better incentives to sign and ratify a climate agreement than the burden-sharing rule which is implicit in the 'Kyoto forever' scenario, a stable agreement cannot generally be achieved, that is, equity seems to enhance the profitability of climate agreements but it does not offset the incentives to free-ride.

Third, we verify whether there exists a transfer mechanism that could help to broaden an initial stable, but partial, coalition achieved by agreeing on an equitable burden-sharing scheme. Our results suggest that transfers can indeed help to broaden a given coalition. However, the grand coalition could not be achieved, at least with the three equity rules considered in this chapter (equal average abatement costs, equal per capita abatement costs and equal abatement costs per unit of GDP).

The only strategy which we showed could achieve a stable global agreement is a policy mix in which global emission trading is coupled with a transfer mechanism designed to offset ex-post incentives to free-ride. This policy mix can achieve a stable global agreement whatever the initial weakly profitable coalition.

As a consequence, our results seem to suggest that an excessive focus on equity rules is not fruitful. It is more effective to minimise overall abatement costs via emission trading and then use the resulting surplus to provide incentives for free-riding countries to join the initial coalition.

The above results are obviously very preliminary. First, we compared only three equity rules. Other criteria could produce different results, even though the equity rules applied in this chapter encompass most of the empirical rules likely to be proposed. Second, and most importantly, all results crucially depend on the specification of the RICE model and on its way of assessing the costs and benefits of emission abatement. It is well known that the RICE model is a very useful but simplified representation of the economic system and that its environmental components are very limited. Therefore, it would be important to check whether our results are robust with respect to different model specifications. In particular, results are sensitive to the specification of the damage function and to the long-run dynamics of the model. A lower perception of damage from climate change in developing countries would reduce the benefits of GHG emission control policies in these countries and therefore their incentives to join a coalition and to contribute to transfer schemes.

APPENDIX

An economic model of international agreements on CO_2 emission reduction

Consider n countries ($n \geq 2$) that interact in a common environment and bargain over emission control of a specific pollutant. Let $W_i(x_1...x_n)$ be a country's welfare function, where x_i, $i=1, 2,..., n$, denotes a vector containing country i's emissions and all other economic variables affecting abatement costs and the environmental damage perceived in each country. The function $W_i(.)$, $i=1, 2,..., n$, captures countries' interaction in a global environment, as welfare depends on all countries' emissions as well as on other transnational variables (that is, trade policy variables). Let $P_i(s)$ denote the value of country i's welfare when it decides to join the coalition s, whereas $Q_i(s)$ is the value of its welfare when country i does not join the coalition s. Let us assume that only one coalition can be formed. Conditions which hold when multiple coalitions form can be found in Yang (2000) and Carraro and Marchiori (2003).

As the focus of this section is to analyse the stability of coalitions, the only argument of the value of the welfare function is the identity and number of cooperating countries. However, it is implicit that all other relevant variables in RICE, including emissions and policy decisions in other countries, enter country i's welfare function. Hence $P_i(\emptyset)$, $i=1, 2,..., n$, is a country's non-cooperative payoff (the non-cooperative Nash equilibrium payoff), whereas $P_i(S)$ is country i's payoff when all countries decide to cooperate (the grand coalition S is formed).

Notice that when a country joins the environmental coalition, it determines its optimal emission level by maximising a function reflecting the agreed-upon burden sharing rule (that is, in the case of the Nash bargaining rule, emissions are determined by maximising the product of the deviation of cooperative countries' emissions from the non-cooperative level). When a country does not join the coalition, it sets emissions by maximising its own welfare function given the emissions levels of all other countries (emissions are therefore defined by its own best-reply function). This behavioural assumption defines the concept of γ-equilibrium (Chander and Tulkens, 1997).

Two conditions must be met for an environmental coalition to be self-enforcing (see, for example, Carraro and Siniscalco, 1993 and Barrett, 1994). First, the coalition must be profitable, that is each country $i \in s$ gains from joining the coalition, with respect to its position when no countries cooperate.

Formally, a coalition s is *profitable* if:

$$P_i(s) \geq P_i(\emptyset), \ \forall \ i \in s. \tag{2.1}$$

Second, no country must have an incentive to free-ride, that is, the coalition s must be stable. More precisely, a country i chooses the cooperative strategy if $P_i(s)$, the country's payoff for belonging to the coalition s, is larger than $Q_i(s\backslash i)$, the country's payoff when it exits the coalition, and lets the other countries sign the cooperative agreement. Hence, $Q_i(s\backslash i) - P_i(s)$, $i \in s$, is a country's incentive to defect from a coalition s, whereas $P_i(s \cup i) - Q_i(s)$, $i \notin s$, is the incentive for a non-cooperating country to join the coalition s.

Thus, a coalition s is *stable* if there is no incentive to free-ride, that is,

$$Q_i(s\backslash i) - P_i(s) < 0 \tag{2.2}$$

for each country i belonging to s; and there is no incentive to broaden the coalition, that is,

$$P_i(s \cup i) - Q_i(s) < 0 \tag{2.3}$$

for each country i which does not belong to s.[16]

It has been shown that under fairly general conditions stable coalitions exist (see Donsimoni et al., 1986). However, this does not satisfactorily address the problem of protecting international commons, because, as has been demonstrated both in the oligopoly and in the environmental literature (see, for example, D'Aspremont et al., 1983; D'Aspremont and Gabszewicz, 1986; Hoel, 1991; Barrett, 1994, 1997; Carraro and Siniscalco, 1993), stable coalitions are generally formed by $j \leq n$ players, where j is a small number, regardless of n.[17] If stable coalitions are small, and countries are symmetric, the impact of their emission reductions on total emissions is likely to be negligible. However, the above-mentioned results mostly concern models in which countries are supposed to be symmetric, that is, they share the same welfare function. More encouraging results can be achieved in the presence of asymmetric countries (Barrett, 1997; Botteon and Carraro, 1997a, 1997b).

The existence of small stable coalitions leads to the following question: can the cooperating countries expand the coalition through self-financed welfare transfers to the remaining players?

The answer provided by the literature and by the practice of international agreements focuses on transfers as means to bribe non-signatory countries. Notice that we are not referring to the possibility of using transfers or side-payments to make the agreement profitable to all countries. This latter issue is discussed, for example, in Chander and Tulkens (1997), Eyckmans and Cornillie (2000) and Yang (2000). Here we start from the necessary condition that the agreement is profitable, and we look at the possibility that transfers increase the stability of the agreement.

In this context, which is discussed in detail in Carraro and Siniscalco (1993), a non-trivial analysis of transfers requires the imposition of constraints on the amount of resources to be transferred: were the transfers unconstrained, all non-signatories could be bribed, but the mechanism would not be credible. Therefore, we assume that: (i) transfers must be self-financed, that is, the total transfer T must be lower than the gain that the committed countries obtain from expanding the coalition; (ii) the move to a larger coalition must be *Pareto-improving*, that is, all countries must increase their welfare vis-à-vis the situation preceding the coalition expansion, and vis-à-vis non-cooperation (the larger coalition must also be profitable).

Under these conditions, however, the theoretical literature has provided a negative result. If countries are symmetric, self-financed transfers cannot induce free-riders to sign the environmental agreement, unless some degree of commitment constrains the strategic choices of cooperating countries.[18] However, in the case of asymmetric countries, transfers can be used to expand the initially stable coalition even in the absence of any forms of commitment (Botteon and Carraro, 1997a).

Let us start by analysing which conditions have to be satisfied in order to induce an additional country to enter a stable coalition. Suppose the coalition s is stable. If its members are committed to cooperation, their joint additional benefit when country j enters the coalition is:

$$\Sigma_i \in {}_s[P_i(s \cup j) - P_i(s)] > 0 \qquad (2.4)$$

The incentive for country j to free-ride from the $s \cup j$ coalition is:

$$Q_j(s) - P_j(s \cup j) > 0 \qquad (2.5)$$

because the coalition $s \cup j$ is not stable. Hence, the coalition $s \cup j$ can be stabilised by a system of transfers if:

$$\Sigma_i \in {}_s[P_i(s \cup j) - P_i(s)] > Q_j(s) - P_j(s \cup j) \tag{2.6}$$

and:

1. there exists a sharing rule such that $P_i(s \cup j) - P_i(s) > 0$ for all $i \in s$.
2. countries belonging to the coalition s are committed to cooperation.

If this latter condition is not satisfied, in the symmetric case transfers cannot expand a stable coalition (Carraro and Siniscalco, 1993). However, in the asymmetric case, transfers may succeed in expanding the stable coalitions s even without any forms of commitment. In the asymmetric case, all countries may have a cost of belonging to the coalition much lower than the cost of exiting it.[19] Formally, $Q_i(s \cup j \backslash i) - P_i(s \cup j)$ may be negative for all $i \in s$. If this is the case, the coalition s $\cup j$ can be stabilised by a system of transfers if:

$$\Sigma_i \in {}_s[P_i(s \cup j) - Q_i(s \cup j \backslash i)] > Q_j(s) - P_j(s \cup j) \tag{2.7}$$

Notice that this latter condition is more restrictive than condition (2.6) because: $P_i(s) < Q_i(s \cup j \backslash i)$, $i \in s$.

NOTES

This chapter has been prepared within the research activities of the CLIMNEG research network. The financial support of the European Commission, Directorate Research, is gratefully acknowledged. The authors are also grateful to Jean Charles Hourcade, Richard Tol and the participants in the Alessandria workshop on 'Game Practice and the Environment' for useful comments. Igor Cersosimo and Jill Weinreich provided useful assistance. The usual disclaimer applies.

Authors' address: Carlo Carraro, Department of Economics, University of Venice, San Giobbe 873, 30121 Venice, Italy. Tel: +39 041 2574166; Fax: +39 041 2574176; E-mail: ccarraro@unive.it.

1. Of course, the recent US decision not to ratify the Kyoto Protocol already suggests that the Kyoto agreement is not stable. However, our analysis is carried out under a long-term horizon and therefore is devoted to analysing long-term incentives to participate in a climate agreement. Short-term decisions may therefore differ from the ones that are optimal according to our modelling framework. See Section 2 for further discussion of this issue.

2. In Section 4 we will discuss why these three criteria are often considered 'equitable' and we will compare these criteria with other equity principles.

3. The 'Kyoto forever' hypothesis is a strong assumption. However, the CO_2 concentration levels implicit in this assumption (if RICE is a good description of the world) coincide with those in the A1B scenario used by the International Panel on Climate Change (IPCC, 2001) which can be considered the 'median' scenario among those currently proposed.

4. In our 'Kyoto forever' scenario, the USA are assumed to comply with the Kyoto Protocol. Therefore, this scenario may lack realism, but it is very useful for analysing the long-term incentive structure which is implicit in the Kyoto Protocol.

5. These remarks should also be useful in clarifying that the wording 'Kyoto agreement' used so far refers to the long-term version of the Kyoto agreement called 'Kyoto forever' scenario or the 'Kyoto forever agreement'.

6. The PANE-equilibrium of the game between the four Annex I countries and the two

Non-Annex I countries of RICE is computed as follows. Annex I countries maximise an aggregate utility function which is the weighted sum of their individual utility functions, where the weights have been computed using the procedure described above, whereas Non-Annex I countries maximise their own utility function, taking as given what the other countries do (see Appendix). In the same way, we also computed all possible PANE-equilibria of the game, whatever the size of the coalition and the identity of its members.

7. The same result has been found in other fields of economics, such as monetary economics (see Rogoff, 1987).
8. Our conclusion differs from the one in Yang (2000) and in Eyckmans and Cornillie (2000) where the 'Kyoto forever agreement' is shown to be weakly profitable (but not strongly profitable unless a transfer scheme is introduced).
9. Recall that in the 'Kyoto forever scenario' Non-Annex I countries have no quantitative emission limit and can therefore free-ride on the abatement of Kyoto signatories.
10. For further details see, for example, Cazorla and Toman (2000), Tol (2001), Rose and Stevens (1993), Rose et al. (1998) and Schmidt and Koschel (1998).
11. For further explanations regarding this distinction see, among others, Rose et al. (1998) and Schmidt and Koschel (1998).
12. This condition is necessary in order to compare the various types of climate agreements with the 'Kyoto forever' scenario. However, as a consequence, the analysis always assumes the same level of stringency and does not verify whether different emission goals, for example, more or less GHG mitigation, could induce different outcomes with respect to coalitional performance.
13. Notice that all these transfer schemes reflect the application of the compensation criterion described in Table 2.6.
14. When introducing emission trading, we explore again the profitability and stability of all possible coalition structures. When Non-Annex I countries are assumed to participate in the trading market, their assigned amount of emission reductions with respect to their BAU emission levels is equal to zero. Therefore, their emission target coincides with their BAU emission level.
15. The results of Propositions 1 and 2 are implicitly shown also in Chander and Tulkens (1995) but for a different definition of stability (usually named coalition unanimity; cf. Tulkens, 1998, and Yi, 1997). In particular, their definition of stability coincides with our definition of profitability.
16. This definition corresponds to that of cartel stability presented in the oligopoly literature (D'Aspremont and Gabszewicz, 1986). A similar definition is also used in Barrett (1994). However, this definition assumes that deviating countries cannot form (or do not find it profitable to form) another coalition, that is, group deviations are not allowed for. This restriction, even if widely accepted, is quite important as shown in Carraro and Marchiori (2003).
17. More satisfactory results are presented in Heal (1994), where a fixed cost of forming the coalition is introduced.
18. Carraro and Siniscalco (1993) prove the following proposition: if no (symmetric) countries can commit to the cooperative strategy, no self-financed transfer from the *j* cooperating countries to the non-cooperating countries can successfully enlarge the original coalition.
19. This is not possible in the symmetric case because the marginal country equates the payoff it receives when it belongs to the coalition with the payoff it would achieve by leaving the coalition.

REFERENCES

Barrett, S. (1994), 'Self-enforcing international environmental agreements', *Oxford Economic Papers*, **46**, 878–94.

Barrett, S. (1997), 'Towards a theory of international environmental co-operation', in C. Carraro and D. Siniscalco (eds), *New Directions in the Economic Theory of the Environment*, Cambridge: Cambridge University Press.

Botteon, M. and C. Carraro (1997a), 'Burden-sharing and coalition stability in environmental negotiations with asymmetric countries', in C. Carraro (ed.), *International Environmental Agreements: Strategic Policy Issues*, Cheltenham: Edward Elgar.

Botteon, M. and C. Carraro (1997b), 'Strategies for environmental negotiations: issue linkage with heterogeneous countries', in N. Hanley and H. Folmer (eds), *Game Theory and the Environment*, Cheltenham: Edward Elgar.

Carraro, C. (1988), 'The implicit objective function of Italian macroeconomic policy', *Economic Modelling*, no. 3, 261–76.

Carraro, C. (1989), 'The tastes of European central bankers', in M. De Cecco and A. Giovannini (eds), *A European Central Bank? Perspectives on Monetary Unification after Ten Years of the EMS*, Cambridge: Cambridge University Press.

Carraro, C. (1997), 'Modelling International Policy Games: Lessons from European Monetary Coordination', *Empirica*, **23**, 163–77.

Carraro, C. (1998), 'Beyond Kyoto: a game-theoretic perspective', in Proceedings of the OCED Workshop on 'Climate Change and Economic Modelling: Background Analysis for the Kyoto Protocol', Paris.

Carraro, C. and C. Marchiori (2003), 'Stable coalitions', in C. Carraro (ed.), *The Endogenous Formation of Economic Coalitions*, Cheltenham: Edward Elgar.

Carraro, C. and D. Siniscalco (1993), 'Strategies for the international protection of the environment', *Journal of Public Economics*, **52**, 309–28.

Cazorla, M. and M. Toman (2000), 'International equity and climate change policy', *RFF Climate Issue Brief*, no. 27, Washington.

Chander, P. and H. Tulkens (1995), 'A core-theoretic solution for the design of cooperative agreements on transfrontier pollution', *International Tax and Public Finance*, **2(2)**, 279–94.

Chander, P. and H. Tulkens (1997), 'The core of an economy with multilateral environmental externalities', *International Journal of Game Theory*, **26**, 379–401.

Chander, P., H. Tulkens, J.P. Van Ypersele and S. Willems (1999), 'The Kyoto Protocol: an economic and game theoretic interpretation', CLIMNEG Working Paper no. 12, CORE, UCL, Louvain.

D'Aspremont, C.A. and J.J. Gabszewicz (1986), 'On the stability of collusion', in G.F. Matthewson and J.E. Stiglitz (eds), *New Developments in the Analysis of Market Structure*, New York: Macmillan Press, pp. 243–64.

D'Aspremont, C.A., A. Jacquemin, J.J. Gabszewicz and J. Weymark (1983), 'On the stability of collusive price leadership', *Canadian Journal of Economics*, **16**, 17–25.

Donsimoni, M.-P., N.S. Economides and H.M. Polemarchakis (1986), 'Stable cartels), *International Economic Review*, **27(2)**, 317–27.

Eyckmans, J. (2001), 'On the farsighted stability of the Kyoto Protocol, some simulation results', ETE Working Paper no. 2001-03, Katholieke Universiteit Leuven, University of Leuven.

Eyckmans, J. and J. Cornillie (2000), 'Efficiency and Equity in the EU Bubble', ETE Working Paper no. 2000-02, Katholieke Universiteit Leuven, University of Leuven.

Eyckmans, J. and H. Tulkens (1999), 'Simulating with RICE coalitionally stable burden sharing agreements for the climate change problem', *FEEM Working Paper* 71–99.

Gilotte, L. (2001), 'Testing Allocation Rules', Report to the European Commission, CIRED.

Heal, G. (1994), 'The formation of environmental coalitions', in C. Carraro (ed.), *Trade, Innovation, Environment*, Dordrecht: Kluwer Academic Publishers.

Hoel, M. (1991), 'Global environmental problems: the effects of unilateral actions taken by one country', *Journal of Environmental Economics and Management*, **20(1)**, 55–70.

Hoel, M. (1992), 'International environmental conventions: the case of uniform reductions of emissions', *Environment and Resource Economics*, **2**, 141–59.

Hourcade, J.C. and L. Gilotte (2001), 'From equity principles to allocation rules', Report to the European Commission, CIRED.

IPCC (2001), *Third Assessment Report and Summary for Policymakers*, Cambridge: Cambridge University Press.

Manne, A. and R. Richels (1999), 'The Kyoto Protocol: a cost-effective strategy for meeting environmental objectives?' in J. Weyant (ed.), 'The cost of the Kyoto Protocol: a multi-model evaluation', Special Issue of the *Energy Journal*.

Nordhaus W.D. and Z. Yang (1996), 'A regional general-equilibrium model of alternative climate-change strategies', *American Economic Review*, **86(4)**.

Rogoff, K. (1987), 'Reputational constraints on monetary policy'. *Carnegie-Rochester Conference Series on Public Policy*, **26**, 141–82.

Rose, A., B. Stevens, J. Edmonds and M. Wise (1998), 'International equity and differentiation in global warming policy: an application to tradable emission permits', *Environment and Resource Economics*, **12(1)**, 25–51.

Rose, A. and B. Stevens (1993), 'The efficiency and equity of marketable permits for CO2 emissions', *Resource and Energy Economics*, **15(1)**, 117–46.

Schmidt, T.F.N. and H. Koschel (1998), 'Climate change policy and burden sharing in the European Union – applying alternative equity rules to a CGE-framework', ZEW Discussion Paper no. 98–12.

Tol, R.S.J. (2001), 'Equitable cost-benefit analysis of climate change policies', *Ecological Economics*, **36**, 71–85.

Tulkens, H. (1998), 'Cooperation versus free-riding in international environmental affairs: two approaches', in N. Hanley and H. Folmer (eds), *Game Theory and the Environment*, Cheltenham: Edward Elgar.

Weyant, J. (ed.) (1999), 'The cost of the Kyoto Protocol: a multi-model evaluation', *Energy Journal*, Special Issue.

Yang, Z. (2000), 'Forming coalitions in international agreements on global climate change', University of Pennsylvania.

Yi, S. (1997), 'Stable coalition structures with externalities', *Games and Economic Behaviour*, **20**, 201–23.

3. Endogenous strategic issue linkage in international negotiations

Carlo Carraro and Carmen Marchiori

1. INTRODUCTION

In recent years, the non-cooperative approach to coalition formation has been adopted to analyse various economic problems (cf. Bloch, 1997; Carraro and Marchiori, 2002; Konishi et al., 1997; Ray and Vohra, 1996, 1997; Yi, 1997). When applying theoretical results on coalition formation to the provision of public goods – and in particular to global environmental agreements – the conclusion is often that no coalition forms at the equilibrium and that, if a non-trivial equilibrium coalition emerges, it is formed by a small number of players (Hoel, 1991, 1992; Carraro and Siniscalco, 1993; Barrett, 1994, 1997; Heal, 1994). This result is the consequence of the presence of strong free-riding incentives that become even stronger in the presence of leakage (that is, when reaction functions are non-orthogonal; cf. Carraro and Siniscalco, 1993).

Different policy strategies have been proposed to increase the number of players who decide to join the equilibrium coalition. Transfers and issue linkage are probably the most popular proposed strategies, even though negotiation rules and treaty design can also be used to achieve equilibria in which large-sized coalitions form at the equilibrium (cf. Carraro, 2001).

In this chapter, we focus on issue linkage. The basic idea of issue linkage is to design a negotiation framework in which countries do not negotiate only on one issue (for instance, the environmental issue), but force themselves to negotiate on two joint issues (for example, the environmental and another interrelated economic issue).

Pioneering contributions on issue linkage are those by Tollison and Willett (1979) and Sebenius (1983). They propose this mechanism to promote cooperation not only on environmental matters, but also on other issues, for example, security and international finance. They also emphasise the increase in transaction costs that can result from the use of issue linkage.

Issue linkage was introduced into the economic literature on international environmental cooperation by Folmer et al. (1993) and by Cesar and

De Zeeuw (1996) to solve the problem of asymmetries among countries. The intuition is simple: if some countries gain from cooperating on a given economic issue whereas other countries gain from cooperating on another, by linking the two issues it may be possible to obtain an agreement that is profitable to all countries.

Issue linkage can also be used to mitigate the problem of free-riding. To do this, negotiations that are affected by free-riding – that is, negotiations concerning public goods – must be linked with negotiations on club or quasi-club goods. The intuition is that the incentives to free-ride on the non-excludable benefits of public good provision can be offset by the incentives to appropriate the excludable benefits coming from providing the club good.

To address the free-riding problem, Barrett (1995, 1997) proposes linking environmental protection to negotiations on trade liberalisation. In this way, potential free-riders are deterred with threats of trade sanctions. In Carraro and Siniscalco (1995, 1997) and Katsoulacos (1997), environmental cooperation is linked to cooperation in research and development (R&D). If a country does not cooperate on the control of the environment, it loses the benefits of technological cooperation. An empirical analysis of this type of issue linkage in the case of climate negotiations is contained in Buchner et al. (2002). Finally, Mohr (1995) and Mohr and Thomas (1998) propose linking climate negotiations to international debt swaps.

These contributions show the *effectiveness of linkage* in increasing the equilibrium number of cooperators on the provision of public goods, but do not investigate the forces which determine the number of issues which could be optimally linked and the related size of the equilibrium coalition (that is, the number of players/countries who cooperate on the linked issues). In a recent work, Alesina et al. (2001) extend the analysis of the effectiveness of issue linkage to the case of heterogeneous countries. One of the most interesting results of their paper is the identification of a trade-off between the size and the scope of a coalition: a coalition where countries cooperate on too many issues may be formed by a few countries, which implies small spillovers among them, whereas coalitions in which cooperation is restricted to few issues may be joined by many countries, thus raising many positive externalities within the coalition. However, the work by Alesina et al. (2001) assumes away the existence of free-riding incentives, which are instead one of the crucial features of the game analysed in this chapter.

In this chapter, we focus on coalitions which can cooperate on at most two issues. The goal of this chapter is neither to check the effectiveness of issue linkage in increasing the number of cooperating countries, nor to identify the number of economic issues that can be optimally linked.

Instead, the goal here is to analyse whether issue linkage belongs to the equilibrium of the game when issue linkage is not exogenously assumed, but players can decide whether or not to link two economic issues on which they know they will have to negotiate.

Let us consider an example. In the case of global environmental issues, incentives to free-ride on emission abatement are strong and cooperation is unlikely. In addition, there is no supra-national authority that can impose the adoption of issue linkage. Negotiating countries therefore decide independently whether or not to link the negotiation on a global environmental problem to the negotiation on a different economic issue. This decision is a strategic choice that players make. A game therefore describes the incentives to link the two issues. This game is also characterised by free-riding incentives. The reason for this is that issue linkage may indeed increase the number of cooperators on the provision of a global environmental good; however, at the same time, issue linkage may reduce the number of cooperators on the second issue (the one linked to the provision of the global environmental good). Hence, even if issue linkage increases the number of signatories – and therefore the amount of global environmental good provided – it may not be an equilibrium outcome.

The crucial question is therefore the following: do players have an incentive to link the negotiations on two different issues instead of negotiating on the two issues separately? Is the choice of issue linkage an equilibrium of the game in which players decide non-cooperatively whether or not to link the negotiations on two different economic issues?

This chapter answers the above questions by analysing a three-stage non-cooperative sequential game. In the first stage, players decide whether or not to link the negotiations on two issues on which they are trying to reach an agreement. If they decide not to link the two issues, in the second stage they decide whether or not to sign either one or both separate agreements. If they decide in favour of issue linkage, in the second stage they decide whether or not to sign the linked agreement. Finally, in the third stage they set the value of their policy variables.

When analysing this game, two cases will be considered: one in which the benefits accruing to the signatories of one of the two separate agreements are perfectly or almost perfectly excludable (cooperators provide a club good), and one in which the degree of excludability is low.

Let us underline that the decision taken in the first stage of the game is analysed assuming the unanimity voting rule. Indeed, the choice of issue linkage can be considered as a negotiation rule whose determination precedes the beginning of actual negotiations and which therefore should be taken with the consensus of all countries involved in the negotiation process. However, the extension to the case of majority voting is straightforward.

The structure of the chapter is as follows. Section 2 introduces the basic definitions and assumptions. Section 3 describes the different cases in which the game will be solved. Section 4 presents the equilibrium of the three-stage game under different degrees of excludability of the club good. Finally, Section 5 discusses the main conclusions of our analysis, possible extensions, and policy implications.

2. DEFINITIONS AND ASSUMPTIONS

Assume n players face the following situation: they decide to either link the two negotiations or not to link them. If the two negotiations are not linked, they subsequently decide whether or not to participate in the first agreement, or in the second agreement, or in both. If the two negotiations are linked, they then decide whether or not to sign the linked agreement.

The game therefore has three stages. In the first stage, the *linkage game* takes place, where the n players decide simultaneously and non-cooperatively whether or not to introduce a rule that forces all players to negotiate on a single agreement in which the two issues are linked. In the second stage, the *coalition game*, they decide simultaneously and non-cooperatively whether or not to sign one of the available treaties (that is, to join a coalition c of cooperating countries). In the third stage, they play the non-cooperative Nash *policy game*, where players that signed the agreement play as a single player and divide the resulting payoff according to a given burden-sharing rule (any of the rules derived from cooperative game theory).

A few assumptions are necessary to simplify our analysis.

A.1 (Uniqueness):   The third stage game, the *policy game,* in which all players decide simultaneously, has a unique Nash equilibrium for any coalition structure.[1]

A.2 (Cooperation):   Inside each coalition, players act cooperatively in order to maximise the coalitional surplus, whereas coalitions (and singletons) compete with one another in a non-cooperative way.

A.3 (Symmetry):   All players are ex-ante identical, which means that each player has the same strategy space in the second stage game.

Assumption A.3 allows us to adopt an equal sharing payoff division rule inside any coalition, that is, each player in a given coalition receives the same payoff as the other members of the coalition. Furthermore, the symmetry assumption implies that a coalition can be identified with its size c. As a consequence, the payoff received by the players only depends on the coalition sizes and not on the identity of the coalition members.

Given the above assumptions, a per-member partition function (partition function hereafter) can be defined. It can be denoted by $p(c; \pi)$, which represents the payoff of a player belonging to the size-c coalition in the coalition structure π. Let $\pi = \{\alpha_{(r)}, \beta_{(s)}, ...\}$ be a coalition structure formed by r size-α coalitions, s size-β coalitions, etc.

A.4 (Issues): Negotiations take place on two, exogenously given, issues (called 'a' and 't' in this chapter). Therefore, there is no trade-off between the size and scope of a coalition.

A.5 (Single coalition): Players are proposed to sign a single agreement. Hence, those who do not sign the agreement cannot propose a different one. From a game-theoretic viewpoint, this implies that only one coalition can be formed, the defecting players playing as singletons. Hence $\pi = \{c, 1_{(n-c)}\}$, where $1_{\{n-c\}}$ denotes the $n-c$ singletons, and the partition (payoff) function can simply be denoted by $P(c)$.

A.6 (Open Membership): Each player is free to join and to leave the coalition without the consensus of the other coalition members.

This assumption enables us to adopt the usual Nash equilibrium concept to identify the equilibrium of the coalition game. Different results could be obtained under exclusive membership or coalition unanimity (cf. Carraro and Marchiori, 2002).

Let us introduce a few definitions. Let c_u^* denote the equilibrium number of players who sign the linked agreement (that is, when issue linkage is chosen in the first stage of the game). Then $P_u(c_u^*)$ is their equilibrium payoff. The remaining $n - c_u^*$ players are the free-riders of the linked agreement. Their equilibrium payoff is $Q_u(c_u^*)$.

If linkage is not adopted, we have two agreements. Let 'a' identify the agreement whose benefits are not excludable (for instance, the environmental agreement), whereas 't' identifies the agreement with (partly) excludable benefits (for example, the agreement on technological cooperation). Then, let c_a^* be the equilibrium number of players who sign the public good agreement, or 'a-agreement', whereas c_t^* is the equilibrium number of signatories of the (quasi) club good agreement, or 't-agreement'. $P_a(c_a^*)$ is the equilibrium payoff of the former, whereas $P_t(c_t^*)$ is the equilibrium payoff of the latter. Finally, free-riders of the 'a-agreement' obtain a payoff equal to $Q_a(c_a^*)$, whereas free-riders of the 't-agreement' obtain $Q_t(c_t^*)$.

These definitions enable us to introduce another useful assumption:

A.7 (Additivity): $P_u(c) = P_a(c) + P_t(c)$, $\forall c$ and $Q_u(c) = Q_a(c) + Q_t(c)$, $\forall c$. Hence, the payoff that can be obtained from linking the two agreements is equal to the sum of the payoffs of the two individual agreements, both for cooperators in the joint agreement and for its free-riders.

Finally, under open membership (Assumption A.6), the following equilibrium concept is adopted:

Equilibrium: A coalition c^* is an equilibrium coalition if it is profitable and stable, where profitability and stability are defined as follows:

Profitability: A coalition c^* is profitable if each cooperating player gets a larger payoff than the one he would get when no coalition forms. Formally:

$$P(c^*) \geq P(0) \tag{3.1}$$

for all players in the coalition c^*, $2 \leq c^* \leq n$.[2]

Stability: A coalition formed by c^* players is stable if on the one hand there is no incentive to free-ride, that is:

$$Q(c^*-1) - P(c^*) \leq 0 \tag{3.2a}$$

and on the other hand there is no incentive to broaden the coalition, that is:

$$P(c^*+1) - Q(c^*) < 0 \tag{3.2b}$$

Notice that, if a coalition c^* is profitable and stable, then no player has an incentive to modify his decision to sign or not to sign the agreement. Hence, c^*, $2 \leq c^* \leq n$, is the outcome of a Nash equilibrium in which each country's strategy set is {sign, not sign}.

In particular, c_u^* identifies the size of the equilibrium coalition when issue linkage is adopted iff:

$$P_a(c_u^*) + P_t(c_u^*) \geq P_a(0) + P_t(0) \tag{3.3a}$$
$$P_a(c_u^*) + P_t(c_u^*) \geq Q_a(c_u^*-1) + Q_t(c_u^*-1) \tag{3.3b}$$
$$P_a(c_u^*+1) + P_t(c_u^*+1) < Q_a(c_u^*) + Q_t(c_u^*) \tag{3.3c}$$

From (3.3a) it is clear that, if the two separate agreements are profitable, then the linked agreement is also profitable. However, a linked agreement may be profitable to all players even when the two separate agreements are profitable only to a fraction of the n players of the game (two different fractions for the two agreements). This is why, as explained in the introduction to this chapter, issue linkage has been proposed to solve the profitability problem (cf. Cesar and De Zeeuw, 1996).

Let us define the structure and the payoffs of the linkage game. If players decide to link the two issues and negotiate on a joint agreement, the equilibrium payoffs are:

$$P_u(c_u^*) = P_a(c_u^*) + P_t(c_u^*) \tag{3.4a}$$

for a signatory of the agreement;

$$Q_u(c_u^*) = Q_a(c_u^*) + Q_t(c_u^*) \tag{3.4b}$$

for a free-rider.

If instead players prefer not to link the two issues, they decide whether or not to participate in two different agreements. In this case, at the equilibrium they obtain the following payoffs:

$$P_a(c_a^*) + P_t(c_t^*) \tag{3.5a}$$

if they decide to cooperate on both issues;

$$P_a(c_a^*) + Q_t(c_t^*) \tag{3.5b}$$

if they cooperate in the 'a-agreement', but they free-ride on the 't-agreement';

$$Q_a(c_a^*) + P_t(c_t^*) \tag{3.5c}$$

if they cooperate in the 't-agreement', but free-ride on the other issue;

$$Q_a(c_a^*) + Q_t(c_t^*) \tag{3.5d}$$

if they free-ride on both issues. Hence, without linkage, there are four 'types' of countries, where the identity of the countries is irrelevant because of symmetry. The structure of the game and its payoffs are summarised in Figure 3.1.

Let us make two final assumptions on how decisions are taken in the first stage of the game.

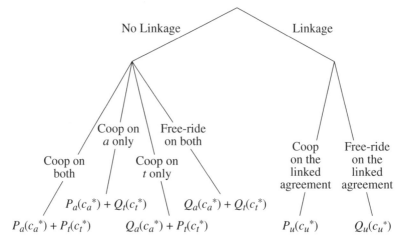

Figure 3.1   The structure of the game

A.8 (Voting):   In the first stage of the game, decisions are taken by unanimous agreement (players set a sort of constitutional rule).[3]

A.9 (Max-min strategy):   In the first stage of the game, a player selects issue linkage only when the worst payoff this choice provides is larger that the one he would get without linkage under any strategy in the second stage of the game (cooperator or non-cooperator, on one issue or two issues).

The idea is that a player votes in favour of linkage only if the worst payoff he gets when the issues are linked is larger than the best payoff he can obtain in the absence of linkage. The equilibrium conditions of the linkage game are then easily obtained by comparing the payoffs summarised in Figure 3.1.

3.   EXCLUDABLE BENEFITS AND PROFITABILITY FUNCTIONS

Before deriving and discussing the conditions under which linking the negotiations on the two economic issues is an equilibrium of the game presented in Section 2, it is important to introduce some additional elements which characterise the structure of the game. As shown below, the equilibrium condition depends, among other things, on two features of the game:

- the degree of excludability of the benefits arising from the agreement (the '*t*-agreement') which is linked to the environmental agreement (the '*a*-agreement');

- the shape of the profitability functions describing the gains achieved by cooperators in the two separate agreements and in the linked agreement.

Let us therefore characterise both the degree of excludability of cooperation benefits and the shape of the profitability functions. Let us use the example of R&D cooperation. In this case, the idea of issue linkage is to link environmental cooperation, which provides non-excludable benefits, with R&D cooperation, which provides excludable, or at least partly excludable, benefits. In this way, the incentive to free-ride on environmental benefits can be offset by the incentive to appropriate the excludable benefits yielded by R&D cooperation.

It is well known that the degree of excludability of R&D and technological innovation may not be perfect. Therefore, in this chapter we consider two basic cases. In the first, the benefits from cooperation on the 't-agreement' are sufficiently excludable to provide incentives for the formation of a grand coalition on this agreement. In the second, a coalition smaller than the grand coalition forms on the 't-agreement', because benefits from cooperation spill over to the free-riders.

Let γ, $\gamma \in [0,1]$, be the degree of excludability of the benefits produced by 't-agreement'. If $\gamma = 1$, then benefits are perfectly excludable and they go only to cooperators. Hence, $Q_t(c_t) = 0$, $\forall c_t \in [2, n]$. If $\gamma = 0$, the benefits produced by cooperators are a public good and go to free-riders as well. In the case of R&D cooperation, γ depends on the possibility of patenting innovations and on the duration and extension of the patent. If $0 < \gamma < 1$, then we have a case of partial excludability. The smaller γ, the larger the benefits achieved by free-riders and hence the larger the function $Q_t(c_t)$ for any given c_t.

Let γ° denote the value of γ such that $P_t(c_t^*) = Q_t(c_t^* - 1)$ when $c_t^* = n$. In words, when $\gamma \geq \gamma^\circ$, the degree of excludability is so high that the benefits from participating in the agreement are larger than the benefits from free-riding for all $2 \leq c_t \leq n$. As a consequence, in this case, if the profitability condition is satisfied for all c_t in the interval $[2, n]$, then the grand coalition forms, that is, all players prefer to sign the 't-agreement' $(c_t^* = n)$.[4] By contrast, when $\gamma < \gamma^\circ$, only a partial coalition forms on the 't-issue', that is, only a subset of countries sign the 't-agreement'. The function $Q_t(c_t)$ for low γ, $\gamma = \gamma^\circ$ and high γ is represented in Figure 3.2.

In the rest of the chapter we will analyse two cases:

Case A: $\gamma^\circ \leq \gamma \leq 1$, that is, the case in which all players would like to sign the 't-agreement' $(c_t^* = n)$;
Case B: $0 < \gamma < \gamma^\circ$, that is, in the case of the 't-agreement' a partial coalition forms $(2 \leq c_t^* < n)$.

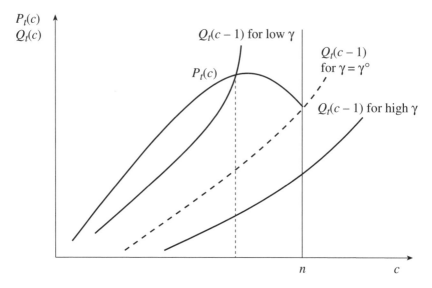

Figure 3.2   Payoff functions for different values of γ

As for the shape of the profitability functions, the following assumption will be used:

A.10 (Incomplete monotonicity):   The payoff functions $P_a(c_a)$, $Q_a(c_a)$, and $Q_t(c_t)$ are assumed to be monotonically increasing in c_a and c_t respectively. The payoff function $P_t(c_t)$ is assumed to be increasing in c_t for $c_t < c_t°$ and monotonically decreasing in c_t for $c_t > c_t°$.

The monotonicity of $P_a(c_a)$, $Q_a(c_a)$, and $Q_t(c_t)$ is a standard assumption in the economic literature on environmental coalition formation (see the surveys by Barrett, 1997; Carraro, 1998; Carraro and Marchiori, 2002). In particular, a monotonic $P_a(c_a)$ implies that the benefits from providing a public good (for example, from abating emissions) increase with the number of countries that participate in the agreement.

As for the payoff function $P_t(c_t)$, we assume that it initially increases with the size of the coalition c and then it decreases (it is hump-shaped). As shown in Carraro and Siniscalco (1997), this is actually the case when the 't-agreement' concerns R&D cooperation and this is generally the case when benefits from cooperation are (partly) excludable. In the case of R&D cooperation, the intuition is as follows. The decision to sign the R&D agreement has two positive effects for signatories: on the one hand, production costs decrease because cooperative R&D makes more efficient technologies available; on the other hand, market share increases because firms with lower costs have a higher market share (a standard Cournot oligopoly is assumed). However, this latter effect becomes smaller and smaller as the coalition size increases and goes to zero when $c_t = n$. Hence, the benefit from belonging to the coalition c_t decreases with the size of c_t when c_t is above a given intermediate value c_t^o.

Notice that, in Case A, if $P_t(c_t^*)$ is hump-shaped, then $P_t(c_t^* = n) \geq P_t(c_t^* + 1)$. Moreover, at the equilibrium $P_t(c_t^* = n) \geq Q_t(c_t^* - 1)$. We also assume for simplicity that, in case A, $P_t(c_t^* + 1) \geq Q_t(c_t^* = n)$. Hence, $Q_t(c_t^*) \leq P_t(c_t^*)$.

The shape of the payoff functions for cooperators and free-riders is shown in Figure 3.3 for Case A ($\gamma^o < \gamma \leq 1$) and in Figure 3.4 for Case B ($0 < \gamma \leq \gamma^o$).

Notice that in Figures 3.3 and 3.4 we represent the case in which $c_a^* < c_t^*$. This reflects the implicit assumption that the equilibrium coalition in the

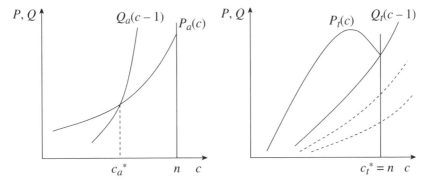

Figure 3.3   Shape of the payoff functions in Case A ($\gamma^o < \gamma \leq 1$)

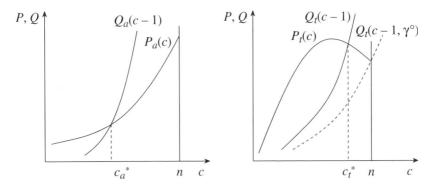

Figure 3.4   Shape of the payoff functions in Case B ($0 < \gamma \leq \gamma^o$)

case of an agreement on a public good is smaller than the equilibrium coalition in the case of an agreement on a (quasi) club good. Indeed, where $c_a^* \geq c_t^*$, the idea of linking the negotiation on the provision of a public good to a different negotiation would be meaningless.

Also notice that the monotonicity of $Q_a(c)$ and $Q_t(c)$ implies the monotonicity of $Q_u(c)$. By contrast, $P_u(c) = P_a(c) + P_t(c)$ can be both monotonic or hump-shaped. However, given Assumption A.10, if $P_u(c)$ is hump-shaped, it is monotonically increasing for $c_u < c_u^o$ and monotonically decreasing for $c_u > c_u^o$, with $c_u^o > c_t^o$.

In order to concentrate on the free-riding problem, let us assume that (i) issue linkage actually increases the number of players who provide the public good, that is:

$$c_u^* > c_a^* \tag{3.6a}$$

and (ii) issue linkage is profitable:

$$P_u(c_u^*) \geq P_u(0) \tag{3.6b}$$

Therefore, let us focus on the stability of the linked agreement. First, we show that c_u^* is smaller than c_t^*, namely that the equilibrium coalition emerging from the linked negotiation is always smaller than the equilibrium coalition in the 't-agreement'.[5]

Proposition 1: *At the equilibrium, $c_u^* \leq c_t^*$, that is, the number of players who participate in the linked agreement is always smaller than or equal to the number of players who participate in the (club good) agreement linked to the public good agreement.*

Proof: The linked agreement is internally stable if $P_u(c_u^*) \geq Q_u(c_u^* - 1)$, that is, if:

$$Q_a(c_u^* - 1) - P_a(c_u^*) \leq P_t(c_u^*) - Q_t(c_u^* - 1) \tag{3.7}$$

When $c_u^* > c_a^*$, the left-hand side of (3.7) is positive because there is an incentive to free-ride on the 'a-agreement' for all $c > c_a^*$. This implies that the right-hand side is also positive, that is, $P_t(c_u^*) > Q_t(c_u^* - 1)$. Therefore, as far as the 't-agreement' is concerned, there is still an incentive to enter the coalition. Hence, c_u^* must be smaller than or equal to the equilibrium coalition size c_t^*, that is, $c_u^* \leq c_t^*$.

The conclusion shown by Proposition 1 holds both in Case A and in Case B. The only difference is that, in Case A, $P_t(c) - Q_t(c - 1)$ is non-negative for

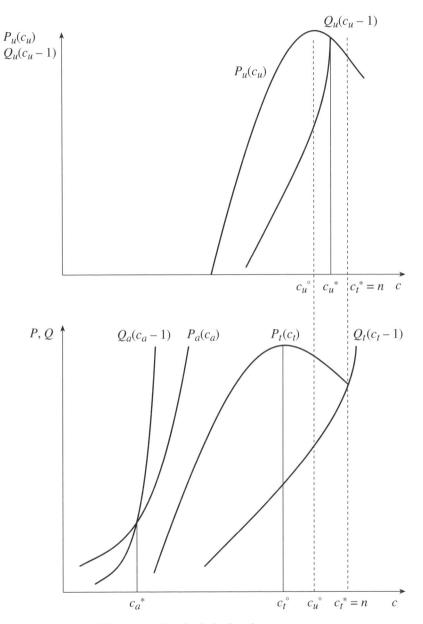

*Figure 3.5   Payoff functions for the linked and separate agreements in
Case A and $c_u^* > c_u^\circ$*

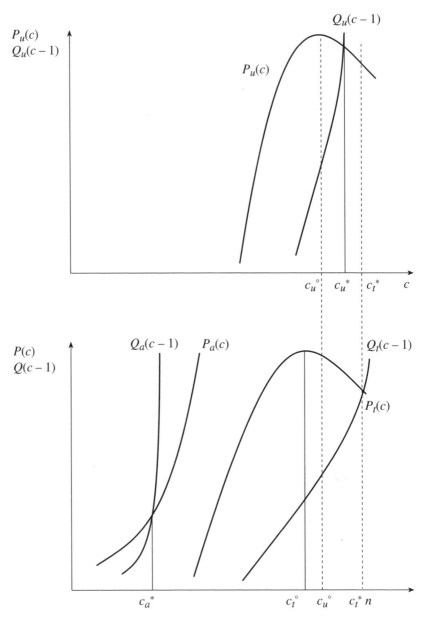

Figure 3.6   Payoff functions for the linked and separate agreements in Case B

all c in the interval $[2, n]$ because this is the condition which implies $c_t^* = n$. Hence, $P_t(c) - Q_t(c-1)$ is obviously non-negative also for $c = c_u^*$. Note that Proposition 1 and the preceding analysis lead to the following ordering:

$$c_a^* < c_u^* \le c_t^* \text{ and } c_t^\circ \le c_u^\circ. \tag{3.8}$$

The payoff functions of the two separate games and of the linked game are shown in Figures 3.5 and 3.6 for Cases A and B respectively. Both figures deal with the situation in which $c_u^* > c_{u'}^\circ$. These figures will be useful to clarify the analysis of the equilibrium of the game.

4. THE EQUILIBRIUM OF THE GAME

4.1 Case A: Linkage with a *Perfect* Club Good

We are now ready to determine players' equilibrium choice in the first stage of the game. In Case A, the situation is simpler, because, if players negotiate only on the 't-agreement', at the equilibrium all countries would like to sign it ($c_t^* = n$). Hence, if players disagree on linkage, either they cooperate on both the 'a-agreement' and the 't-agreement', or they free-ride only on the first one. Their payoff is therefore $P_a(c_a^*) + P_t(c_t^*)$ or $Q_a(c_a^*) + P_t(c_t^*)$, where $P_a(c_a^*) + P_t(c_t^*) \le Q_a(c_a^*) + P_t(c_t^*)$ because the monotonicity of $P_a(c_a)$ and conditions (3.2a) and (3.2b) imply $P_a(c_a^*) \le Q_a(c_a^*)$. As a consequence:

Proposition 2: *Assume A.1 to A.10 hold and $\gamma^\circ < \gamma \le 1$, that is, $c_t^* = n$. If (i) $P_u(c_u)$ is monotonic in the interval $[2, n]$; or (ii) $c_u^* < c_u^\circ$; or (iii) $c_u^* < c_u^\circ$, $c_u^\circ < n$, and $P_t(c_u^*) - Q_t(c_u^*)$ is smaller than $Q_a(c_u^*) - P_a(c_u^*) > 0$, then players adopt issue linkage under unanimity voting if:*

$$[P_a(c_u^*) - Q_a(c_a^*)] > [P_t(c_t^* = n) - P_t(c_u^*)] \tag{3.9}$$

If instead (iv) $c_u^* > c_u^\circ$, $c_u^\circ < n$ and $P_t(c_u^*) - Q_t(c_u^*)$ is positive and larger than $Q_a(c_u^*) - P_a(c_u^*)$; or (v) $c_u^* = n > c_{u'}^\circ$ the condition for players to adopt issue linkage becomes:

$$[Q_a(c_u^*) - Q_a(c_a^*)] > [P_t(c_t^* = n) - Q_t(c_u^*)] \tag{3.10}$$

Proof: If $P_u(c_u)$ is monotonic or $P_u(c_u)$ is hump-shaped with $c_u^* < c_u^\circ$, then at the equilibrium $P_u(c_u^* + 1) \ge P_u(c_u^*)$, which implies $P_u(c_u^*) = P_a(c_u^*) + P_t(c_u^*) < Q_u(c_u^*) = Q_a(c_u^*) + Q_t(c_u^*)$ because of (3.2a) and (3.2b). Hence, all players vote for issue linkage if $P_u(c_u^*) = P_a(c_u^*) + P_t(c_u^*)$ – the worst payoff they can get under issue linkage – is larger than $Q_a(c_a^*) + P_t(c_t^*)$ – the largest payoff they get without linkage. Hence, (3.9) must hold. If $P_u(c_u)$ is hump-shaped with $c_u^* \geq c_u^\circ$, $c_u^\circ < n$, then $Q_u(c_u^*)$ may be smaller than $P_u(c_u^*)$. If not, (3.9) holds again. $Q_u(c_u^*)$ is smaller than $P_u(c_u^*)$ if $P_t(c_u^*) - Q_t(c_u^*) > Q_a(c_u^*) - P_a(c_u^*)$. Notice that $Q_a(c_u) - P_a(c_u) > 0$ at $c = c_u^*$, because $c_a^* < c_u^*$. Hence, a necessary condition for $Q_u(c_u^*) < P_u(c_u^*)$ is $P_t(c_u^*) - Q_t(c_u^*) > 0$, which holds because $c_u^* < c_t^*$. As a consequence, if $P_t(c_u^*) - Q_t(c_u^*) > Q_a(c_u^*) - P_a(c_u^*) > 0$, all players vote in favour of issue linkage when $Q_u(c_u^*) = Q_a(c_u^*) + Q_t(c_u^*)$ – the worst payoff they can get under issue linkage – is larger than $Q_a(c_a^*) + P_t(c_t^*)$ – the largest payoff they get without linkage. Hence, (3.10) must hold. Finally, when $c_u^* = n$, there is no incentive to defect for any $c_u \leq n$. Hence, $P_u(c_u^*) > P_t(c_u^* + 1) > Q_u(c_u^*)$. As a consequence, $Q_u(c_u^*) = Q_a(c_u^*) + Q_t(c_u^*)$ must be larger than $Q_a(c_a^*) + P_t(c_t^*)$, that is, (3.10) must hold (Q.E.D.).

How can conditions (3.9) and (3.10) be interpreted? $[P_a(c_u^*) - Q_a(c_a^*)]$ – the left-hand side of (3.9) – represents the gain or loss that a free-rider on the '*a*-agreement' achieves from joining the expanded coalition. It can also be written as $[P_a(c_u^*) - P_a(c_a^*)] - [Q_a(c_a^*) - P_a(c_a^*)]$, where the first term is the increased gain that a cooperator on the '*a*-agreement' achieves from expanding the coalition, whereas the second term is a free-rider's relative gain when a coalition c_a^* forms. $[P_t(c_t^*) - P_t(c_u^*)]$ is the possible gain or loss that goes to a cooperator in the '*t*-agreement' when the coalition size moves from c_t^* to c_u^*. Hence, (3.9) says that *the gain (loss) that a free-rider on the '*a*-agreement' achieves from joining the expanded coalition must be larger (smaller) than the gain (loss) that goes to a cooperator in the '*t*-agreement' when the coalition size moves from c_t^* to c_u^*.*

Condition (10) has a different interpretation. $[Q_a(c_u^*) - Q_a(c_a^*)]$ is the gain that goes to a free-rider when more players cooperate on the provision of a public good. $[P_t(c_t^*) - Q_t(c_u^*)] = [P_t(c_t^*) - P_t(c_u^*)] + [P_t(c_u^*) - Q_t(c_u^*)]$ is the possible gain or loss that goes to a cooperator in the '*t*-agreement' when the coalition size moves from c_t^* to c_u^*, plus the excess benefits of cooperation when $c_u^* < c_t^*$ (recall that $P_t(c) > Q_t(c)$ for all $c < c_t^* = n$, because the agreement concerns a perfect club good). Hence, issue linkage is chosen by all players if *the gain that goes to a free-rider when more players cooperate in the provision of a public good is larger than the excess benefits of cooperation when $c_u^* < c_t^*$ plus the gain (loss) that goes to a cooperator in the '*t*-agreement' when the coalition size moves from c_t^* to c_u^*.*

4.2 Case B: Linkage with an *Imperfect* Club Good

Let us now consider the second case, in which the club good issue linked to the public good issue is an imperfect club good. This implies that the benefits from cooperation on the '*t*-agreement' which spill over to free-riders are strong enough to induce some players not to join the coalition. Hence, when players negotiate on the '*t*-agreement' only, the equilibrium coalition c_t^* is not the grand coalition, that is, $c_t^* < n$.

In this context, it is still important to adopt issue linkage as a strategy to increase the coalition size on the '*a*-agreement' because $c_a^* < c_t^*$. Hence, issue linkage helps players to achieve a coalition c_u^* larger than c_a^*, but smaller than c_t^* (Proposition 1). However, the benefits of a larger coalition on the '*a*-agreement' must be traded off with the loss of a smaller coalition in the '*t*-agreement'.

The first step to determine the equilibrium of the game is the analysis of the payoffs of the four types of players that emerge in the second stage of the game. We need to compare:

- $P_a(c_a^*) + P_t(c_t^*)$, the payoff of a cooperator in both separate agreements;
- $P_a(c_a^*) + Q_t(c_t^*)$, the payoff of a player who cooperates in the '*a*-agreement' but free-rides on the other one;
- $Q_a(c_a^*) + P_t(c_t^*)$, the payoff of a player who cooperates in the '*t*-agreement' but free-rides on the other one;
- $Q_a(c_a^*) + Q_t(c_t^*)$, the payoff of a free-rider on both separate agreements.

First, notice that $P_a(c_a^*) + P_t(c_t^*) < Q_a(c_a^*) + P_t(c_t^*)$ and $P_a(c_a^*) + Q_t(c_t^*) < Q_a(c_a^*) + Q_t(c_t^*)$ because the monotonicity of $P_a(c)$ implies $P_a(c_a^*) < Q_a(c_a^*)$. Hence, the largest payoff in the case of two separate agreements is the one in which a player free-rides on both agreements iff:

$$P_t(c_t^*) < Q_t(c_t^*) \tag{3.11}$$

In the rest of this chapter we will use (3.11), which says that a free-rider on the '*t*-agreement' achieves a larger payoff than a cooperator in the same agreement. This is reasonable if the degree of appropriability of the benefits from cooperation in the '*t*-agreement' is sufficiently low. We assume that this is the case for $\gamma < \gamma^\circ$.

Then, the conditions for issue linkage to be an equilibrium strategy are described by the following Proposition:

Proposition 3: *Assume A.1 to A.10 hold, $0 \leq \gamma < \gamma^\circ$, that is, $c_t^* < n$, and $P_t(c_t^*) < Q_t(c_t^*)$. If (i) $P_u(c_u)$ is monotonic in the interval [2, n]; or (ii) $c_u^* < c_u^\circ$; or (iii) $c_u^* \geq c_u^\circ$, $c_u^* < n$, and $P_t(c_u^*) - Q_t(c_u^*)$ is smaller than $Q_a(c_u^*) - P_a(c_u^*) > 0$, then players adopt issue linkage under unanimity voting iff condition (3.12) holds, that is:*

$$[P_a(c_u^*) - Q_a(c_a^*)] > [Q_t(c_t^*) - P_t(c_u^*)] \tag{3.12}$$

If $c_u^* > c_u^o$, $c_u^o < n$, and $P_t(c_u^*) - Q_t(c_u^*)$ is positive and larger than $Q_a(c_u^*) - P_a(c_u^*)$, the condition for issue linkage to be adopted becomes:

$$[Q_a(c_u^*) - Q_a(c_a^*)] > [Q_t(c_t^*) - Q_t(c_u^*)] \tag{3.13}$$

Proof: If $P_u(c_u)$ is monotonic or $P_u(c_u)$ is hump-shaped with $c_u^* < c_u^o$, then at the equilibrium $P_u(c_u^* + 1) \geq P_u(c_u^*)$, which implies $P_u(c_u^*) = P_a(c_u^*) + P_t(c_u^*) < Q_u(c_u^*) = Q_a(c_u^*) + Q_t(c_u^*)$ because of (3.2a and 3.2b). Hence, all players vote for issue linkage if $P_u(c_u^*) = P_a(c_u^*) + P_t(c_u^*)$ – the worst payoff they can get under issue linkage – is larger than $Q_a(c_a^*) + Q_t(c_t^*)$ – the largest payoff they get without linkage. Hence, (3.12) must hold.

If $P_u(c_u)$ is hump-shaped with $c_u^* \geq c_u^o$, $c_u^o < n$, then $Q_u(c_u^*)$ may be smaller than $P_u(c_u^*)$. If not, (3.12) holds again. $Q_u(c_u^*)$ is smaller than $P_u(c_u^*)$ if $P_t(c_u^*) - Q_t(c_u^*) > Q_a(c_u^*) - P_a(c_u^*)$. Notice that $Q_a(c_u) - P_a(c_u) > 0$ at $c = c_u^*$, because $c_a^* < c_u^*$. Hence, a necessary condition for $Q_u(c_u^*) < P_u(c_u^*)$ is $P_t(c_u^*) - Q_t(c_u^*) > 0$, which holds for $c_u^* < c_t^*$. As a consequence, if $P_t(c_u^*) - Q_t(c_u^*) > Q_a(c_u^*) - P_a(c_u^*) > 0$, all players vote in favour of issue linkage when $Q_u(c_u^*) = Q_a(c_u^*) + Q_t(c_u^*)$ – the worst payoff they can get under issue linkage – is larger than $Q_a(c_a^*) + Q_t(c_t^*)$ – the largest payoff they get without linkage. Hence, (3.13) must hold **(Q.E.D.)**.

The interpretation of this Proposition goes as follows. Again we have two conditions for issue linkage to be chosen by all players in the first stage of the game. Consider the first one. The right hand side of (3.12) – $[Q_t(c_t^*) - P_t(c_u^*)]$ – is the loss from reducing the coalition on the 't-agreement' from c_t^* to c_u^* (Proposition 1 has shown that $c_t^* \geq c_u^*$). This loss can be written as $Q_t(c_t^*) - P_t(c_u^*) = [Q_t(c_t^*) - Q_t(c_u^*)] - [P_t(c_u^*) - Q_t(c_u^*)]$ where the first term represents a free-rider's loss when they get fewer benefits from a smaller coalition, whereas the second term represents the excess benefit of cooperation when $c_u^* < c_t^*$.

The left-hand side of (3.12) is the same as the left-hand side of (3.9). Hence, it represents the gain or loss which a free-rider on the 'a-agreement' achieves when joining the expanded coalition. It can also be written as $[P_a(c_u^*) - P_a(c_a^*)] - [Q_a(c_a^*) - P_a(c_a^*)]$. The positivity of $Q_t(c_t^*) - P_t(c_u^*)$ implies that (3.12) holds if $P_a(c_u^*) - Q_a(c_a^*)$ is also positive, that is, if *the increased gain which a cooperator on the 'a-agreement' achieves from expanding the coalition is larger than a free-rider's relative gain when a coalition c_a^* forms.*

This is only a necessary condition. The sufficient condition says that *the increased gain which a cooperator on the 'a-agreement' (for example, a signatory of an environmental agreement) achieves from expanding the coalition from c_a^* to c_u^*, plus the excess benefit of cooperation on the 't-agreement' when $c_u^* < c_t^*$, must be larger than a free-rider's relative gain when a coalition c_a^* forms plus the loss that a free-rider suffers because of the smaller spillovers from the reduced cooperation on the 't-agreement'.*

The second condition – the inequality (3.13) – is new and says that *the benefits enjoyed by a free-rider on the 'a-agreement' when the coalition size increases must be larger than the loss suffered by a free-rider on the 't-agreement' when the number of signatories of the 't-agreement' decrease from c_t^* to c_u^** (recall that benefits from cooperation spill over to free-riders in the case of the '*t*-agreement' also).

5.   SUMMARY AND CONCLUSIONS

The previous section has identified four conditions under which all players of the game prefer to negotiate on two linked issues rather than on the two issues separately. In order to simplify the message which can be derived from Propositions 2 and 3, let us assume that free-riders on the linked agreement are better off than cooperators $[P_u(c_u^*) < Q_u(c_u^*)]$. This is the most frequent case in coalition theory. Then, issue linkage is the equilibrium strategy under unanimity voting if:

$$[P_a(c_u^*) - Q_a(c_a^*)] > [Q_t(c_t^*) - P_t(c_u^*)]$$

in the case of an imperfect club good ($c_t^* < n$), or

$$[P_a(c_u^*) - Q_a(c_a^*)] > [P_t(c_t^* = n) - P_t(c_u^*)]$$

in the case of a perfect club good ($c_t^* = n$).

What policy message can be derived from these inequalities? First, let us underline a necessary condition for issue linkage to be adopted in the first stage of the game. A free-rider on the public good agreement who enters the coalition on the linked agreement must get a higher payoff $[P_a(c_u^*) > Q_a(c_a^*)]$. This is a prerequisite without which issue linkage is not chosen. Hence, public good (for example, environmental) benefits provided by a larger coalition must be perceived as sufficiently large.

Then, there is the necessary and sufficient condition. A free-rider on the public good agreement who enters the coalition on the linked agreement must not only increase his payoff, but this positive change must be larger than the loss a player may suffer because the club good coalition becomes smaller, (this is particularly clear in condition (3.9) but it is also true in (3.12).

This highlights the trade-off that players face when deciding whether or not to adopt issue linkage. Consider again the example of an environmental negotiation linked to a negotiation on R&D cooperation. On the one hand, players would like to reap the benefits provided by a larger environmental coalition. On the other hand, they know that though issue linkage increases the number of environmental cooperators, it also decreases the participants in the R&D cooperation agreement. Hence, environmental benefits could be offset by technological losses.

A similar argument holds when free-riders on the linked agreement are worse off than cooperators $[P_u(c_u^*) > Q_u(c_u^*)]$. In this case the conditions for issue linkage to be adopted under unanimity voting are:

$$[Q_a(c_u^*) - Q_a(c_a^*)] > [Q_t(c_t^*) - Q_t(c_u^*)]$$

in the case of an imperfect club good ($c_t^* < n$), or

$$[Q_a(c_u^*) - Q_a(c_a^*)] > [P_t(c_t^* = n) - Q_t(c_u^*)]$$

in the case of a perfect club good ($c_t^* = n$).

There is no necessary condition to be stressed, because the monotonicity of $Q_a(c_a)$ implies $Q_a(c_u^*) > Q_a(c_a^*)$. The necessary and sufficient condition says that the gain $[Q_a(c_u^*) - Q_a(c_a^*)]$ that a free-rider achieves when free-riding on a larger public good agreement must be larger than the loss a player may suffer because the club good coalition becomes smaller.

As a consequence, when proposing or advocating issue linkage, policy-makers must be careful in assessing two crucial elements. The first crucial element is the relative change of the coalition sizes $c_u^* - c_a^*$ and $c_t^* - c_u^*$. The greater $c_u^* - c_a^*$ and the smaller $c_t^* - c_u^*$, the larger the likelihood that conditions (3.12) (or (3.9)) and (3.13) (or (3.10)) be satisfied. The second crucial element is the relative change in the players' payoffs. The greater the increased benefits induced by greater cooperation on the public good issue, the greater the likelihood that issue linkage be adopted. Similarly, the smaller the loss from a reduced cooperation on the '*t*-agreement', the greater the likelihood that issue linkage be adopted.

Notice that these conditions neglect the likely increase of transaction costs when negotiating on two linked issues. However, introducing transaction costs would be trivial. They would simply be added to the right-hand side of conditions (3.12), (3.9), (3.13) and (3.10).

Finally, let us note that all equilibrium conditions become less restrictive in the presence of majority voting and when the degree of excludability of technological benefits is high (γ is large).

NOTES

The authors are grateful to two anonymous referees, Scott Barrett, Sergio Currarini, Domenico Siniscalco and to the participants at the Sixth Coalition Theory Workshop held in Louvain and at the Second World Congress of Environmental Economists held in Monterey for helpful comments and suggestions. Corresponding author: Carlo Carraro, Department of Economics, University of Venice, San Giobbe 873, 30121, Venice, Italy. Fax: +39 041 2349176. E-mail: ccarraro@unive.it.

1. See Carraro and Marchiori (2002) for an explanation of this and the following assumptions.
2. In the case of symmetric countries, this condition is fairly trivial: it simply means that a country's choice must be rational and that, if a coalition is profitable for one country, it is profitable for all other ones.
3. The extension of our results to the case in which first-stage decisions are taken with majority voting is straightforward.
4. Notice that, when $\gamma > \gamma°$, all coalitions c_i where $2 \le c_i \le n$ satisfy the internal stability condition (3.2a), but not the external stability condition (3.2b). In this case, all players want to join the coalition. Hence, we assume that the equilibrium is achieved when $c_i = n$.
5. A similar result is also obtained in Alesina et al. (2001).

REFERENCES

Alesina, A., I. Angeloni and F. Etro (2001), 'The political economy of unions', NBER Working Paper, December 2001.

Barrett, S. (1994), 'Self-enforcing international environmental agreements', *Oxford Economic Papers*, **46**, 878–94.

Barrett, S. (1995), 'Trade restrictions in international environmental agreements', London Business School.

Barrett, S. (1997), 'Towards a Theory of International Cooperation', in C. Carraro and D. Siniscalco (eds), *New Directions in the Economic Theory of the Environment*, Cambridge: Cambridge University Press.

Bloch, F. (1997), 'Noncooperative models of coalition formation in games with spillovers', in C. Carraro and D. Siniscalco (eds), *New Directions in the Economic Theory of the Environment*, Cambridge: Cambridge University Press.

Buchner, B., C. Carraro, I. Cersosimo and C. Marchiori (2002) 'Back to Kyoto? US participation and the linkage between R&D and climate cooperation', FEEM Working Paper no. 22.02, Milan.

Carraro, C. (1998), 'Environmental conflict, bargaining and cooperation', in J. van den Bergh, *Handbook of Natural Resources and the Environment*, Cheltenham: Edward Elgar.

Carraro, C. (2001), 'Institution design for managing global commons', paper presented at the Fourth FEEM-IDEI-INRA Conference on Energy and Environmental Economics, Toulouse, 3–4 May, 2001 and at the International Conference 'Game Practice and the Environment', Alessandria, 12–13 April 2002.

Carraro, C. and C. Marchiori (2002), 'Stable coalitions', in C. Carraro (ed.), *The Endogenous Formation of Economic Coalitions*, Cheltenham: Edward Elgar.

Carraro, C. and D. Siniscalco (1993), 'Strategies for the international protection of the environment', *Journal of Public Economics*, **52**, 309–28.

Carraro, C. and D. Siniscalco (1995), 'Policy coordination for sustainability: commitments, transfers, and linked negotiations', in I. Goldin and A. Winters (eds), *The Economics of Sustainable Development*, Cambridge: Cambridge University Press.

Carraro, C. and D. Siniscalco (1997), 'R&D cooperation and the stability of international environmental agreements', in C. Carraro (ed), *International Environmental Agreements: Strategic Policy Issues*, Cheltenham: Edward Elgar.

Cesar, H. and A. De Zeeuw (1996), 'Issue linkage in global environmental problems', in A. Xepapadeas (ed.), *Economic Policy for the Environment and Natural Resources*, Cheltenham: Edward Elgar.

Folmer, H., P. van Mouche and S. Ragland (1993), 'Interconnected games and international environmental problems', *Environmental Resource Economics*, **3**, 313–35.

Heal, G. (1994), 'The formation of environmental coalitions', in C. Carraro (ed.), *Trade, Innovation, Environment*, Dordrecht: Kluwer Academic Publisher.

Hoel, M. (1991), 'Global environmental problems: the effects of unilateral actions taken by one country', *Journal of Environmental Economics and Management*, **20** **(1)**, 55–70.

Hoel, M. (1992), 'International environmental conventions: the case of uniform reductions of emissions', *Environmental and Resource Economics*, **2**, 141–59.

Katsoulacos, Y. (1997), 'R&D spillovers, R&D cooperation, innovation and international environmental agreements', in C. Carraro (ed.), *International Environmental Agreements: Strategic Policy Issues*, Cheltenham: Edward Elgar.

Konishi, H., M. Le Breton and S. Weber (1997), 'Stable coalition structures for the provision of public goods', in C. Carraro and D. Siniscalco (eds), *New Directions in the Economic Theory of the Environment*, Cambridge: Cambridge University Press.

Mohr, E. (1995), 'International environmental permit trade and debt: the consequences of country sovereignty and cross-default policies', *Review of International Economics*, **3**, 1–19.

Mohr, E. and J.P. Thomas (1998), 'Pooling sovereign risks: the case of environmental treaties and international debt', *Journal of Development Economics*, **55**, 173–90.

Ray, D. and R. Vohra (1996), 'A theory of endogenous coalition structure', mimeo, Department of Economics, Brown University and Boston University.

Ray, D. and R. Vohra (1997), 'Equilibrium binding agreements', *Journal of Economic Theory*, **73**, 30–78.

Sebenius J.K. (1983), 'Negotiation arithmetic: adding and subtracting issues and parties', *International Organisation*, **37(2)**, 281–316.

Tollison, R.D. and T.D. Willett (1979), 'An economic theory of mutually advantageous issue linkages in international negotiations', *International Organisation*, **33(4)**, 425–49.

Yi, S. (1997), 'Stable coalition structures with externalities', *Games and Economic Behaviour*, **20**, 201–23.

4. Kyoto and beyond Kyoto climate policy: comparison of open-loop and feedback game outcomes

Juan Carlos Císcar and Antonio Soria

1. INTRODUCTION

From the start of the industrial revolution human-induced activities have warmed the Earth's atmosphere. The combustion of fossil fuels and changes in land use have gradually increased the concentration of greenhouse gases (GHG) in the atmosphere, which has altered the global climate.[1] The 1997 Kyoto Protocol on climate change[2] sets for the first time binding GHG emission reduction targets to developed countries (known in the protocol as Annex B countries). GHG emissions in the Annex B countries are to be reduced by 5.2% in 2010, with respect to the 1990 emission levels. Developing countries (the non-Annex B countries) do not have mitigation goals.

Most studies assessing climate policies, and in particular the Kyoto Protocol, have considered a *static* framework in the sense that countries act once and at the same time deciding their policies for all future periods (the Kyoto commitment period and the beyond Kyoto decades). The information structure of this simultaneous game is known in the literature as open-loop, and leads to the *open-loop Nash equilibrium*. Such a static approach has been predominant in the numerical economic literature dealing with climate change policy. OECD (1999), Nordhaus and Boyer (2000), Peck and Teisberg (1999), and Manne and Richels (1999) study the 'Kyoto forever' hypothesis. This scenario assumes that the climate policy beyond Kyoto keeps *constant* the Kyoto emission target of the Annex B region forever, while the non-Annex B region does not reduce emissions at all in the foreseeable future.

In Císcar and Soria (2002) the Kyoto forever assumption is removed thanks to the application of a *dynamic*, multi-stage sequential game framework, indeed allowing a prospective analysis of the climate policy scenarios. The dynamic sequential method is based on a game in extensive form (also known as decision trees), a method that has not been applied so far to the climate policy literature, to the best of our knowledge.[3] A difference game is used to analyse the climate policy prospects.[4] Regions can dynamically and strategically react to the opponent's past moves, by choosing at each stage their best policy among a set of policy options, and are not constrained by the Kyoto forever hypothesis. From the point of view of the information structure of the game framework, the Nash outcome is derived under a dynamic information structure. At any stage, whenever a player decides his strategy and consequently takes an action, he knows the history of the past moves of all players to that stage. This kind of equilibrium is known in the literature as *feedback Nash equilibrium*, because the information on past actions may affect the strategy of the player.[5]

A fundamental assumption when selecting the second approach is that this dynamic interaction between players may be of relevance to the game outcome. The goal of this chapter is precisely to assess this point, by comparing the outcomes under the open-loop and feedback game frameworks. Depending on the characteristics of the game under consideration one or another kind of information structure might be more appropriate. In the climate change issue one would expect that the real situation is closer to a feedback information structure, because players do not set their policies simultaneously and for all future periods. The current situation is that a group of countries (Annex B) has committed to mitigation efforts to be implemented in a delimited time period (2000–2010). It seems then more reasonable to assume the feedback information structure, and therefore to derive the feedback Nash outcome.

Another even more fundamental reason for implementing the feedback approach is that it yields a *dynamically consistent* equilibrium, that is, there is no incentive to deviate from the equilibrium path. With a feedback structure players can change their strategies at any period depending on the past evolution of the game.[6] Therefore by construction the feedback equilibrium is dynamically consistent.

The crucial question of interest in this discussion is whether the feedback information structure assumption affects the game outcome. There are some theoretical results in this respect. Van der Ploeg and de Zeeuw (1992) build a multi-country model with environmental damage due to the stock accumulation of the pollutant. These authors study the design of Pigouvian taxes within this differential game context.[7] For the particular case of quadratic functions they show that the steady-state level of the stock pollutant in the feedback Nash equilibrium is higher than that in the open-loop Nash equilibrium.[8] These authors defend the use of the feedback concept not only because it is more realistic, but also because the use of the open-loop assumption underestimates the damage to the environment when there is no coordination of environmental policies.[9] The fact that the validity of the previous theoretical result is subject to certain assumptions on the damage and objective functions of the model prevents it from being a general result, that is, applicable to any model specification.

The remainder of this chapter is organised as follows. Section 2 presents the main theoretical elements upon which the open-loop and feedback frameworks are compared. Section 3 proposes a numerical model to perform the comparison in a particular context. Section 4 concludes by summarising the main findings of this chapter.

2. OPEN-LOOP AND FEEDBACK GAME OUTCOMES: THE METHODOLOGICAL AND THEORETICAL BACKGROUND

The methodology follows a strand of the literature that couples two key elements: integrated assessment models (IAM) of the climate and the economy, and a game context.[10] The idea is to use a framework that takes into account the most relevant relationships between the systems involved in the analysis of climate policy: the socio-economic, climatic (both captured by the IAM) and international policy-making systems (captured by the game context). Table 4.1 shows the main elements. As will be seen below, the IAM selected studies the regional mitigation policies within a cost-benefit framework.[11]

Table 4.1   The elements of the IAM-game architecture

	Systems	Interaction Channels	Assumptions
IAM	Socio-economic Climatic	Coupling of both systems through the environmental externality	Optimality, rationality
Game	International policy-making	Strategic interactions	Rationality

It is assumed that regions behave rationally. Each region seeks to optimise its own individual welfare, subject to a series of constraints. Regions are identified with a group of countries that agree to implement a common climate policy.

The optimal policy of one region is interdependent with the optimal policy of the other regions, due to the climate change externality. The outcome of the interaction between regions will be different according to the kind of interregional strategic relationships. If direct negotiation is excluded the framework is that of a non-cooperative multi-region optim-isation model. Each region is maximising its own welfare independently of the actions of the other regions. A cooperative framework considers direct negotiations between regions. The methodology integrates these strategic interactions between regions, by applying game theory developments.

The previously noted static, single-stage approach and what is known as the coalition paradigm have been the standard treatments undertaken in the literature so far.[12] Nevertheless, given that the actual future negotiation process is sequential in nature – like past negotiation rounds on trade policy – a *multi-stage sequential* approach seems more appropriate. Each region decides its optimal magnitude of the choice variables (the climate policy) in each of the periods of time – or stages – within the planning horizon. The optimal sequential action will inform about what to do concerning climate change policy in each of the future decades. This is indeed a dis-crete-time optimisation problem. Table 4.2 shows an example for the case of two regions deciding their policy for three temporal periods, for example, decades.

Table 4.2   Example of sequential game

	Player	Decision over period	Policy Options at the stage
Stage 1	region 1	1	{No, low or high mitigation}
Stage 2	region 2	1	{No, low or high mitigation}
Stage 3	region 1	2	{No, low or high mitigation}
Stage 4	region 2	2	{No, low or high mitigation}
Stage 5	region 1	3	{No, low or high mitigation}
Stage 6	region 2	3	{No, low or high mitigation}

In stage 1, region 1 chooses its policy for period 1 from a set of available policy options, that is, several GHG mitigation efforts, such as no, low or high mitigation. In the next stage, region 2 decides its policy for period 1, reacting to the decision previously taken by region 1. In stage 3, region 1 decides its policy for period 2, taking into account the policy implemented by region 1 in the previous stage. The process continues up to stage 6.

The game in extensive form with final payoffs, graphically represented by a tree structure with several nodes and branches, shows the order of play and the information available to each player at the time of his decision. Following Başar and Olsder (1999), if the *order of play* in which decisions are made is of significance, the game can be called dynamic. When there is a dynamic context with many players, these authors talk of 'dynamic game theory'.

Furthermore, the final payoffs are a function of *the information structure* of the game. If at each decision node the players know the previous moves of the game then the information structure is feedback. In this case the game can also be called sequential. On the contrary, if players do not know the previous moves, that is, players act once and independently of each other, the information structure is called open-loop. At this point, it is worth giving a more systematic characterisation of what is called the dynamic, sequential approach. Throughout this chapter various terms will refer to the same game approach or framework:

- Feedback information structure (versus open-loop information structure);
- Sequential (versus simultaneous);
- Multi-stage (versus one-shot);
- Dynamic (versus static).

Solving open-loop models analytically is easier than feedback ones. However the more realistic feedback structure can be numerically imposed easily if each player optimises by taking into account the previous moves of the game.

The benefits of the feedback approach are not only its realism but also its property of *dynamic consistency*. The optimal plan at the initial period (set under an open-loop scheme) may no longer be optimal at a future time, even without new information becoming available. With a feedback structure the optimal plan can be modified over time. The backward induction resolution procedure of the sequential game guarantees by definition that it is dynamically consistent.

Another advantage of the proposed sequential framework is its flexibility for the analysis of the post-Kyoto climate policies. Authors have usually assumed that the Kyoto Protocol emission limits will be kept forever. With the sequential approach this assumption can be overcome because regions are allowed to decide in each of the post-Kyoto periods their optimal policy among a set of policy options.

These advantages come at the cost of having intensive computation requirements. The IAM needs to be numerically solved for all the combinations of policy options for all regions. In this respect, Figure 4.1 gives an overview of this sequential methodology, and shows the role played by the IAMs and game framework. There is a decision tree, a game in extensive form, with as many branches as the number of policy options in each decision node (the same number for all stages) at the power of the number of stages. In the previous example, the number of branches would be $3^6 = 729$. Each branch then sets particular climate policies for all regions in all the periods of the planning horizon. An IAM is used to compute the payoffs that each region gets at the end of each branch (known as terminal payoffs). The game outcome is derived when the game framework is applied to the payoffs for all branches. The GHGAME Excel add-in,[13] designed for the SIADCERO research project, has been used to this end in this chapter.

The most natural equilibrium concept that can be applied to this game framework is the Nash equilibrium. Assuming that at each node the region is implementing a best reply reaction function, the Nash outcome is derived by backward induction.

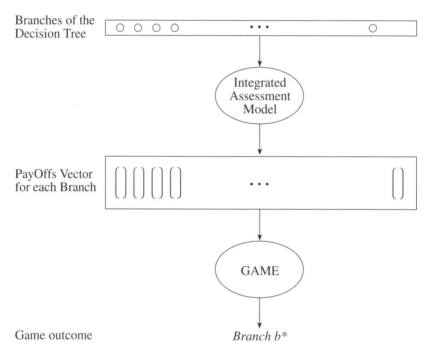

Figure 4.1   Overview of the sequential methodological framework

3.   OPEN-LOOP AND FEEDBACK GAME OUTCOMES: SOME EMPIRICAL RESULTS

3.1   The IAM-Game Setup

After having seen the theoretical game framework, in this section a concrete IAM and non-cooperative game are selected and applied, in very simple terms, to the current international discussions on climate policies.[14]

In order to numerically compute the payoffs a simple two-region IAM has been used.[15] It is largely based on the Dynamic Integrated model of the Climate and the Economy (DICE model; see Nordhaus, 1994), a global model, and its regional version: the Regional Integrated model of Climate and the Economy (RICE model; see Nordhaus and Yang, 1996). The model is an extension of the Ramsey growth model,[16] and compares the costs of reducing GHG emissions with the benefits derived from avoiding the damage caused by those emissions on the economic and natural systems. Each region optimises a utility function that depends on the present value of the consumption flows, the control variables being the savings rate and the GHG mitigation rate. The model consists of several equations representing the climate system. Moreover, it is assumed that there is a process of technology diffusion over time from the developed region to the developing one. The dynamic path of Total Factor Productivity (TFP) is the driving force of economic convergence.[17] The dynamic optimisation problem is not amenable to an analytical solution and therefore numerical methods are used.

The game has two players, identified as the two main sets of countries in the Kyoto Protocol: Annex B countries and non-Annex B countries. Five sequential stages are considered in the proposed game set-up. Figure 4.2 shows who moves when.

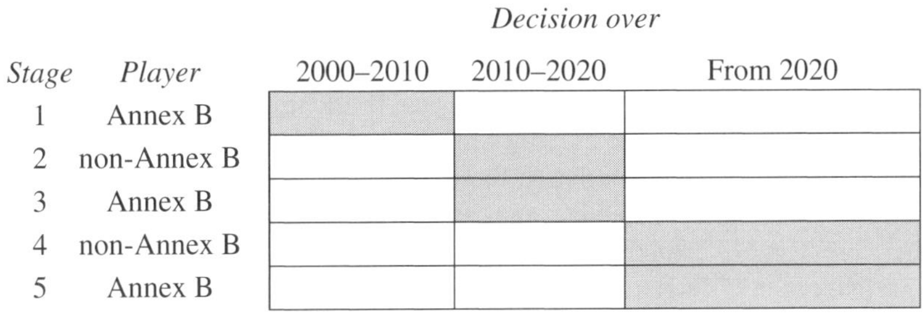

Decision over

Stage	Player	2000–2010	2010–2020	From 2020
1	Annex B	▓▓▓		
2	non-Annex B		▓▓▓	
3	Annex B		▓▓▓	
4	non-Annex B			▓▓▓
5	Annex B			▓▓▓

Figure 4.2.   Who moves when

The stages are described in the following:

- Stage 1: Kyoto Protocol (2000–2010), the Annex B region moves. The Annex B region decides its climate policy for the period 2000–2010.[18]
- Stage 2: Post-Kyoto (2010–2020), the non-Annex B region moves. By 2010 it is assumed that there will be another negotiation round on the climate policy for the period 2010–2020. Non-Annex B countries will be able to assess the extent to which the Kyoto commitment has been fulfilled and, accordingly, decide on the most appropriate policy to adopt.

- Stage 3: Post-Kyoto (2010–2020), the Annex B region moves. In a third sequential period immediately after the previous decision is taken, the Annex B region will decide its policy for the period 2010–2020. Therefore, developed countries can modify their policy depending on the actual reaction of developing countries to their actual emission control effort in the Kyoto Protocol. In this way a flexible post-Kyoto policy is foreseen, instead of assuming a fixed policy equivalent to the Kyoto absolute mitigation target.
- Stage 4: from 2020, the non-Annex B region moves. From 2020 for the sake of simplicity it is assumed that the non-Annex B region decides on a policy to be pursued in perpetuity.
- Stage 5: from 2020, the Annex B region moves. The next Annex B region move is assumed to take place immediately after the previous non-Annex B decision in full knowledge that the non-Annex B choice would be maintained perpetually. The Annex B policy is also assumed to be forever and definitive from 2020.

It is supposed that the costs of non-compliance are infinite, and so a region always meets its GHG commitments.

A key feature of the chosen IAM is that the GHG mitigation effort is defined with respect to a baseline scenario in which no mitigation measures are implemented. In the original DICE model the mitigation rate is continuous. For this game application it has been made discrete in order to compute the respective payoffs of the tree branches. In each stage of the game, a region can decide its policy among a set of three GHG mitigation policy options (always relative to the baseline): 0, 5 and 10 per cent reductions. Since the game has five stages and three policy options in each stage, there are $3^5 = 243$ branches in the tree. An iterative algorithm has been followed in order to determine the final set of policy options. If from the game outcome the chosen policy in a stage is 10 per cent (that is, in the upper bound of the range of policy options), a new set of policies is considered in another series of model runs: 5, 10 and 15 per cent. The idea is to have the final game outcome in the *interior* of the policy options range (for example, for the 0, 5, 10 per cent range, the interior outcome would be 5 per cent), but for the case when the chosen policy is do-nothing (that is, no GHG mitigation).

3.2   Results

The open-loop Nash outcome can be derived from the game in normal or matrix form, where all the combinations of the possible choices for both players are represented. Table 4.3 shows this matrix and the corresponding payoffs. Annex B can play do-nothing, mitigate by 5 per cent or

Table 4.3 Normal form of the game with utility payoffs

Stage			non-Annex B								
1	3	2 (5|4)	5%			10%			15%		
(Annex B)			5%	10%	15%	5%	10%	15%	5%	10%	15%
0	0	0	1.76	2.53	3.30	1.93	2.69	3.46	2.08	2.85	3.62
			2.52	2.93	0.86	2.44	2.86	0.78	1.66	2.07	0.00
		5%	2.18	2.95	3.72	2.34	3.11	3.89	2.50	3.25	4.01
			6.86	7.29	5.24	6.78	7.22	5.16	6.00	6.47	4.49
		10%	0.81	1.59	2.35	0.98	1.75	2.52	1.13	1.91	2.69
			11.22	11.67	9.70	11.15	11.59	9.60	10.36	10.83	8.80
	5%	0	1.84	2.61	3.38	2.00	2.76	3.54	2.16	2.93	3.70
			3.56	3.98	1.91	3.45	3.87	1.79	2.70	3.12	1.05
		5%	2.25	3.03	3.80	2.41	3.17	3.96	2.56	3.34	4.12
			7.91	8.34	6.29	7.80	8.29	6.17	7.10	7.50	5.44
		10%	0.88	1.67	2.45	1.05	1.82	2.61	1.22	1.99	2.75
			12.31	12.72	10.69	12.17	12.61	10.58	11.41	11.87	9.93
	10%	0	1.42	2.18	2.95	1.57	2.34	3.11	1.75	2.51	3.29
			4.61	5.03	2.96	4.50	4.91	2.84	3.79	4.21	2.14
		5%	1.83	2.55	3.38	1.98	2.76	3.52	2.16	2.92	3.71
			8.95	9.29	7.34	8.85	9.28	7.29	8.13	8.61	6.52
		10%	0.44	1.24	2.01	0.60	1.39	2.18	0.78	1.58	2.35
			13.41	13.77	11.79	13.28	13.70	11.64	12.57	12.96	10.95

Table 4.3 (continued)

Annex B			non-Annex B								
Stage 1	Stage 3	Stage 2 (5\4)	5%			10%			15%		
			5%	10%	15%	5%	10%	15%	5%	10%	15%
5%	0	0	1.84	2.61	3.38	2.01	2.78	3.55	2.17	2.94	3.71
10%	0	0	3.72	4.15	2.07	3.65	4.07	2.00	2.91	3.32	1.25
5%	0	5%	2.25	3.03	3.80	2.42	3.20	3.97	2.59	3.36	4.13
10%	0	5%	8.10	8.51	6.46	7.99	8.43	6.38	7.25	7.69	5.63
5%	0	10%	0.89	1.65	2.45	1.06	1.83	2.62	1.23	2.00	2.78
10%	0	10%	12.44	12.96	10.86	12.37	12.84	10.79	11.61	12.07	10.04
5%	5%	0	1.92	2.69	3.46	2.09	2.86	3.63	2.25	3.02	3.79
10%	5%	0	4.78	5.19	3.12	4.70	5.12	3.05	3.95	4.37	2.30
5%	5%	5%	2.34	3.11	3.86	2.50	3.26	4.05	2.67	3.44	4.22
10%	5%	5%	9.12	9.56	7.60	9.07	9.51	7.43	8.30	8.74	6.69
5%	5%	10%	0.96	1.73	2.53	1.12	1.90	2.67	1.31	2.08	2.86
10%	5%	10%	13.53	14.03	11.91	13.47	13.94	11.94	12.67	13.12	11.10
5%	10%	0	1.50	2.27	3.04	1.66	2.43	3.20	1.83	2.60	3.37
10%	10%	0	5.82	6.24	4.17	5.75	6.17	4.10	5.00	5.42	3.35
5%	10%	5%	1.91	2.69	3.46	2.08	2.85	3.63	2.23	3.02	3.79
10%	10%	5%	10.18	10.61	8.56	10.09	10.53	8.48	9.41	9.79	7.75
5%	10%	10%	0.53	1.30	2.09	0.71	1.49	2.25	0.87	1.64	2.44
10%	10%	10%	14.62	15.07	13.02	14.47	14.92	12.96	13.76	14.27	12.16

non-Annex B

Stage 1	Stage 3	Stage 2 5\4	5%			10%			15%		
			5%	10%	15%	5%	10%	15%	5%	10%	15%
Annex B 10%	0	0	1.29	2.06	2.83	1.46	2.23	3.00	1.62	2.39	3.16
			4.95	5.36	3.29	4.87	5.29	3.21	4.12	4.54	2.47
		5%	1.71	2.48	3.25	1.87	2.65	3.41	2.04	2.81	3.59
			9.29	9.72	7.68	9.21	9.65	7.63	8.46	8.91	6.86
		10%	0.32	1.12	1.90	0.51	1.29	2.07	0.68	1.45	2.23
			13.75	14.11	12.09	13.58	14.04	12.01	12.84	13.29	11.27
	5%	0	1.37	2.14	2.91	1.54	2.31	3.08	1.70	2.47	3.24
			5.99	6.41	4.34	5.91	6.33	4.26	5.17	5.59	3.52
		5%	1.79	2.56	3.33	1.95	2.72	3.50	2.11	2.89	3.65
			10.33	10.79	8.74	10.26	10.70	8.65	9.55	9.95	7.98
		10%	0.43	1.18	1.98	0.58	1.35	2.14	0.76	1.54	2.31
			14.70	15.24	13.14	14.68	15.16	13.11	13.88	14.34	12.33
	10%	0	0.95	1.72	2.49	1.11	1.88	2.65	1.28	2.05	2.82
			7.04	7.46	5.39	6.96	7.38	5.31	6.22	6.64	4.57
		5%	1.35	2.14	2.91	1.53	2.29	3.08	1.68	2.47	3.24
			11.41	11.83	9.79	11.32	11.80	9.70	10.63	11.01	8.96
		10%	0.00	0.76	1.53	0.17	0.94	1.73	0.33	1.11	1.89
			15.76	16.28	14.28	15.68	16.14	14.11	14.93	15.40	13.38

by 10 per cent in the three stages in which it moves. The non-Annex B region can mitigate by 5 per cent, 10 per cent or 15 per cent.[19] Since the Annex B region moves three times (Kyoto, post-Kyoto and forever) and the non-Annex B region twice (post-Kyoto and forever), then the Annex B has $3^3 = 27$ possible choices, and the non-Annex B $3^2 = 9$ choices. The game matrix has then 27 rows and nine columns. In each cell of this matrix, the payoff for the Annex B region appears in the first line and that of the non-Annex B region in the second.

The payoffs are the utility levels in the optimum normalised by the minimum value for each region. The numbers in shaded cells represent the *reaction function* of each player, that is, what his best reply is given each of the possible moves of the other player. The intersection of the reaction functions of both players (marked with a circle in Table 4.3) yields the Nash open-loop equilibrium: the Annex B region mitigates by 5 per cent in all its stages, and the non-Annex B region mitigates by 5 per cent in the post-Kyoto period and by 10 per cent in the forever period.

The feedback outcome is the same as that obtained with the open-loop information structure. Therefore, it seems that the kind of information structure does not matter (in the sense that the results in this particular game are independent of the information structure), a somehow unexpected result. This may be due not only to the particular IAM used and to the calibration of the model parameters, but also to the way the game is defined and solved.

When another payoff definition is taken into consideration this vision changes. Instead of using the utility values, the game can be solved with cardinal payoffs. In another series of numerical exercises the game has been solved with a different payoff definition: the sum of the discounted consumption flows up to the year 2200. The remaining of the IAM and game framework is the same. The normal form of the game appears in Table 4.4.

Table 4.5 represents the results obtained from the consumption payoff definition for the two possible information structures.

With consumption payoffs and under the open-loop information case, Annex B always mitigates by 5 per cent and non-Annex B by 15 per cent (see the outcome marked with a circle in Table 4.4). However, when a player can react to past moves of the other player, that is, under the feedback information structure, the equilibrium is different. Table 4.5 presents both the open-loop and feedback outcomes. Annex B mitigates more in the Kyoto period, by 10 per cent. The reaction of the non-Annex B region in the post-Kyoto period is to mitigate less, by 10 per cent, which could be interpreted as free-rider behaviour.[20] It could be argued that the Annex B region anticipates this reaction of the non-Annex B region, and consequently in order to offset it, decides to mitigate more in the Kyoto period.

Table 4.4 Normal form of the game with consumption payoffs

| Stage | | | | non-Annex B | | | | | | | | |
| 1 | 3 | 2 | 5\4 | 5% | | | 10% | | | 15% | | |
				5%	10%	15%	5%	10%	15%	5%	10%	15%
Annex B 0	0	0	0	44.420	55.835	67.301	46.528	58.046	69.531	48.799	60.197	71.662
				0.000	5.739	5.668	0.902	6.677	6.387	0.754	6.435	6.311
				53.542	64.682	76.022	55.681	67.099	78.145	57.984	65.187	41.008
				15.117	21.078	21.065	15.759	22.038	21.734	15.698	21.532	22.129
				39.395	51.156	49.440	40.839	52.126	57.042	43.562	52.181	64.832
				29.729	35.692	36.540	30.947	36.581	36.860	31.092	36.642	36.907
	5%	5%	5%	46.400	57.860	69.310	48.560	59.933	71.385	50.756	62.300	73.639
				2.509	8.116	8.337	3.484	9.318	9.166	3.332	9.099	9.081
				54.303	66.861	76.276	56.033	56.234	80.698	46.765	71.738	81.917
				17.772	23.850	23.076	18.828	24.604	24.347	18.693	24.550	24.494
				29.362	52.800	65.175	40.239	54.509	67.569	45.504	56.849	38.885
				32.681	38.844	38.744	33.963	39.602	39.191	33.278	39.063	39.550
	10%	10%	10%	43.744	55.230	66.698	45.928	57.387	68.868	48.186	59.624	71.133
				5.289	11.093	10.952	6.087	11.851	11.724	5.996	11.846	11.524
				52.771	49.586	76.019	54.092	65.882	64.538	57.684	56.714	80.143
				20.380	27.363	26.168	21.022	27.089	27.040	21.099	27.254	26.502
				1.201	50.181	52.332	17.549	48.294	63.404	20.137	54.515	62.646
				35.829	41.014	41.601	36.605	41.949	42.226	36.419	41.881	42.063

Table 4.4 (continued)

Stage 1	Stage 3	Stage 2	5\4	non-Annex B								
				5%			10%			15%		
				5%	10%	15%	5%	10%	15%	5%	10%	15%
Annex B 5%	0	0	0	46.851	58.268	69.749	49.034	60.472	71.952	51.245	62.674	74.119
			5%	2.782	8.588	8.195	3.411	9.492	9.240	3.075	9.446	9.137
			10%	47.889	67.676	78.089	58.412	69.686	81.231	60.220	73.005	83.112
		5%	0	18.046	23.708	23.756	18.696	24.433	24.336	18.848	24.117	24.439
			5%	41.137	34.199	64.949	41.711	52.660	67.821	45.343	57.871	68.931
			10%	32.577	38.711	39.015	34.027	39.881	39.607	33.416	39.207	39.485
		10%	0	48.793	60.225	71.711	50.945	62.444	73.927	53.140	64.642	76.122
			5%	4.912	11.082	11.228	6.431	11.951	11.849	6.302	11.932	11.926
			10%	58.128	68.392	53.353	53.105	74.464	83.750	62.390	73.742	85.044
	10%	0	0	20.482	26.228	26.807	21.307	27.082	27.195	20.952	26.853	27.335
			5%	32.487	24.523	67.228	30.113	34.963	29.115	47.469	59.924	72.120
			10%	35.690	41.994	41.204	36.604	42.457	42.712	36.342	42.340	42.526
		5%	0	46.160	57.585	69.153	48.498	59.866	71.360	50.625	62.070	73.564
			5%	8.009	13.754	13.800	8.979	14.586	14.599	8.763	14.627	14.607
			10%	51.773	67.129	78.723	57.474	69.318	80.332	45.375	70.558	80.794
		10%	0	23.182	28.949	28.956	24.029	29.849	29.443	24.319	29.991	29.473
			5%	12.941	22.976	50.352	41.056	54.927	48.102	37.887	26.306	67.804
			10%	38.218	43.387	44.347	39.098	45.112	45.249	39.278	44.992	44.921

non-Annex B

Stage			5%			10%			15%		
1	3	5\4	5%	10%	15%	5%	10%	15%	5%	10%	15%
Annex B 10%	0	0	44.320	55.752	67.230	46.459	57.938	69.435	48.668	60.149	71.635
			5.597	11.470	11.191	6.202	12.189	12.066	6.334	12.131	12.022
		5%	52.915	64.823	74.958	55.145	67.230	70.578	57.941	69.127	80.688
			20.328	26.517	26.244	21.378	27.402	27.530	21.398	27.105	27.082
		10%	0.000	49.845	60.544	40.740	51.307	64.649	42.507	55.147	66.902
			35.769	41.589	41.377	36.248	42.378	42.702	36.431	42.140	42.336
	5%	0	46.264	57.701	69.185	48.468	59.921	71.397	50.667	62.109	73.600
			8.221	13.822	13.782	8.717	14.929	14.761	8.950	14.446	14.573
		5%	55.438	61.637	75.771	57.401	68.601	81.309	54.665	71.017	62.139
			23.591	28.996	29.572	24.537	29.765	29.923	24.042	29.707	30.073
		10%	41.242	25.512	63.587	34.195	34.636	57.534	45.609	57.098	66.686
			38.303	44.440	44.625	39.633	45.181	45.198	39.258	45.002	45.375
	10%	0	43.724	55.169	66.646	45.908	57.366	68.851	48.122	59.557	71.061
			10.820	16.597	16.140	11.678	17.517	17.337	11.327	17.468	17.208
		5%	45.998	63.762	74.272	52.193	55.021	78.047	43.326	68.899	80.008
			26.080	31.719	31.921	26.805	33.052	32.553	26.857	32.757	32.545
		10%	38.253	34.009	24.147	40.366	51.476	64.425	42.985	54.840	65.150
			41.111	47.176	47.051	41.487	47.776	47.374	41.482	47.271	47.580

Table 4.5 Nash open-loop and feedback outcomes: consumption payoffs

Stage	Period	Region	Open-loop	Feedback
1	Kyoto	Annex B	5	10
2	Post-Kyoto	non-Annex B	15	10
3		Annex B	5	5
4	Forever	non-Annex B	15	15
5		Annex B	5	5

This interpretation is at the heart of the feedback Nash equilibrium concept and is logically related to the backward induction procedure implemented to solve the game.

Furthermore, one key characteristic of the games so far discussed should be noted at this point. In the game with utility payoffs, all the subgames always have the same outcome as that of the Nash outcome, for both the open-loop and feedback cases. Players implement a 'constant strategy' or constant decision rule: they always choose the same action or move irrespective of what the other player has made in the previous stages.[21] This could be interpreted in the following way: the Nash equilibrium path is very stable. Any player will always choose the Nash equilibrium action for any possible action the other player follows.

On the contrary, the game with consumption payoffs does not yield constant strategies. Table 4.6 presents all the possible subgames and the corresponding outcomes[22] for the feedback information structure. Subgame number one is the feedback Nash outcome, that is, the outcome of the whole game. In the table figures in shaded cells represent the assumed previous regional policies leading to each subgame. For instance, subgame number two would be the game outcome if Annex B did nothing in the Kyoto period (instead of 10 per cent mitigation in the Nash equilibrium). What happens in the following two stages seems logical. Both regions do more (with respect to the feedback outcome, subgame number one) in the post-Kyoto period, compensating the inaction of the Annex B region in the Kyoto period.

It is worth studying subgame number three: this would be the game outcome if Annex B mitigated by 5 per cent in the Kyoto period, as in the open-loop equilibrium (instead of 10 per cent mitigation in the feedback equilibrium). If the Annex B region reduces emissions by 5 per cent, as in the open-loop framework, then the non-Annex B region reacts by mitigating less (by 5 per cent, instead of by 10 per cent in the feedback equilibrium) to which the Annex B region responds with more mitigation (by 10

Table 4.6   All the subgame outcomes for the case of consumption payoffs

Sub-Game	Annex B Kyoto	non-Annex B Post Kyoto	Annex B Post Kyoto	non-Annex B For ever	Annex B For ever	Leaf
1	10%	10%	5%	15%	5%	206
2	0%	15%	10%	15%	5%	80
3	5%	5%	10%	15%	5%	107
4	10%	10%	5%	15%	5%	206
5	0%	15%	10%	15%	5%	26
6	0%	10%	5%	15%	5%	44
7	0%	5%	10%	15%	5%	80
8	5%	5%	10%	15%	5%	107
9	5%	10%	5%	15%	5%	125
10	5%	15%	5%	15%	5%	152
11	10%	5%	5%	15%	5%	179
12	10%	10%	5%	15%	5%	206
13	10%	15%	5%	10%	5%	230
14	0%	5%	0%	10%	5%	5
15	0%	5%	5%	10%	5%	14
16	0%	5%	10%	15%	5%	26
17	0%	10%	0%	10%	5%	32
18	0%	10%	5%	15%	5%	44
19	0%	10%	10%	10%	5%	50
20	0%	15%	0%	10%	5%	59
21	0%	15%	5%	10%	5%	68
22	0%	15%	10%	15%	5%	80
23	5%	5%	0%	15%	5%	89
24	5%	5%	5%	10%	5%	95
25	5%	5%	10%	15%	5%	107
26	5%	10%	0%	10%	5%	113
27	5%	10%	5%	15%	5%	125
28	5%	10%	10%	10%	5%	131
29	5%	15%	0%	15%	5%	143
30	5%	15%	5%	15%	5%	152
31	5%	15%	10%	10%	5%	158
32	10%	5%	0%	10%	5%	167
33	10%	5%	5%	15%	5%	179
34	10%	5%	10%	15%	5%	188
35	10%	10%	0%	15%	5%	197
36	10%	10%	5%	15%	5%	206
37	10%	10%	10%	15%	5%	215
38	10%	15%	0%	10%	5%	221
39	10%	15%	5%	10%	5%	230
40	10%	15%	10%	10%	5%	239

Table 4.6   (continued)

Sub-Game	Annex B Kyoto	non-Annex B Post Kyoto	Annex B Post Kyoto	non-Annex B For ever	Annex B For ever	Leaf
41	0%	5%	0%	5%	5%	2
42	0%	5%	0%	10%	5%	5
43	0%	5%	0%	15%	5%	8
44	0%	5%	5%	5%	5%	11
45	0%	5%	5%	10%	5%	14
46	0%	5%	5%	15%	5%	17
47	0%	5%	10%	5%	5%	20
48	0%	5%	10%	10%	0%	22
49	0%	5%	10%	15%	5%	26
50	0%	10%	0%	5%	5%	29
51	0%	10%	0%	10%	5%	32
52	0%	10%	0%	15%	5%	35
53	0%	10%	5%	5%	5%	38
54	0%	10%	5%	10%	0%	40
55	0%	10%	5%	15%	5%	44
56	0%	10%	10%	5%	5%	47
57	0%	10%	10%	10%	5%	50
58	0%	10%	10%	15%	0%	52
59	0%	15%	0%	5%	5%	56
60	0%	15%	0%	10%	5%	59
61	0%	15%	0%	15%	0%	61
62	0%	15%	5%	5%	0%	64
63	0%	15%	5%	10%	5%	68
64	0%	15%	5%	15%	5%	71
65	0%	15%	10%	5%	5%	74
66	0%	15%	10%	10%	0%	76
67	0%	15%	10%	15%	5%	80
68	5%	5%	0%	5%	5%	83
69	5%	5%	0%	10%	5%	86
70	5%	5%	0%	15%	5%	89
71	5%	5%	5%	5%	5%	92
72	5%	5%	5%	10%	5%	95
73	5%	5%	5%	15%	0%	97
74	5%	5%	10%	5%	5%	101
75	5%	5%	10%	10%	5%	104
76	5%	5%	10%	15%	5%	107
77	5%	10%	0%	5%	5%	110
78	5%	10%	0%	10%	5%	113
79	5%	10%	0%	15%	5%	116
80	5%	10%	5%	5%	5%	119

Table 4.6 (continued)

Sub-Game	Annex B Kyoto	non-Annex B Post Kyoto	Annex B Post Kyoto	non-Annex B For ever	Annex B For ever	Leaf
81	5%	10%	5%	10%	5%	122
82	5%	10%	5%	15%	5%	125
83	5%	10%	10%	5%	5%	128
84	5%	10%	10%	10%	5%	131
85	5%	10%	10%	15%	5%	134
86	5%	15%	0%	5%	5%	137
87	5%	15%	0%	10%	5%	140
88	5%	15%	0%	15%	5%	143
89	5%	15%	5%	5%	5%	146
90	5%	15%	5%	10%	5%	149
91	5%	15%	5%	15%	5%	152
92	5%	15%	10%	5%	0%	154
93	5%	15%	10%	10%	5%	158
94	5%	15%	10%	15%	5%	161
95	10%	5%	0%	5%	5%	164
96	10%	5%	0%	10%	5%	167
97	10%	5%	0%	15%	5%	170
98	10%	5%	5%	5%	5%	173
99	10%	5%	5%	10%	5%	176
100	10%	5%	5%	15%	5%	179
101	10%	5%	10%	5%	5%	182
102	10%	5%	10%	10%	5%	185
103	10%	5%	10%	15%	5%	188
104	10%	5%	0%	5%	5%	191
105	10%	10%	0%	10%	5%	194
106	10%	10%	0%	15%	5%	197
107	10%	10%	5%	5%	5%	200
108	10%	10%	5%	10%	5%	203
109	10%	10%	5%	15%	5%	206
110	10%	10%	10%	5%	5%	209
111	10%	10%	10%	10%	0%	211
112	10%	10%	10%	15%	5%	215
113	10%	15%	0%	5%	5%	218
114	10%	15%	0%	10%	5%	221
115	10%	15%	0%	15%	5%	224
116	10%	15%	5%	5%	5%	227
117	10%	15%	5%	10%	5%	230
118	10%	15%	5%	15%	0%	232
119	10%	15%	10%	5%	0%	235
120	10%	15%	10%	10%	5%	239
121	10%	15%	10%	15%	5%	242

per cent, instead of by 5 per cent in the feedback equilibrium). It seems that the Annex B region to some extent compensates its own less active climate policy of the Kyoto period with more action in the post-Kyoto period. The non-Annex B region itself decides to mitigate less in that period once it observes, and consequently takes into account, the lower mitigation effort of the Annex B region in the Kyoto period. In fact this subgame shows *the temporal inconsistency of the open-loop outcome.*

Other interesting interpretations could be extracted from the analysis of Table 4.6. For instance, subgame number 14 shows the consequences of the inaction of the Annex B region in both the Kyoto and post-Kyoto periods. The non-Annex B region decides to be less active in the forever period: reduce emissions by 10 per cent (instead of by 15 per cent in the feedback Nash outcome, subgame number one).

Whether there exist constant strategies therefore might be one of the reasons explaining the fact that the open-loop and feedback outcomes cases differ.

Another interpretation of the results relates to the comparison of the outcomes derived with the two different kinds of payoffs (see Table 4.7). With *consumption* payoffs the policies chosen in each stage for both players

Table 4.7   Nash open-loop and feedback outcomes: utility and consumption payoffs

Stage	Period	Region	Utility Payoffs		Consumption Payoffs	
			Open-loop	Feedback	Open-loop	Feedback
1	Kyoto	Annex B	5	5	5	10
2	Post-Kyoto	non-Annex B	5	5	15	10
3		Annex B	5	5	5	5
4	Forever	non-Annex B	10	10	15	15
5		Annex B	5	5	5	5

are always either the same or with more mitigation than in the game with utility payoffs. In particular, the non-Annex B region always mitigates more with respect to the utility payoff game, both in the open-loop and feedback cases. The concavity assumption of the utility function[23] could explain this. The same gain in consumption in a certain future decade because of higher mitigation today is more valued with a consumption payoff function than with a utility function, leading to more mitigation efforts.

4. CONCLUSIONS

In Císcar and Soria (2002) the authors introduced the *sequential* or *feedback* approach in order to model regional climate policies. In this chapter we go further by comparing the standard approach in the literature, *simultaneous* or *open-loop*, with the sequential approach. Moreover, our study explores the implications of using the simultaneous approach in terms of the *time consistency* of climate policies.

With utility payoffs the information structure of the game, whether dynamic (that is, feedback) or static (that is, open-loop), does not affect the game Nash outcome. This is to some extent an unexpected result given the real characteristics of international talks on climate policy. We believe that a game with players taking decisions sequentially is realistic and therefore a well-defined game should meet this dynamic requirement. Yet the numerical results do not confirm this point. It rather seems that each region does not react to the previous moves of the other region. It keeps on doing the same (*constant strategy*) as if it had planned all future actions before the first move.

On the contrary, when the game is solved using consumption payoffs it seems that the information available to the players does matter for the game outcome. The dynamic game outcome does not coincide with the static one. In particular, the outcomes for the Kyoto and post-Kyoto periods do change. The open-loop strategy approach leads to a *dynamically inconsistent* equilibrium.

It might seem less rigorous to use the consumption payoffs because the optimisation problem of each branch of the tree is computed by maximising the utility levels, and not the consumption variable. From the policymakers perspective, however, it could be argued that when solving the game the consumption considerations, cardinal by definition, are more relevant than the utility levels. A kind of compromise between rationality of decision makers when choosing their strategies, and economic theory when solving the optimisation problem may be found in this way, but of course subject to some degree of controversy.

A methodological conclusion would be that whether the open-loop and feedback equilibria are the same should be checked in any numerical exercise in order to guarantee the crucial dynamic consistency property of the feedback equilibrium.

NOTES

Work performed in partial fulfilment of the Strategic Integrated Assessment of Dynamic Carbon Emission Reduction Policies (SIADCERO) research project, partially financed by the European Commission (DG Research), contract number ENG3-12999-00011. The authors would like to thank Elena Múgica and two anonymous referees for their comments and suggestions. The views expressed are those of the authors, and do not necessarily reflect those of the European Commission.

1. See IPCC (2001).
2. See Oberthür and Ott (1999).
3. Valverde et al. (1999) study the sequential nature of climate change negotiations under uncertainty with the influence diagrams method.
4. See Petit (1990) and de Zeeuw and van der Ploeg (1991) for the theory and applications in other domains.
5. For a formal analysis of these game concepts, including the closed-loop information structure case, see Başar and Olsder (1999).
6. See the discussion on this respect of de Zeeuw and van der Ploeg (1991).
7. The differential game refers to a game in which players choose over a continuous variable. In difference games, the ones used to implement the sequential approach, players optimise over a discrete variable.
8. This at first would imply that the degree of mitigation of the pollutant in a feedback Nash equilibrium is lower than that of an open-loop Nash equilibrium.
9. In this respect, using the open-loop model in the analysis of international pollution problems underestimates the gains from cooperation.
10. See, for example, Peck and Teisberg (1995), Nordhaus and Yang (1996), Císcar and Soria (2000), Bosello *et al.* (2001), Buchner et al. (2001), Eyckmans and Tulkens (2001), and Buchner et al. (2002).
11. This does not explicitly consider the equity implications of the problem, nor the details of how to implement and achieve the mitigation goals. This is to some extent a necessary simplification in order to keep the complexity of the numerical exercises within the current computation possibilities.
12. Some authors have applied a two-stage approach (for example, Buchner et al., 2002), between the standard one-stage approach of the literature and the multi-stage perspective proposed in this chapter.
13. See Forgó et al. (2001).
14. It is not at all straightforward to determine the complex process of international negotiations on climate change for the coming decades. The approach here proposed is *one* possible way of modelling the future international 'rounds' on climate policy, which seems reasonable given the likely sequential nature of the political negotiations and the resulting decisions. Indeed, the framework is purely sequential. Alternative cases combining simultaneous and sequential decisions could be envisaged.
15. A more detailed description of the model appears in Císcar and Soria (2002).
16. See, for instance, chapter 2 of Barro and Sala-i-Martin (1995).
17. See Bernard and Jones (1996).
18. It is implicitly assumed that in the period 2000–2010 non-Annex B countries will not take measures to reduce emissions, given their lack of commitment in the Kyoto Protocol.
19. With a 0, 5, 10 per cent range of policy options, the game outcome of the non-Annex B region is 10 per cent for both the post-Kyoto and forever periods, therefore at the upper limit of the range of policy options. The game was then solved, applying the noted iterative algorithm, with a 5, 10, 15 per cent range.
20. Indeed, some authors have obtained analogous empirical results. For the acid rain problem Mäler and de Zeeuw (1998) derive numerically a similar but rather small effect.
21. Following de Zeeuw and van der Ploeg (1991) this is called subgame perfectness. The Nash equilibrium for the whole game remains a Nash equilibrium for every subgame starting from any decision node after the first node of the game. In this respect the

dynamic consistency property is less strong than the subgame perfectness one, as noted by these authors, because subgame perfectness implies in addition that there is no deviation from any point off the equilibrium path either.
22. This table is computed by the GHGAME software developed in the SIADCERO project (see Forgó et al., 2001, available at http://energy.jrs.es/pages/finished/projects.htm).
23. The utility level is equal to the population times the logarithmic of per capita consumption.

REFERENCES

Barro, R.J. and X. Sala-i-Martin (1995), *Economic Growth*, New York: McGraw-Hill, Inc.

Başar, T. and G.J. Olsder (1999), *Dynamic Noncooperative Game Theory*, 2nd edn, SIAM Classics in Applied Mathematics 23, Philadelphia: SIAM – Society for Industrial and Applied Mathematics.

Bernard, A. and C. Jones (1996), 'Comparing apples to oranges: productivity convergence and measurement across industries and countries', *American Economic Review*, **86**, 1216–38.

Bosello, F., B. Buchner, C. Carraro and D. Raggi (2001), 'Can equity enhance efficiency? Lessons from the Kyoto Protocol', FEEM Working Paper 49.01, Milan.

Buchner, B., C. Carraro and I. Cersosimo (2001), 'On the consequences of the U.S. withdrawal from the Kyoto/Bonn Protocol', FEEM Working Paper 102.01, Milan.

Buchner, B., C. Carraro, I. Cersosimo and C. Marchiori (2002), 'Back to Kyoto? US participation and the linkage between R&D and climate cooperation', FEEM Working Paper 22.02, Milan.

Císcar, J.C. and A. Soria (2000), 'Economic convergence and climate policy', *Energy Policy*, **28**, 749–61.

Císcar, J.C., and A. Soria (2002), 'Prospective analysis of beyond Kyoto climate policy: a sequential game framework', *Energy Policy*, **30(15)**, 1327–35.

Eyckmans, J. and H. Tulkens (2001), 'Simulating coalitionally stable burden sharing agreements for the climate change problem', CLIMNEG Working Paper 18, Université Catholique de Louvain, Belgium.

Forgó, F., J. Fülop and M. Prill (2001), 'GHGAME: an Excel add-in for computation with game theoretic models in the SIADCERO project. User's guide', Deliverable D4b. Internal Report of the partially EC-funded SIADCERO project. ORDBUES and MTA-SZTAKI.

IPCC (2001), *Climate Change 2001. The Scientific Basis*, IPCC Third Assessment Report: Contributions of IPCC Working Group I, Cambridge: Cambridge University Press.

Mäler, K.-G. and A. de Zeeuw (1998), 'The acid rain differential game', *Environmental and Resource Economics*, **12(2)**, 167–84.

Manne, A. and R. Richels (1999), 'The Kyoto Protocol: a cost-effective strategy for meeting environmental objectives?' *The Energy Journal*, 1999 special issue, 1–24.

Nordhaus, W.D. (1994), *Managing the Global Commons. The Economics of Climate Change*, Cambridge: The MIT Press.

Nordhaus, W.D. and J. Boyer (2000). *Warming the World. Economic Models of Global Warming*, London: The MIT Press.

Nordhaus, W.D. and Z. Yang (1996), 'A regional general equilibrium model of alternative climate change strategies', *American Economic Review*, **86(4)**, September, 741–65.

Oberthür, S. and H.E. Ott (1999), *The Kyoto Protocol. International Climate Policy for the 21st Century*, Berlin: Ecologic, Springer.

OECD (1999), *Action against Climate Change. The Kyoto Protocol and Beyond*, Paris: Organisation for Economic Cooperation and Development (OECD).

Peck, S.C. and T.J. Teisberg (1995), 'International CO_2 emissions control: an analysis using CETA', *Energy Policy*, **23**, 297–308.

Peck, S.C. and T.J. Teisberg (1999), 'CO_2 emissions control agreements: incentives for regional participation', *The Energy Journal*, 1999 special issue, 367–90.

Petit, M.L. (1990), *Control Theory and Dynamic Games in Economic Policy Analysis*, Cambridge: Cambridge University Press.

van der Ploeg, F. and A.J. de Zeeuw (1992), 'International aspects of pollution control', *Environmental and Resource Economics*, **2**, 117–39.

Valverde, J., H.D. Jacoby and G.M. Kaufman (1999), 'Sequential climate decisions under uncertainty: an integrated framework', *Journal of Environmental Modelling and Assessment*, **4**, 87–101.

de Zeeuw, A.J. and F. van der Ploeg (1991), 'Difference games and policy evaluation: a conceptual framework', *Oxford Economic Papers*, **43**, 612–36.

PART II

Sharing environmental costs

5. Cost sharing in a joint project[1]
Stef Hendrikus Tijs and Rodica Brânzei

1. INTRODUCTION

Cooperation is an essential part of human interaction. Environmental problems in particular call for cooperation. Game theory can contribute to smoothing cooperation by developing attractive and transparent rules for the allocation of costs or rewards among the participants in joint projects. There is a huge literature dealing with cost sharing problems using game theory. For surveys see Tijs and Driessen (1986) and Young (1994).

In this chapter we consider situations where agents plan to cooperate in a complex project. The agents have to decide about the form of the project and about the associated cost sharing. Both facets depend on the relevant costs and the budgets (which we identify with the willingness to pay and the rewards) of the agents for the different forms which the project may finally take. Our model can be used, for example, for the following: cooperation in irrigation systems (cf. Aadland and Kolpin, 1998; Kolpin and Aadland, 2001), airport landing networks (cf. Brânzei et al., 2002; Koster et al., 2001, Littlechild and Thompson, 1977; Potters and Sudhölter, 1999), railway networks with facilities (Fragnelli et al., 2000; Norde et al., 2002), and also car pooling, sharing a clubhouse and sharing playing-fields by different clubs and so on. In an irrigation system the wishes of the participants differ and are determined by the position of the pieces of land owned by the participants. In a railway system intercity trains will require different facilities from local trains and so on. In an airport landing network the wishes of the participants depend on the size of their aircraft and the flights on offer.

To simplify our task in this chapter we suppose from now on that there is a collection of basic units (components) such that each feasible project consists of a subset of these components, and such that the cost of such a feasible project is equal to the sum of the costs of the components involved. Further we suppose that the benefits increase if the set of components involved increases. In railway projects the basic units are tracks between two neighbouring railway stations and available facilities at the railway stations. In irrigation systems and in airport landing systems the basic units are ditch pieces and landing strip pieces, respectively.

The outline of this chapter is as follows. In Section 2 we introduce the formal model of a joint project situation and a related cooperative game. Sufficient conditions are given which guarantee that the game is a convex game. In Section 3 we describe for a structured joint project a flexible procedure that is based on the decomposition of its related cost sharing problem into a finite number of simple cost sharing problems to which cost sharing rules from the taxation literature can be applied. Different aspects regarding this procedure and its relation to the related cooperative TU-game are discussed.

2. JOINT PROJECT SITUATIONS AND JOINT ENTERPRISE GAMES

A *joint project situation* is a tuple $<N, A, c, F, (R)_{i \in N}>$ where N is the set of agents involved in the cooperation, A is the set of basic units, $c : A \rightarrow R_+$ the cost function, $F \subset 2^A$ the set of feasible projects, and $R_i : F \rightarrow R_+$ the reward function of agent $i \in N$. In the following we suppose (J.1) and (J.2), with

(J.1) $\phi \in F$ and $R_i(\phi) = 0$ for each $i \in N$.

(J.2)   If $\pi_1, \pi_2 \in F$ and $\pi_1 \subset \pi_2$, then $R_i(\pi_1) \leq R_i(\pi_2)$ for each $i \in N$ (*Monotonicity*).

We will say that F is a *lattice* if (J.3) holds, with

(J.3)   If $\pi_1, \pi_2 \in F$, then $\pi_1 \cap \pi_2 \in F$, $\pi_1 \cup \pi_2 \in F$ (*Lattice property*).

We suppose that the agents choose a feasible optimal project π_1 where

$$\pi_1 \in argmax_{\pi \in F} \left(\sum_{i \in N} R_i(\pi) - c(\pi) \right) \text{ and } c(\pi) = \sum_{a \in \pi} c(a). \text{ To solve the cost}$$

sharing problem, or equivalently, to solve the problem of dividing the total

benefit $\sum_{i \in N} R_i(\pi_1) - c(\pi_1)$, the related cooperative game $<N, v>$, which we

call the *joint enterprise game*, may be helpful, where for the coalition $S \in 2^N$, the worth $v(S)$ is equal to

$$\max_{\pi \in F} \left(\sum_{i \in S} R_i(\pi) - c(\pi) \right).$$

Then one can use for this joint enterprise game standard solutions such as the Shapley value (Shapley, 1953), the nucleolus (Schmeidler, 1969) or the τ-value (Tijs, 1981) to solve the benefit allocation problem. When the game is convex the Shapley value is especially appealing, because in this case the core is large and the Shapley value is the barycentre of the core. Recall (cf. Shapley, 1971) that a game $<N,v>$ is a *convex game* if for all S, $T \in 2^N$: $v(S \cup T) + v(S \cap T) \geq v(S) + v(T)$. In Theorem 2.1 sufficient conditions are given in a joint project situation to guarantee that the corresponding joint enterprise game is convex. A role is played here by the supermodularity property of R_i for each $i \in N$, if F is a lattice. Recall that $R_i : F \rightarrow R_+$ is a *supermodular function* if

$$R_i(\pi_1 \cup \pi_2) + R_i(\pi_1 \cap \pi_2) \geq R_i(\pi_1) + R_i(\pi_2).$$

In general, a joint enterprise game is not necessarily convex. Even the core $C(V)$ may be empty (cf. Feltkamp et al., 1996).

Example 2.1. (A connection problem) Consider the graph $<V, A>$ with vertex set $\{v_0, v_1, v_2, v_3\}$ and arc set $A = \{a_1, a_2, a_3, a_4\}$ with $a_1 = \langle v_0, v_1 \rangle$, $a_2 = \langle v_1, v_2 \rangle$, $a_3 = \langle v_2, v_3 \rangle$, and $a_4 = \langle v_0, v_3 \rangle$. Suppose agent i wants to connect v_0 with v_i, via a path, where $i \in N = \{1, 2, 3\}$ and the cost of using an arc a equals $c(a) = 10$. Suppose that $F = 2^A$ and that a correct connection corresponds to a benefit 12 for the involved agent. Then this situation corresponds to the joint project situation $<N, A, c, 2^A, (R_i)_{i \in N}>$, where $R_i(\pi) = 12$ if π contains a path connecting v_i with v_0 and $R_i(\pi) = 0$ otherwise. The corresponding joint enterprise game $<N, v>$ is given by $v(\{1\}) = v(\{3\}) = 2$, $v(\{2\}) = 0$, $v(\{1, 2\}) = v(\{1, 3\}) = v(\{2, 3\}) = 4$, and $v(N) = 6$. The Shapley value of this game equals $(2\frac{1}{3}, 1\frac{1}{3}, 2\frac{1}{3})$ and is unequal to the unique core element $(2, 2, 2)$. The game is not convex because $v(\{1, 2\}) + v(\{2, 3\}) > v(\{1, 2, 3\}) + v(\{2\})$. Note that $F = 2^A$ is a lattice but $R_2 : F \rightarrow R_+$ is not supermodular: $R_2(\pi_1) + R_2(\pi_2) = 24 > 12 = R_2(\pi_1 \cap \pi_2) + R_2(\pi_1 \cup \pi_2)$ with $\pi_1 = \{a_1, a_2\}$ and $\pi_2 = \{a_3, a_4\}$.

Now we arrive at the main result of this section.

Theorem 2.1. *Let $<N, v>$ be the cooperative joint enterprise game corresponding to the joint project situation $<N, A, c, F, (R_i)_{i \in N}>$. Suppose that F is a lattice and that $R_i : F \rightarrow R_+$ is supermodular for each $i \in N$. Then $<N, v>$ is a convex game.*

Proof.   Take $S, T \in 2^N$. Let $\alpha \in F$ and $\beta \in F$ be such that

(i) $\sum\limits_{i \in S} R_i(\alpha) - c(\alpha) = v(S), \sum\limits_{i \in T} R_i(\beta) - c(\beta) = v(T)$.

Note that from (J.2) it follows
(ii) $R_i(\alpha) \leq R_i(\alpha \cup \beta)$ for $i \in S \backslash T$
(iii) $R_i(\beta) \leq R_i(\alpha \cup \beta)$ for $i \in T \backslash S$,

and from the supermodularity of R_i

(iv) $R_i(\alpha) + R_i(\beta) \leq R_i(\alpha \cup \beta) + R_i(\alpha \cap \beta)$ for $i \in S \cap T$.

Adding the inequalities in (ii), (iii) and (iv) we obtain

(v) $\sum\limits_{i \in S} R_i(\alpha) + \sum\limits_{i \in T} R_i(\beta) \leq \sum\limits_{i \in S \cup T} R_i(\alpha \cup \beta) + \sum\limits_{i \in S \cap T} R_i(\alpha \cap \beta)$.

Note that the additivity of the cost function implies

(vi) $c(\alpha) + c(\beta) = c(\alpha \cup \beta) + c(\alpha \cap \beta)$.

Since $\sum\limits_{i \in S \cup T} R_i(\alpha \cup \beta) - c(\alpha \cup \beta) \leq v(S \cup T)$ and $\sum\limits_{i \in S \cap T} R_i(\alpha \cap \beta) - c(\alpha \cap \beta) \leq$

$v(S \cap T)$, we obtain from (i), (v), and (vi):

(vii) $v(S) + v(T) \leq v(S \cup T) + v(S \cap T)$.

Hence, $<N, v>$ is a convex game. ∎

Remark 2.1. One can easily see that the game $<N, v>$ is still convex if in Theorem 2.1 we weaken the additivity condition for the cost function by assuming that the cost function is submodular. The proof of this generalization is the same, except in (*vi*) the equality is changed into the inequality $c(\alpha) + c(\beta) \geq c(\alpha \cup \beta) + c(\alpha \cap \beta)$.

Let us call a function $R_i : F \rightarrow R$ a *one-step reward function* if there is a $b_i > 0$ and a $\pi_i \in F$ such that $R_i(\pi) = b_i$ if $\pi_i \subset \pi$ and $R_i(\pi) = 0$ otherwise.
    If F is a lattice, then a one-step reward function is supermodular. From Theorem 2.1 we obtain then the following corollary.

Corollary 2.2. *Let $<N, v>$ be the joint enterprise game corresponding to the joint project situation $<N, A, c, 2^A, (R_i)_{i \in N}>$ and suppose that the reward functions R_i are one-step reward functions. Then $<N, v>$ is a convex game.*

A proof of Corollary 2.2 can also be found in Koster et al. (2002).

The next corollary of Theorem 2.1 deals with tree-based joint project situations. We will say that a *joint project situation* $<N, A, c, F, (R_i)_{i \in N}>$ is *based on the tree* $<V, A>$, with root $v_0 \in V$, if the basic units are the arcs of the tree, and if each feasible project consists of the arcs of a subtree of $<V, A>$ with root v_0.

Note that F is a lattice for tree-based joint project situations.

Corollary 2.3. *Let $<N, v>$ be the joint enterprise game corresponding to the tree-based joint project situation $<N, A, c, F, (R_i)_{i \in N}>$ and suppose that the reward functions R_i are one-step reward functions. Then $<N, v>$ is a convex game.*

A special case of Corollary 2.3, where the underlying tree is a rooted line graph, was proved in Brânzei et al. (2002).

3. STRUCTURED JOINT PROJECTS AND SIMPLE COST SHARING RULES

In this section we want to describe how well-known cost sharing rules applied to simple cost sharing problems can be helpful in solving in an appealing and transparent manner the reward sharing problem related to structured joint project situations. Here *a simple cost sharing problem* is a tuple $<N, c, b>$, where N is the set of agents, $c > 0$ is the cost to be paid by the agents and $b \in R_+^N$, the maximal contribution vector, where b_i is the maximum contribution to c which agent $i \in N$ is willing to pay that satisfies the condition $c \leq \sum_{i \in N} b_i$. A cost sharing rule T assigns to problems of the form $<N, c, b>$ with $0 < c \leq \sum_{i \in N} b_i$ a vector $T(N, c, b) \in R^N$, where $0 \leq T_i(N, c, b) \leq b_i$ for each $i \in N$ and $\sum_{i \in N} T_i(N, c, b) = c$. Well known from the taxation literature (Young, 1987) and the bankruptcy literature (Aumann and Maschler, 1985) are the cost sharing rules PROP (the proportional rule) and CEC (the constrained equal contribution rule). For each $i \in N$, $PROP_i(N, c, b) = (\Sigma b_j)^{-1} b_i c$, and $CEC_i(N, c, b) = \min(b_i, \alpha)$, where $\alpha \in R_+$ is the unique real number such that $\sum_{i \in N} \min(b_i, \alpha) = c$.

So, according to the proportional rule, the cost c is divided among the players proportionally to their individual maximal contribution b_i to c, while the constrained equal contribution rule assigns to the players with $b_i \geq \alpha$ a cost contribution share of α and for the other players, with $b_i < \alpha$, a cost share equal to their individual maximal contribution b_i to c.

Let $<N, A, c, F, (R_i)_{i \in N}>$ be a joint project situation such that $c(a)>0$ for all $a \in A$. Let $\hat{\pi}$ be a fixed optimal project (for the whole group of agents) with m units involved. Further, let T be a fixed cost sharing rule for simple cost sharing problems. For each $a \in \hat{\pi}$ we denote by $\Delta R(a)$ the vector in R^N with the i-th coordinate given by $\Delta_i R(a) = R_i(\hat{\pi}) - R_i(\hat{\pi} \setminus \{a\}) \geq 0$, where $R_i(\hat{\pi} \setminus \{a\})$ equals $\max\{R_i(\pi) | \pi \in F, \pi \subseteq \hat{\pi} \setminus \{a\}\}$. By $B(a)$ we denote the set $\{i \in N | \Delta_i R(a) > 0\}$ of beneficiaries from unit a. Note that $B(a) \neq \phi$ for each $a \in \hat{\pi}$ since $c(a) > 0$ and $\hat{\pi}$ is optimal.

We say that $\hat{\pi}$ is a *structured joint project*, or equivalently, that the given *joint project situation is structured* w.r.t. $\hat{\pi}$, if for all $a, b \in \hat{\pi}$ with $a \neq b$ we have only one of the following three possibilities:

$$B(a) \cap B(b) = \phi; \ B(a) \supset B(b); \ B(b) \supset B(a)$$

(where $P \supset Q$ means that Q is a proper subset of P).

For a structured joint project $\hat{\pi}$ we propose a flexible procedure which consists in applying an agreed upon standard cost sharing rule to each simple cost sharing problem corresponding to a basic unit $a \in \hat{\pi}$.

First, a feasible ordering σ of $\hat{\pi}$ has to be found according to which the costs of the basic units of $\hat{\pi}$ will be one by one distributed over the agents in N. To find such an ordering of $\hat{\pi}$ we construct a rooted tree $<W, L>$ with vertex set $W = \{v_0\} \cup \{B(a) | a \in \hat{\pi}\}$, where v_0 is the root of the tree, and the set L of arcs is described as follows: $<v_0, B(a)> \in L$ for $a \in \hat{\pi}$ iff there is no $a' \in A$ such that $B(a') \supset B(a)$, that is, those beneficiaries' sets are connected with the root v_0 which are maximal with respect to the partial order of inclusion; for each $a, b \in \hat{\pi}$, $a \neq b$, the ordered pair $<B(a), B(b)>$ will be an element in L iff $B(a) \supset B(b)$ and there is no $c \in \hat{\pi}$, $c \neq a$, $c \neq b$ such that $B(a) \supset B(c) \supset B(b)$. We call $<W, L>$ the *beneficiary tree* corresponding to $\hat{\pi}$.

Further, by using the beneficiary tree $<W, L>$ we construct an ordering $\sigma = <a_1, a_2 \dots a_m>$ of the m basic units of $\hat{\pi}$ such that:

(i) $B(a_1)$ is an endpoint of the beneficiary tree $<W, L>$ that is, there is no $a \in \hat{\pi}$ with $B(a_1) \supset B(a)$;
(ii) $B(a_2)$ is an endpoint of the reduced beneficiary tree $<W \setminus \{B(a_1)\}$, $L \setminus \{\langle v, B(a_1)\rangle\}>$, obtained by removing the leaf $\{B(a_1)\}$ and the arc $\langle v, B(a_1)\rangle$, where v is the predecessor of $B(a_1)$ in the beneficiary tree $<W, L>$;
(iii) $B(a_3)$ is an endpoint of the smaller beneficiary tree obtained by removing the leaf $B(a_2)$ (and the corresponding arc) from the tree $<W \setminus \{B(a_1)\}, L \setminus \{\langle v, B(a_1)\rangle\}>$, and so on.

Such an ordering σ of $\hat{\pi}$ which is obtained by the 'leaf by leaf' approach described above has the property that for k, l with $k < l$ we have

$$B(a_k) \subset B(a_l) \text{ if } B(a_k) \cap B(a_l) \neq \phi. \tag{5.1}$$

We use the feasible ordering σ obtained as described above to solve the cost sharing problem corresponding to $\hat{\pi}$ by solving a sequence of m simple cost sharing problems, namely $<N, c(a_1), b^1>$, $<N, c(a_2), b^2>$,...,$<N, c(a_m), b^m>$, where for $r \in \{1, 2,..., m\}$,

$$b^r = R(\hat{\pi}) - R(\hat{\pi}_r) - \sum_{k \in P_r} T(N, c(a_k), b^k). \tag{5.2}$$

Here $P_r = \{k \in \{1,..., r-1\} | B(a_k) \subset B(a_r)\}$ and $\hat{\pi}_r = \hat{\pi} \backslash (\{a_r\} \cup \{a_k | k \in P_r\})$.

We next show that all the cost sharing problems associated with the (basic) units in $\hat{\pi}$ with respect to the ordering σ are simple cost sharing problems. Since $\hat{\pi}$ is optimal

$$\sum_{i \in N} R_i(\hat{\pi}) - c(\hat{\pi}) \geq \sum_{i \in N} R_i(\hat{\pi}_r) - c(\hat{\pi}_r).$$

This implies that

$$0 \leq \sum_{i \in N} (R_i(\hat{\pi}) - R_i(\hat{\pi}_r)) - \sum_{k \in \hat{\pi} \backslash \hat{\pi}_r} c(a_k). \tag{5.3}$$

From (5.2) we obtain

$$\sum_{i \in N} b_i^r = \sum_{i \in N} (R_i(\hat{\pi}) - R_i(\hat{\pi}_r)) - \sum_{k \in P_r} c(a_k). \tag{5.4}$$

By combining (5.3) and (5.4) one obtains

$$\sum_{i \in N} b_i^r \geq c(a_r)$$

which expresses the fact that for each $r \in \{1,..., m\}$, $<N, c(a_r), b^r>$ is a simple cost sharing problem.

Given an ordering $\sigma = <a_1,..., a_m>$ and a cost sharing rule T, the final reward vector, denoted by $\psi(\hat{\pi}, T, \sigma)$, is obtained by solving the above sequence of m simple cost sharing problems, so $\psi(\hat{\pi}, T, \sigma) = R(\hat{\pi}) - \sum_{r=1}^{m} T(N, c(a_r), b^r)$. Note that $\psi(\hat{\pi}, T, \sigma) \geq 0$ and

$$\sum_{i \in N} \sum_{r=1}^{m} T_i(N, c(a_r), b^r) = \sum_{r=1}^{m} \sum_{i \in N} T_i(N, c(a_r), b^r) = \sum_{r=1}^{m} c(a_r).$$

Let us illustrate the procedure with two examples.

Example 3.1. Consider the joint project situation $<N, A, c, F, (R_i)_{i \in N}>$ where $N = \{1, 2, 3, 4\}$, $A = \{a_1, a_2, a_3\}$, $c(a_1) = c(a_2) = c(a_3) = 10$, $F = 2^A$ and $R_i(\phi) = R_i(\{a_1\}) = R_i(\{a_2\}) = R_i(\{a_1, a_2\}) = 0$, $i \in N$; $R_1(\{\pi\}) = 7$, if $a_3 \in \pi$, $R_2(\{a_3\}) = R_2(\{a_3, a_2\}) = 2$, $R_2(\{a_3, a_1\}) = R_2(\{a_1, a_2, a_3\}) = 8$; $R_3(\{a_3\}) = R_3(\{a_3, a_2\}) = 1$, $R_3(\{a_1, a_3\} = R_3(\{a_1, a_2, a_3\} = 7$; $R_4(\{a_3\}) = R_4(\{a_1, a_3\}) = 0$, $R_4(\{a_3, a_2\}) = R_4(\{a_1, a_2, a_3\}) = 18$.

Then $\hat{\pi} = A$ is the unique optimal plan.

(i) Note that $\Delta R(a_1) = R(\hat{\pi}) - R(\{a_2, a_3\}) = (7, 8, 7, 18) - (7, 2, 1, 18) = (0, 6, 6, 0)$, $B(a_1) = \{2, 3\}$; $\Delta R(a_2) = R(\hat{\pi}) - R(\{a_1, a_3\}) = (7, 8, 7, 18) - (7, 8, 7, 0) = (0, 0, 0, 18)$, $B(a_2) = \{4\}$; $\Delta R(a_3) = R(\hat{\pi}) - R(\{a_1, a_2\}) = (7, 8, 7, 18) - (0, 0, 0, 0) = (7, 8, 7, 18)$; $B(a_3) = N$. This implies that the joint project situation is structured w.r.t. $\hat{\pi}$.

The corresponding rooted tree $<W, L>$ is given by $W = \{0, v_1, v_2, v_3\}$, with $v_1 = B(a_3)$, $v_2 = B(a_1)$, $v_3 = B(a_2)$, and $L = \{<0, v_1>, <v_1, v_2> <v_1, v_3>\}$.

(ii) The suitable orderings of A with respect to the rooted tree are $\sigma = <a_1, a_2, a_3>$ and $\sigma' = <a_2, a_1, a_3>$. First, we take the ordering σ. Further we take the proportional rule PROP to solve our three simple cost sharing problems. Then we obtain

$$PROP(N, c(a_1), b^1) = PROP(N, c(a_1), \Delta R(a_1))$$
$$= PROP(N, 10, (0, 6, 6, 0)) = (0, 5, 5, 0),$$
$$PROP(N, c(a_2), b^2) = PROP(N, c(a_2), \Delta R(a_2))$$
$$= PROP(N, 10, (0, 0, 0, 18)) = (0, 0, 0, 10),$$
$$PROP(N, c(a_3), b^3) = PROP(N, c(a_3), R(\hat{\pi}) - \sum_{r=1}^{2} PROP(N, c(a_r), b^r))$$
$$= PROP(N, 10, (7, 8, 7, 18) - (0, 5, 5, 0) - (0, 0, 0, 10))$$
$$= PROP(N, 10, (7, 3, 2, 8)) = (3.5, 1.5, 1, 4).$$

Hence $\psi(\pi, PROP, \sigma) = (7, 8, 7, 18) - (0, 5, 5, 0) - (0, 0, 0, 10) - (3.5, 1.5, 1, 4) = (3.5, 1.5, 1, 4)$.

(iii) The cooperative game $<N, v>$ corresponding to the above joint project situation is given by $N = \{1, 2, 3\}$, $v(N) = \sum_{i \in N} R_i(\hat{\pi}) - \sum_{r=1}^{3} c_r(a_r)$ $= 10$, $v(\{1, 4\}) = 5$, $v(\{1, 2, 3\}) = 2$, $v(\{1, 2, 4\}) = 7$, $v(\{1, 3, 4\}) = 6$, $v(\{2, 3, 4\}) = 3$, and $v(S) = 0$ for the other coalitions. Note that $<N, v>$ is a convex game and that $\psi(\pi, PROP, \sigma) \in C(v)$.

(iv)　We describe now two interactive situations which lead to the above joint project situation.

(a)　Suppose four clubs 1, 2, 3, 4 share the use of playing-fields a_1, a_2, a_3. These fields need maintenance at a cost of 10 units per year for each field. The rewards of the members are given by R_1, R_2, R_3, R_4 above. From these rewards one can conclude that member 1 uses only field a_3, player 4 uses only fields a_2 and a_3, and players 2 and 3 use mainly $\{a_1, a_3\}$ but profit also a little from the presence of a_2.

(b)　One can also think of a situation of four farmers sharing an irrigation system consisting of ditches a_1, a_2, a_3 which have to be maintained, where farmer 1 only profits from a_3, farmer 4 only from $\{a_3, a_2\}$ and farmers 2 and 3 mainly from $\{a_3, a_1\}$.

Example 3.2.　Let us reconsider the connection problem from Example 2.1, which is a joint project situation not based on a tree. For this problem there are two optimal projects for N, namely $\hat{\pi}_1 = \{a_1, a_3, a_4\}$ and $\hat{\pi}_2 = \{a_4, a_2 a_1\}$ which correspond to the two minimum cost spanning trees. Each such a project is a structured joint project. We concentrate now on $\hat{\pi}_1$ and on the proportional rule $T = PROP$. Since $\Delta R(a_1) = (12, 0, 0)$, $\Delta R(a_3) = (0, 12, 0)$, $\Delta R(a_4) = (0, 12, 12)$, the beneficiary tree $<W, L>$, with $W = \{0, B(a_1), B(a_3), B(a_4)\}$, and $L = \{<0, B(a_4)>, <0, B(a_1)>, <B(a_4), B(a_3)>\}$ is obtained, where $B(a_1) = \{1\}$, $B(a_3) = \{2\}$, and $B(a_4) = \{2, 3\}$. Note that this beneficiary tree is isomorphic to the minimum spanning tree corresponding to $\hat{\pi}_1$ (the points v_0, v_1, v_2, v_3 correspond to the points 0, $B(a_1)$, $B(a_3)$, $B(a_4)$, respectively, and the arcs $\langle v_0, v_1\rangle$, $\langle v_3, v_2\rangle$, $\langle v_0, v_3\rangle$ correspond to $<0, B(a_1)>$, $<B(a_3), B(a_4)>$, $<0, B(a_4)>$).

Given $\hat{\pi}_1$, T and the ordering $\sigma_1 = <a_1, a_3, a_4>$ the reward vector $\psi(\hat{\pi}_1, T, \sigma_1) = (2, \frac{4}{7}, 3\frac{3}{7}) = (12, 12, 12) - (10, 0, 0) - (0, 10, 0) - PROP(N, 10, (0, 2, 12))$ results. This reward vector is equal to $\psi(\hat{\pi}_1, T, \sigma_2)$ and to $\psi(\hat{\pi}_1, T, \sigma_3)$, where $\sigma_2 = <a_3, a_1, a_4>$ and $\sigma_3 = <a_3, a_4, a_1>$. If we had decided in favour of the project $\hat{\pi}_2$, the benefit vector would, for symmetry reasons, have been equal to $(3\frac{3}{7}, \frac{4}{7}, 2)$ for each of the orderings $\sigma_4 = <a_2, a_4, a_1>$, $\sigma_5 = <a_2, a_1, a_4>$ and $\sigma_6 = <a_4, a_2, a_1>$. For $T^1 = CEC$ we obtain $\psi(\hat{\pi}_1, T^1, \sigma_1) = (2, 0, 4)$, $\psi(\hat{\pi}_2, T^1, \sigma_1) = (4, 0, 2)$. Note that the benefit vectors are not in the core $C(v) = \{(2, 2, 2)\}$ of the corresponding cooperative game.

We conclude with some remarks on our procedure and its relation with our main result in Section 2.

Remark 3.1.　Our procedure proposes a subtle way, namely the 'leaf by leaf' approach of the beneficiary tree, to find a feasible ordering $\sigma = (a_1, ...,$

a_m) of $\hat{\pi}$ according to which the costs $c(a_1),...,c(a_m)$ of the basic units of $\hat{\pi}$ have to be distributed over the agents in N via simple cost sharing problems and the chosen cost sharing rule T. Property (5.1) of such an ordering σ guarantees that the corresponding reward $\psi(\hat{\pi}, T, \sigma)$ is found by applying our procedure. However, if one arbitrarily chose an ordering σ which did not satisfy (5.1) it might happen that the related procedure failed during the process of decomposition into simple cost sharing problems because at a certain stage k the corresponding cost to be distributed exceeds the available related benefit b^k. Consider, for example, the structured joint project situation w.r.t. $\hat{\pi}_1$ in Example 3.2, the rule $T = PROP$, but the ordering σ_4 $= (a_4, a_3, a_1)$ which, clearly, does not satisfy (5.1). Then $PROP(N, c(a_4), b^1)$ $= PROP(N, 10, (0, 12, 12)) = (0, 5, 5)$. The next problem to be considered is $(N, c(a_3), b^2) = (N, 10, (0, 12 - 5, 0)) = (N, 10, (0, 7, 0))$ which is *not* a simple cost sharing problem because the available benefit is smaller than the cost to be covered. This fact is due to agent 2 who has a low benefit versus the cost structure of the project. Here we say that a structured joint project situation w.r.t. $\hat{\pi}$ is with low benefits if there is at least one agent i whose benefit is smaller than the sum of the costs of the basic units of $\hat{\pi}$ in which the agent is involved (in our example: $12 < 10 + 10$). Structured joint project situations with large benefits can always be approached by decomposing the cost sharing problem corresponding to an optimal joint project into simple cost sharing problems by using an arbitrary ordering. Our procedure is to be considered especially suitable for structured joint projects with low benefits.

Remark 3.2. An optimal joint project $\hat{\pi}$ determines an ordering of treatment of basic units (leaf by leaf in the beneficiary tree). There may be many orderings which satisfy conditions (i), (ii), and (iii) (see Example 3.1). One can prove that all such orderings lead to the same benefit for each of the agents involved. In a tree-based joint project situation the obtained benefit sharing vector is even independent of the optimal project with which one starts, and it is a core element of the corresponding cooperative game. This is not the case in general as we learn from Example 3.2.

Remark 3.3. For non-structured joint projects one can also try to solve the cost sharing problem by decomposing it in simple cost sharing problems. However, during this decomposition process it is quite possible that at a certain node one does not arrive at a simple cost sharing problem, since the costs are higher than the available (low) budget. It could be a topic of further research to develop here a more subtle decomposition procedure than the above one.

Remark 3.4. Another attractive approach to solving the cost sharing problem in a joint project situation is a non-cooperative approach. This line is followed in Brânzei et al. (2002) for generalized airport problems. Extensions to the problems in this chapter will be of interest.

Remark 3.5. It could be a topic of further research to find an axiomatic support for our procedure. Sources of inspiration for this could be Aumann and Maschler (1985), Herrero and Villar (2001), Moulin and Shenker (1992b).

Remark 3.6. The procedure described in this section has some similarity with the serial cost sharing method in Moulin and Shenker (1992a). There, the problem of cost sharing in a joint production situation is first solved for the agents with the lowest demand, then for those with the second lowest demand, and so on. In our procedure a basic unit with a small set of beneficiaries is treated earlier than a unit with more beneficiaries.

NOTES

1. This chapter is dedicated to Michael Maschler on the occasion of his 75th birthday. The authors appreciate the thorough comments and suggestions made by two anonymous referees on the earlier versions of this chapter.

REFERENCES

Aadland, D. and V. Kolpin (1998), 'Shared irrigation costs: an empirical and axiomatic analysis', *Mathematics of Social Sciences*, **35**, 203–18.
Aumann, R.J. and M. Maschler (1985), 'Game theoretic analysis of a bankruptcy problem from the Talmud', *Journal of Economic Theory*, **36**, 195–213.
Brânzei, R., E. Inarra, S. Tijs and J. Zarzuelo (2002), 'Cooperation by asymmetric agents in a joint project', CentER DP 2002–15, Tilburg University, The Netherlands, to appear in the *Journal of Public Economy Theory*.
Feltkamp, V., J. Kuipers and S. Tijs (1996), 'Vertex weighted Steiner tree games', Report M 96-07, Department of Mathematics, Maastricht University, The Netherlands.
Fragnelli, V., I. Garcia–Jurado, H. Norde, F. Patrone and S. Tijs (2000), 'How to share railways infrastructure costs', in F. Patrone, I. Garcia–Jurado and S. Tijs, (eds), *Game Practice: Contributions from Applied Game Theory*, Boston: Kluwer Academic Publishing, pp. 91–101.
Herrero, C. and A. Villar (2001), 'The three musketeers: four classical solutions to bankruptcy problems', *Mathematical Social Sciences*, **42**, 307–28.
Kolpin, V. and D. Aadland (2001), 'Environmental determination of cost sharing – an application to irrigation', Report, Department of Economics, University of Oregon.

Koster, M., E. Molina, Y. Sprumont and S. Tijs (2001), 'Sharing the cost of a network: core and core allocations', *International Journal of Game Theory*, **30**, 567–99.

Koster, M., H. Reijnierse and M. Voorneveld (2003), 'Voluntary contribution to multiple public projects', *Journal of Public Economic Theory*, **5** (1), 25–49.

Littlechild, S.C. and G.F. Thompson (1977), 'Aircraft landing fees: a game theory approach', *The Bell Journal of Economics*, **8**, 186–204.

Moulin, H. and S. Shenker (1992a), 'Serial cost sharing', *Econometrica*, **60**, 1009–37.

Moulin, H. and S. Shenker (1992b), 'Average cost pricing versus serial cost sharing: An axiomatic comparison', *Journal of Economic Theory*, **64**, 178–201.

Norde, H., V. Fragnelli, I. Garcia–Jurado, F. Patrone and S. Tijs (2002), 'Balancedness of infrastructure cost games', *European Journal of Operational Research*, **136**, 635–54.

Potters, J. and P. Sudhölter (1999), 'Airport problems and consistent allocation rules', *Mathematical Social Sciences*, **38**, 83–102.

Schmeidler, D. (1969), 'The nucleolus of a characteristic function game', *SIAM Journal of Applied Mathematics*, **17**, 1163–70.

Shapley, L.S. (1953), 'A value for n-person games', *Annals of Mathematics Studies*, **28**, 307–17.

Shapley, L.S. (1971), 'Cores of convex games', *International Journal of Game Theory*, **1**, 11–26.

Tijs, S.H. (1981), 'Bounds for the core and the τ-value', in O. Moeschlin and D. Pallaschke (eds), *Game Theory and Mathematical Economics*, Amsterdam: North Holland, 123–32.

Tijs, S. and T. Driessen (1986), 'Game theory and cost allocation problems', *Management Science*, **32**, 1015–28.

Young, H.P. (1987), 'On dividing an amount according to individual claims or liabilities', *Mathematics of Operations Research*, **12**, 398–414.

Young, H.P. (1994), 'Cost allocation', chapter 34 in R.J. Aumann and S. Hart (eds), *Handbook of Game Theory*, vol. II, Amsterdam: North Holland, pp. 1193–235.

6. A model for cooperative inter-municipal waste collection: cost evaluation toward fair cost allocation[1]

Stefano Moretti

1. INTRODUCTION

Some countries in the EU have a very large number of small municipalities with individual responsibility for managing municipal waste. These are frequently too small to be able to develop a waste management system (wms) that meets the high standards demanded by EU legislation at an affordable cost. In this case, as the *Handbook on the Implementation of EC Environmental Legislation* (European Commission, 2000) suggests, inter-municipal cooperation can be very beneficial in achieving groupings that are large enough to make the wms affordable. Indeed, due to economies of scale, imposed by the need for specialist staff and facilities (Tickner and McDavid, 1986; Antonioli et al., 2000), the size of inter-municipal areas tends to expand (European Commission, 2000). From this follows the usefulness of a tool capable of efficiently reorganizing the wms as the inter-municipal area where the service has to be supplied is in the process of enlargement.

On the other hand, efficiency cannot be the sole criterion which has to be considered in order to make decisions on this topic. In fact the overall supply cost must still be met by single municipalities, which are not interested in paying more than the amount they would have paid if they had been organized in different groupings. Roughly speaking, the overall cost must be shared among municipalities in a fair way in order to foster cooperation among them (Ferrari et al., 2001).

The aim of this chapter is to propose a possible approach to tackling the decision problem arising from the above considerations. In order to achieve this goal, first of all we point out a method to provide an ex-ante quantitative valuation of facilities and specialist staff (and their costs) needed for collecting waste in new emerging inter-municipal contexts. More precisely, we offer a theoretical model for the assessment of the cost that each sub-group of the inter-municipal group should support in order to develop a wms on its own territory. Such a model is depicted in Section 2. In Section 3, implementation of the model is briefly described in the programming language Visual Basic 6.0. Section 4 is devoted to a comparison of data yielded by the model with real data provided by an Italian waste management company (Crocco, 2001) and the results of a simulation on a new inter-municipal group are presented. On the basis of the results provided by this simulation, some cost allocation issues discussed from a game-theoretical point of view are presented in Section 5.

Before introducing Section 2, we would like to stress two important additional features of the model:

- This model works with a 'relatively' small set of data. This means that from our point of view, the model is a good compromise between the precision of results and the flexibility in collecting information necessary to comply with the dynamism of the context (continuous enlargement of the inter-municipal groupings);
- This model is the first step of a wider decision-making model for inter-municipal waste management (Ferrari et al., 2001) founded on game-theoretical arguments (Young, 1995).

Finally, note that no discussion on disposal services in waste management is provided. Usually, as emerged from meeting with Italian waste managers (Crocco, 2001), disposal sites are chosen with respect to social, political and normative constraints rather than on the basis of monetary efficiency. On the other hand, all the waste disposal managers we met stated that the overall disposal cost in inter-municipal contexts was usually shared in proportion to the waste production of each single municipality. These factors persuaded us to focus our efforts in the direction of waste collection. Anyway, we believe that the disposal of waste should also be considered for a more accurate description of the problem. For instance, the location of the disposal site has important effects: close proximity is profitable (lower transportation costs); on the other hand, further is better (in terms of environmental damage, traffic, smog and so on).

2. THE THEORETICAL MODEL

Currently, in a wide number of municipalities in Italy, the prevailing method of collecting non-recyclable solid waste is curbside collection. In curbside collection programmes, residents set out unsorted non-recyclable materials in containers placed at the curb. Collection crews of one, two or three persons load the materials onto collection vehicles in order to carry them to the disposal site. Containers can be grouped in collecting isles, usually from one to five containers per isle.

The aim of this model is to provide an evaluation of the quantity of facilities and staff demanded to supply waste collection procedures in an inter-municipal area. In order to do this, we describe the context where this service is supplied, that is, the area of a municipality or the overall area of an inter-municipal group, as an urban territory divided into classes of sub-zones (called simply *zones*); each class differs with respect to the kind of collection service supplied in it, which is in turn a function of qualitative characteristics like architectural constraints, socioeconomic needs and so on. In this way we intend separately to perform calculations concerning different urban zones in order to better meet the effective needs of each zone (shopping centre, historical centre, periphery and so on).

In the following we will refer to these different types of zone by the attribute *type* (for brevity, we will often use letters to represent these attributes). The same arguments hold for other kinds of variables of the model, such as containers and vehicles. A summary of the data structure demanded by the model is shown in the following lists of input items.

Input data for each type of zone:

Δt_d^z: time needed to go from the zone of type z to the disposal site, discharge waste material and come back (*min*);

Δt_s^z: time spent at the stop signs and traffic lights on the zone of type z (*min*);

d_z: average density of the waste material set out in the zone of type z (Kg/m^3)

Max_z: maximum number of days within two successive emptying operations of the containers in the zone of type z;

Q_z: average daily production rate of waste in the zone of type z ($kg \ day^{-1}$).

Input data for each type of container:

a_b^z: number of containers of type b per collecting isle in the zone of type z;

c_b: initial cost of the container of type b (*euro*);

D_z^b: distance between two collecting isles of containers of type b in the zone z (*m*);

f_b^z: empty rate of the container of type b in the class zone z (*collection routes/day*);

l_b: expected life of the container of type b (*years*);
r_b^z: percentage of capacity of the container of type b that the waste management wish not to exceed as amount of garbage stored into the container in the zone z;
V_b: geometrical volume of the container of type b (m^3).

Input data for each type of vehicle:

c_v :   initial cost of the vehicle of type v (*euro*);
Δt_v^b: average time needed to load material placed inside a single container of type b into a collection vehicle of type v (*min*);
Δt_v: time length of a working turn for the vehicle of type v (*hours*);
l_v :   expected life of the vehicle of type v (*years*);
L_v: maximum average speed of the vehicle of type v (*Km hour^{-1}*);
Q_v: volume of the vehicle of type $v(m^3)$;
R_v: compaction ratio of the vehicle of type v;
s_v: number of persons demanded as crew of the vehicle of type v;
w_v: annual wage for a single employee working as crew member of the vehicle of type v (*euro*).

In the case of inter-municipal groups, the model also needs to identify zones in different municipalities which can be considered, on the basis of the previous information structure, to belong to the same class. So far, such identification is affected by the subjective criterion of the decision-maker. However, we intend to improve our model by defining an objective criterion which could be implemented as a computer program, in order automatically to classify zones with respect to similarities among them.

Finally, the model also requires the following input parameter:

Δt^z: time requested to visit all the zones in the same class z following the shortest connection path connecting the different municipalities (*hours*).

From Section 2.1 to Section 2.5 all the outputs generated by the model will be explained step by step. After that, a summary of all those outputs – translated into cost items – will be introduced in Section 2.6 as the inter-municipal cost function to be considered when tackling the cost sharing problem.

2.1   Determination of the Number of Containers

The calculation of n_b^z (number of containers of type b) needed for waste collection in the class of zones of type z inside a municipal area or inside the area of an inter-municipal group, is performed on the basis of the following equation (Kaulard and Massarutto, 1997):

$$n_b^{\bar{z}} = \frac{Q_z \, Max_z}{d_z r_b^{\bar{z}} \, V_b} \tag{6.1}$$

Note that the value Max_z depends on the container empty rate in the given area. For example, let us suppose the container empty rate has a daily frequency. This means that containers are emptied six days in a week (excluding Sunday), that is $Max_z = 2$ days. In this context, on Monday the amount of garbage going into containers is double the average amount achieved during the working days.

2.2 Determination of the Capacity of the Vehicles

We are not intending to solve the problem of finding an optimal route encompassing all the collecting isles in a given area. In our opinion the complexity of collecting the information needed to solve such a problem in order to obtain more accurate results is too expensive compared with the benefits obtained from a model flexibly adaptable to changeable situations. Moreover, we guess that an optimal collecting route already exists in each zone as a consequence of the choices made by past managements in response to criteria of optimality (for example, finding the shortest path), but also taking into consideration the socioeconomic requirements of the community. In our opinion such choices cannot leave out of consideration the very long process of dialogue between the community and the management, which in turn can be modelled only with great difficulty.

In order to calculate the number of vehicles needed to complete a route, we must calculate the maximal number of containers whose content can be removed by a vehicle on a single journey before discharging its load at the disposal site. In other words n_v^{bz} represents the carrying capacity (in terms of number of containers of type b whose content can be removed) of a vehicle of type v in a zone of type z and it is calculated by the following equation

$$n_v^{bz} = \frac{Q_v \, R_v}{V_b \, r_v^{bz}} \tag{6.2}$$

Note that as a matter of fact we implicitly assume that vehicles of type v are able, in zone z, to load waste material only from containers of type b (for example, due to mechanical constraints of the vehicle facilities in handling the containers).

The compaction ratio R_v of a vehicle of type v has been computed as the ratio between the volume of waste material collected from the containers and the volume occupied by the same quantity of waste material after it has been compacted by the compactor device of the vehicles.

2.3 Determination of the Overall Time to Complete a Route

The route time is defined as the time required to serve a given collection route, from the first to the last collecting isle of the overall area covered by all the zones in the same class. It includes the time required to travel between isles of containers, to wait at stop signs and traffic lights and to collect materials that have been left out.

It is possible to determine the travel time $\Delta t_{D_z^b}$ (*min*) between two stops (that is, collecting isles) on the collection route by means of the following non-linear empirical relationship (Everett et al., 1998) that is a function of the stop-to-stop distances during the collection:

$$\Delta t_{D_z^b} = 0.06 \frac{D_z^b}{L_v(1 - e^{kD_z^b})} \qquad (6.3)$$

More precisely, the maximum average speed L_v is the average speed attainable between stops that are separated by a large distance and k is a calculated coefficient (*metre^{-1}*) representing the rate at which the average speed approaches the maximum average speed.

Given the capacity of a collection vehicle in terms of number of containers n_v^{bz} provided by equation (6.2), the total time $\Delta t_{D_{Journey_v}^b}$ (*hours*) demanded by a vehicle of type v to perform a single journey, loading as much waste material as possible, going to the disposal site, discharging waste material and coming back to zone z, is given by the following relation:

$$\Delta t_{D_{Journey_v}^b} = \frac{1}{60} \left((\frac{n_v^{bz}}{\alpha_b^z} - 1) \cdot \Delta t_{D_z^b} + n_v^{bz} \cdot \Delta t_v^b + \Delta t_s^z + \Delta t_d^z \right) \qquad (6.4)$$

Here Δt_v^b and Δt_d^z can be derived via linear regression from field data (Everett et al., 1998). Finally, the overall route time $\Delta t_{Route_v}^{bz}$ (*hours*) is simply obtained by the following relationship:

$$\Delta t_{Route_v}^{bz} = \frac{n_b^z}{n_v^{bz}} \cdot \Delta t_{Journey_v}^{bz} + \Delta t^z \qquad (6.5)$$

Note that n_b^z / n_v^{bz} equals the number of journeys to the disposal site required for a vehicle of type v to empty all n_b^z containers of type b (by equation (6.1)) in a zone of type z following the collection route.

2.4 Determination of the Number of Collection Vehicles

A working turn for a collection vehicle v is the number of hours that the vehicle v must work in a single day. Hence, the number of working turns demanded to complete a collection route is yielded by the following equation:

$$\hat{n}_{wv}^{bz} = \frac{\Delta t_{Route_v}^{bz}}{\Delta t_v} \tag{6.6}$$

Since $\hat{n}_{wv}^{bz}$ is the number of working turns required for vehicles of type v to empty all containers of type b on the collection route in the area covering all zones of type z in the inter-municipal group, it is obvious that the number of vehicles required to completely empty all containers of type b in the same area in a period of exactly one day is given by just $\hat{n}_{wv}^{bz}$. Indeed, the number N_v^{bz} of vehicles v required on the waste collection route (with the demanded frequency f_b^z) in the class of zones of type z is achieved by the following equation

$$N_v^{bz} = \hat{n}_{wv}^{bz} \cdot f_b^z \tag{6.7}$$

2.5 Determination of Annual Costs

The annual amortization for vehicles and containers has been calculated using the following formula (Kaulard and Masarutto, 1997):

$$\hat{c}_f = c_f \frac{r(1+r)^{lf}}{(1+r)^{lf} - 1} \tag{6.8}$$

where f can be either a vehicle of type v or a container of type b and r is the general rate of profit.

Maintenance costs on vehicles and containers are supposed to be equal to 10 per cent of the investment costs (Kaulard and Massarutto, 1997).

Finally, keeping in mind the work hours for personnel and the number of persons demanded as crew for a certain type of vehicles, we calculated the total wage W_v for staff corresponding to each vehicle employed.

2.6 Determination of the Inter-Municipal Annual Cost

Consider a finite set N of municipalities. Then the total cost $c(N)$ provided by the model for waste collection in the inter-municipal area in N is the following:

$$c(N) = \sum_{z \in B} (\sum_{b \in B} \lceil \sum_{i \in N} n_b^z(i) \rceil \bar{c}_b + \sum_{v \in V} \lceil \sum_{i \in N} N_v^{bz}(i) \rceil \bar{c}_v) + c^*(N) \qquad (6.9)$$

where Z, B and V are finite sets whose elements stand for types of zones, containers and vehicles, respectively; $n_b^z(i)$ is the number of containers of type b needed for zone z inside municipality i as provided by equation (6.1); N_v^{bz} is the number of vehicles v required for a zone of type z in the municipality i as provided by equation (6.7).

The two numbers $\bar{c}_b$ and $\bar{c}_v$ stand for the total annual cost related to each container of type b and each vehicle of type v respectively. More precisely, $\bar{c}_b = \hat{c}_b + 0.1c_b$ and $\bar{c}_v = \hat{c}_v + 0.1c_v + W_v$, where $\hat{c}_b$ and $\hat{c}_v$ are the annual amortization (by equation (6.8)) for each container of type b and each vehicle of type v respectively, and the addends $0.1c_b$ and $0.1c_v$ are the maintenance costs for container b and vehicle v, respectively, as suggested by Kaulard and Massarutto (1997). Finally the value W_v is the total annual cost for all the employees required as crew of the vehicle of type v.

Note that we use the standard convention $\lceil x \rceil$, with $x \in \mathcal{R}$, in order to symbolize the smallest integer number larger than or equal to x. In other words, the model shows economies of scale for waste collection as the result of savings in terms of devices (that is, containers, vehicles and staff) which derive from the partial use of the devices employed by each single municipality on its own.

For instance, consider two municipalities, 1 and 2, and suppose the model provides the value $N_v^{bz}(1) = 0.6$ and $N_v^{bz}(2) = 1.3$, with $z \in Z$, $b \in B$, $v \in V$; this means that municipality 1 according to the model, needs at least $\lceil 0.6 \rceil = 1$ vehicle of type v to perform waste collection by itself, whereas municipality 2 demands at least $\lceil 1.3 \rceil = 2$ vehicles of type v for its own territory. On the other hand, if municipalities 1 and 2 join together, the minimum number of vehicles of type v demanded for waste collection performed in cooperation equals $\lceil 0.6 + 1.3 \rceil = \lceil 1.9 \rceil = 2$.

Finally the term $c^*(N)$, with $c^*(N) \geq 0$, stands for the incremental cost due to a possible (but not necessary) increase of the number of vehicles related to the distances between municipalities. In fact distances between municipalities increase the overall route time $\Delta t_{Route_v}^{bz}$ and this increase could directly affect the number of vehicles needed to collect waste as calculated by equation (6.7). For the sake of completeness, we state that equation (6.9) equals zero if N is the empty set.

3. SOFTWARE IMPLEMENTATION

The model described in Section 2 has been implemented via the Visual Basic 6.0 programming language. The main features of the software are the

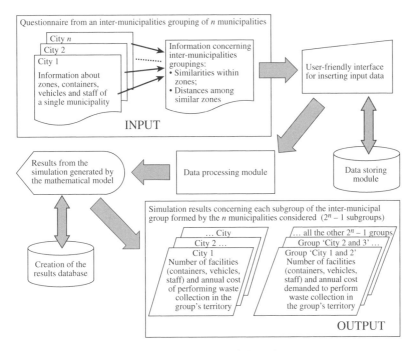

Figure 6.1   A short description of our model implementation

user-friendly interface which efficiently allows the handling of a great deal of data coming from questionnaires, and the simple procedure of introducing indications of similarities among zones in different municipalities. Moreover, the facility automatically to create an MS Access database containing the results provided by the output of the simulation has been integrated into the same environment. A very short description of the software is given in Figure 6.1. Computer programs in Java language have also been used to deal with the cost sharing problem (see Section 5.). So far, such programs have not yet been integrated into the software implementation of the theoretical model described in Section 2. As a first step in this direction, a special method of computation will be introduced in Section 5.1.

4.   SIMULATION RESULTS

4.1   Model Validation

We carried out a validation test via a simulation performed on data concerning the waste collection context of the city of Tortona (Italy). Input data introduced in Section 2 were reported in our questionnaire by the management staff of the ASMT S.p.a. (Crocco, 2001). ASMT S.p.a. is a Joint-stock company which manages the non-recyclable solid waste collection of Tortona and some other municipalities near to this city. In order to explain how to complete the questionnaire correctly, another questionnaire completed on the basis of an imaginary inter-municipal situation was sent with the questionnaire to be completed. Just to sketch out the dimension of the collection context we considered, we provide in Table 6.1 a few parameters concerning the situation during the year 2000. Simulation results yielded by our model are summarized in Table 6.2.

Table 6.1   Selected data concerning the wms of Tortona in 2000

Municipality name	Tortona
Inhabitants	26826
Urban area	$10^8 m^2$
Waste production	$15.5 \cdot 10^6 Kg$
Types of zone	Centre, periphery
Percentage of production in the centre	70
Percentage of production in the periphery	30
Number of types of containers	5
Location of the disposal site	Very close to the city

Table 6.2   Cost values provided by the model for waste collection in Tortona

Cost item	Cost amount (Euro)
Total annual amortizement for containers	61970
Total annual amortizement for vehicles	114650
Annual cost for maintenance of containers	40280
Annual cost for maintenance of vehicles	58360
Annual cost for staff	640920
Total cost	916180

Comparison between data yielded by the simulation and data actually owned by the management of ASMT showed a very good level of approximation in estimating all the cost items except for the maintenance cost of the vehicles. In fact, that kind of cost was overestimated by about 15–20 per cent in the simulation.

4.2 A Simulation on a New Inter-municipal Group

In this section we give an example of a simulation for the determination of the annual costs of an inter-municipal group of three municipalities. Tortona is still one of the municipalities involved and the other two are smaller municipalities quite close to Tortona: Castelnuovo Scrivia and Pontecurone.

Actually, ASMT is already providing the collection service in the municipalities of Castelnuovo Scrivia and Pontecurone, but the same methodology could be used by ASMT management to evaluate the increment in collection costs resulting from a possible enlargement of the ASMT operational area to a new urban territory. In Table 6.3 we briefly outline the scale of the waste collection arrangements in each single municipality in the grouping considered.

Table 6.3   Selected data concerning the inter-municipal grouping

City	Inhabitants	Waste collected (tons)	Area ($10^4 \, m^2$)
Tortona	26 826	15 500	9 929
Castelnuovo S.	5 762	2 774	4 542
Pontecurone	4 008	2 218	2 981
Total	36 596	20 492	17 452

In Figure 6.2 a sketch map of the inter-municipal group is shown. The number near each connection represents the average time taken by vehicles to cover the distance between the two most far-flung zones of the municipalities at the ends of the connection. Results given by the simulation are summarized in Table 6.4. Obviously, in this case it was not possible to make a comparison between data from simulation and real data, since the actual cost supported by each single intermediate sub-grouping of municipalities is unknown. Anyway, note that results provided by the model show economies of scale well known in the literature (Tickner and McDavid, 1986; Antonioli et al., 2000), in particular in contexts with fewer than 200 to 300 000 inhabitants (see also Biagi and Massarutto, 2001). In Antonioli et al. (2000), a parametric method of finding a proxy for the total cost of a wms is described. Such a method starts from the analysis of a database of balance sheets coming from companies operating in waste management. However, in their approach Antonioli et al. were not able to separate collection costs from disposal costs; further, they considered only public companies, excluding other kinds of management. Finally, the numerical parameters they found do not seem sufficiently to explain the cost variability observed as a matter of fact (Biagi and Massarutto, 2001).

Table 6.4   Total annual cost for each group of municipalities (from equation (6.9))

Group of municipalities	Total cost (Euro)
Tortona	916180
Castelnuovo S.	463260
Pontecurone	455510
Tortona – Castelnuovo	1112960
Tortona – Pontecurone	1030330
Castelnuovo S. – Pontecurone	476690
Tortona – Castelnuovo S. – Pontecurone	1236910

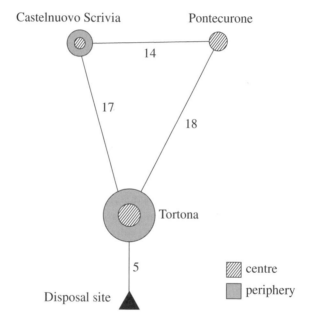

Figure 6.2   Time taken by vehicles to cover the respective distance (min.)

5. COST ALLOCATION

In this section we are going to tackle the cost sharing problem as a cooperative cost game (von Neumann and Morgenstern, 1944; Young, 1995). Recall that a cooperative cost game is an ordered pair $\langle N, c \rangle$, where $N = \{1, 2,..., n\}$ is the set of players and $c : 2^N \rightarrow \mathcal{R}^+$ is the characteristic cost function, which assigns to each coalition $S \in 2^N$ (that is, any subset of N, including N itself and all the one-element subsets) a real number $c(S)$, and where $c(\varnothing) = 0$.

As stated in Section 2, given a set N of n municipalities, equation (6.9) directly determines the characteristic cost function when applied to each subset of N. In general, there are many other situations in which the total number of facilities required by a coalition is provided by the smallest integer greater than or equal to the sum of the demands of all the individuals (for example, some travel agencies requiring portions of a bus). Fragnelli et al. (2001), defining the class of *bus games*, studied this kind of situation from the game-theoretical point of view.

In our case, supposing $B = \{b_1, ..., b_p\}$, $V = \{v_1, ..., v_q\}$, and $Z = \{z_1, ..., z_r\}$ to be, respectively, the set of containers, the set of vehicles and the set of zones in equation (6.9), then the characteristic cost function can be expressed as the linear combination of the games $\langle N, u_{b1}^{z1}\rangle, ..., \langle N, u_{b1}^{zr}\rangle, ..., \langle N, u_{bp}^{z1}\rangle, ..., \langle N, u_{bp}^{zr}\rangle, ...,$ $\langle N, u_{v1}^{z1}\rangle, ..., \langle N, u_{v1}^{zr}\rangle, ..., \langle N, u_{vp}^{z1}\rangle, ..., \langle N, u_{vp}^{zr}\rangle, \langle N, a\rangle, \langle N, c^*\rangle$ with the coefficients $\underbrace{(\bar{c}_{b1}, ..., \bar{c}_{b1})}_{r\ times}, ..., \underbrace{(\bar{c}_{bp}, ..., \bar{c}_{bp})}_{r\ times}, \underbrace{(\bar{c}_{v1}, ..., \bar{c}_{v1})}_{r\ times}, ..., \underbrace{(\bar{c}_{vq}, ..., \bar{c}_{vq})}_{r\ times}, 1, 1$, where $\langle N, u_{b1}^{z1}\rangle, ...,$

$\langle N, u_{b1}^{zr}\rangle, ..., \langle N, u_{bp}^{z1}\rangle, ..., \langle N, u_{bp}^{zr}\rangle, \langle N, u_{v1}^{z1}\rangle, ..., \langle N, u_{v1}^{zr}\rangle, ..., \langle N, u_{vp}^{z1}\rangle, ..., \langle N, u_{vp}^{zr}\rangle$, are $r \cdot p + r \cdot q$ bus games (Fragnelli et al., 2001) with, for each $S \subseteq N$, $j = 1, ...,$

p, $k = 1, ..., q$, $l = 1, ..., r$, $u_{bj}^{zl}(S) = \lceil \sum_{i \in S} (n_{bj}^{zl}(i) - \lfloor n_{bj}^{zl}(i) \rfloor) \rceil$, $u_{vk}^{zl}(S) = \lceil \sum_{i \in S} (N_{vk}^{bzl}(i) - $

$\lfloor N_{vk}^{bzl}(i) \rfloor) \rceil$, and where $\lfloor x \rfloor$, $x \in \mathbb{R}$, is the largest integer smaller than or equal to x; finally, $\langle N, c^*\rangle$ is the game obtained by the term c^* of equation (6.9) applied to each $S \subseteq N$, and $\langle N, a\rangle$ is the additive game with characteristic

cost function $a(S) = \sum_{i \in S} \left[\sum_{z \in Z} \left(\sum_{b \in B} \lfloor n_b^z(i) \rfloor \bar{c}_b + \sum_{v \in V} \lfloor N_v^{bz}(i) \rfloor \bar{c}_v \right) \right]$, $S \subseteq N$.

In particular, with regard to the simulation, the cost sharing problem was already shaped in the previous section: the set of players is $M = \{Tortona,$ *Castelnuovo S., Pontecurone*$\}$ and the characteristic cost function $g(S)$, $S \subseteq M$, has been displayed in Table 6.4.

As we pointed out previously, joining a larger coalition is profitable due to cost saving. Then, it is reasonable to expect that the coalition M will be effectively formed by players (that is, the municipalities). Now, assuming that this happens, the municipalities will have the total cost ( )g (M) to divide. In order to guarantee cooperation, municipalities should not disagree on how the total cost will be allocated among them.

On this topic, a basic concept in game theory is the *core* of a game. Recall that an *allocation* is a vector $x \in \mathbb{R}^N$. A *core allocation* of $\langle N, c\rangle$ is an allocation satisfying

- Efficiency: $\sum_{i=1}^{n} x_i = c(N)$,

- Stability: $\sum_{i \in S} x_i \leq c(S)$ for each $S \in 2^N$.

The core (Gillies, 1953) of $\langle N, c \rangle$ is denoted by Core(N, c) and consists of all core allocations.

The efficiency property states that the whole cost supported by the large coalition has to be shared among the players. Moreover, by means of the stability property, if $x \in$ Core(N, c), then no coalition $S \subset N$ has an incentive to split off if x is the proposed cost allocation in N, since the total amount $x(S) = \sum_{i \in S} x_i$ allocated to S is not larger than the amount $c(S)$ which they should pay by forming the sub-coalition. In other words, allocations not in the core will reasonably be considered unacceptable for any players.

We examined a sample of 13 different consortia of municipalities which manage inter-municipal waste collection in Italy (Ferrari et al., 2001). Summarizing, the three main cost sharing rules employed by the consortia correspond to a division among the municipalities proportional to three different indicators: the number of inhabitants, the amount of waste collected and the territorial extent (that is, the area of each municipality), respectively. The cost allocations obtained performing these 'common in practice' rules on the game $\langle M, g \rangle$ are reported in Table 6.5 (values are in euros).

Table 6.5 'Common in practice' rules of cost allocation

Allocation by: Municipality:	Inhabitants	Waste collected	Area
Tortona	906 700	935 590	703 720
Castelnuovo S.	194 750	167 440	321 910
Pontecurone	135 470	133 880	211 280
Total	1 236 910	1 236 910	1 236 910

It is easy to check that the allocation by number of inhabitants does not satisfy the stability property for the coalition {*Tortona, Pontecurone*}; allocation by amount of waste collected does not satisfy the stability property either in the coalition {*Tortona, Pontecurone*} nor for {*Tortona*} itself; finally the allocation by territorial extent does not satisfy the stability property for the coalition {*Castelnuovo S., Pontecurone*}.

The idea of the core is not the only idea suggested by the theory. Another basic concept is the idea of a *one-point solution* for games: a map which assigns to each game with n players a unique allocation of the game. In other words, a one-point solution of a given game is the unique allocation which conforms to requested principles (axioms), and moreover exists always (not necessarily in the core of the game). One of the most famous one-point solutions is the *Shapley value* (Shapley, 1953). A basic property of this solution is that it takes into consideration the role of each player in increasing (or decreasing) the cost of each coalition (for a detailed introduction to the Shapley value in cost allocation see also Shapley, 1971; Young, 1995). Roughly speaking, given a cooperative game, the Shapley value provides an allocation satisfying the efficiency property and moreover conforming to three distinct ideas: the allocation is invariant under the renaming of the players; if the characteristic cost function can be broken down into different categories (for example, the *cost of the containers* and the *cost of the vehicles*) then the Shapley value of the cooperative game equals the sum of the Shapley values calculated in the games based on the single categories; finally, someone should not be charged for a cost element he does not use (for example, if a municipality does not use any vehicles which are demanded from others in the same coalition, then he should pay nothing for them). Shapley in 1953 proved that for each fixed set of players N there exists a uniquely efficient one-point solution ϕ defined for all cost functions c on N which conforms to the previous three ideas. Moreover, he provided the following formula to compute such an allocation, for each $i \in N$:

$$\phi_i(c) = \sum_{S \subseteq N \setminus \{i\}} \frac{s!(n-s-1)!}{n!}(c(S \cup \{i\}) - c(S)) \tag{6.10}$$

where s and n are the cardinality, respectively, of the coalitions S and N and the value $c(S \cup \{i\}) - c(S)$ is called the marginal contribution of player i to the coalition S.

For the game $\langle M, g \rangle$ the Shapley value has been displayed in Table 6.6. One can check that the Shapley value belongs to Core (M, g).

In order to understand the connections between the core and the Shapley value for a general cost function provided by our model, the following theorem should be taken into consideration:

Table 6.6   Shapley value and nucleolus (costs in euros)

Municipality	Shapley value	Nucleolus
Tortona	762890	808940
Castelnuovo S.	259610	255300
Pontecurone	214420	172670
Total	1236910	1236910

Theorem (Shapley, 1971): *The core of every cooperative cost game with concave characteristic cost function is non-empty and contains the Shapley value.*

Here a characteristic cost function c of a cooperative cost game $\langle N, c \rangle$ is called concave if $c(S \cup \{i\}) - c(S) \geq c(T \cup \{i\}) - c(T)$ for all $i \in N$ and all S, T $\in 2^N$ with $S \subseteq T \subseteq N \setminus \{i\}$. In our case, the characteristic cost function g of the game $\langle M, g \rangle$ is not concave (consider, for example, the marginal contribution of Tortona to the coalition $\{Pontecurone\}$, that is, $1\ 030\ 330 - 455\ 510 = 574\ 820$ and the marginal contribution of Tortona to the coalition $\{Castelnuovo\ S., Pontecurone\}$, that is, $1\ 236\ 910 - 476\ 690 = 760\ 220$). Therefore, taking into account the previous theorem by Shapley (1971), in general we cannot guarantee that, for a cooperative cost game with characteristic cost function provided by our model, the Shapley value belongs to the core of the game. On the other hand, so far the simulations performed by means of our model have only yielded cooperative cost games whose Shapley values stay in the corresponding cores, similarly to what happens for the game $\langle M, g \rangle$ as we pointed out above.

Finally, let us note that different one-point solutions, which conform to other ideas and with other properties, could also be considered for tackling the cost allocation problem. For example the nucleolus (Schmeidler, 1969) always belongs to the core – if non-empty – of the corresponding cooperative cost game (in Table 6.6 we also display the nucleolus of the game $\langle M, g \rangle$). As already pointed out, some considerations related to the axiomatic characterization would seem to suggest a very appropriate use of the Shapley value as allocation rule in inter-municipal situations. Moreover, there is also another practical reason to adopt the Shapley value instead of other theoretical solution concepts: the existence of a simple method for its calculation in this special class of games.

5.1 An Efficient Method to Calculate the Shapley Value

Consider a cooperative cost game $\langle N, c \rangle$, where N is a finite set of municipalities and c is the characteristic cost function provided by equation (6.9) in each subset of N. Then, by additivity, the Shapley value of the game $\langle N, c \rangle$ is the following:

$$\phi_j(c) = \phi_j(c - c^*) + \phi_j(c^*) \tag{6.11}$$

for each $j \in N$.

Consider $\phi_j(c - c^*), j \in N$. Then by equations (6.9) and (6.10)

$$\phi_j(c - c^*) =$$

$$= \sum_{S \subseteq N\setminus\{j\}} \frac{s!(n-s-1)!}{n!} \sum_{z \in Z} \left[\sum_{b \in B} \left(\lceil \Sigma_{i \in S \cup \{j\}} n_b^{\bar{z}}(j) \rceil - \lceil \Sigma_{i \in S} n_b^{\bar{z}}(j) \rceil \right) \bar{c}_b \right. \tag{6.12}$$

$$\left. + \sum_{v \in V} \left(\lceil \Sigma_{i \in S \cup \{j\}} N_v^{bz}(i) \rceil - \lceil \Sigma_{i \in S} N_v^{bz}(i) \rceil \right) \bar{c}_v \right]$$

Note that the amount $\lceil \Sigma_{i \in S \cup \{j\}} n_b^{\bar{z}}(j) \rceil - \lceil \Sigma_{i \in S} n_b^{\bar{z}}(j) \rceil$, with $b \in B$, $z \in Z$, $S \subseteq N \setminus \{j\}$, and $j \in N$, takes values in the set $\{\lceil n_b^{\bar{z}}(j) \rceil, \lfloor n_b^{\bar{z}}(j) \rfloor\}$. Similarly, the quantity $\lceil \Sigma_{i \in S \cup \{j\}} N_v^{bz}(i) \rceil - \lceil \Sigma_{i \in S} N_v^{bz}(i) \rceil$, with $v \in V$, $z \in Z$, $S \subseteq N \setminus \{j\}$ and $j \in N$, takes values in the set $\{\lceil N_v^{bz}(j) \rceil, \lfloor N_v^{bz}(j) \rfloor\}$.

Actually, in many real applications, where municipalities are neighbouring and the time to travel from one municipality to another is very short, c^* can be neglected. On those special cases, equation (6.12) can easily be used to compute $\phi_j(c)$, $j \in N$, comparing $\sum_{i \in S} n_b^{\bar{z}}(i) - \lfloor \sum_{i \in S} n_b^{\bar{z}}(i) \rfloor$, for each $S \subseteq N \setminus \{j\}$, with $n_b^{\bar{z}}(j) - \lfloor n_b^{\bar{z}}(j) \rfloor$ (and $\sum_{i \in S} N_v^{bz}(i) - \lfloor \sum_{i \in S} N_v^{bz}(i) \rfloor$, for each $S \subseteq N \setminus \{j\}$, with $N_v^{bz}(j) - \lfloor N_v^{bz}(j) \rfloor$), as shown in the following example.

Example 5.1 *Consider a game $\langle \{1, 2, 3\}, c \rangle$ with 1, 2 and 3 as neighbouring municipalities and where c has been obtained by equation (6.9) with $c^*(S) = 0$ for each $S \subseteq N$. Then, by additivity, the Shapley value of the game is*

$$\phi_j(c) = \phi_j(\check{c}) + \phi_j(\tilde{c}) \tag{6.13}$$

where

$$\check{c}(S) = \sum_{z \in Z} \left(\sum_{b \in B} \lceil \sum_{i \in S} n_b^{\bar{z}}(i) \rceil \bar{c}_b \right) \tag{6.14}$$

and

$$\tilde{c}(S) = \sum_{z \in Z} \left(\sum_{v \in V} \lceil \sum_{i \in S} N_v^{bz}(i) \rceil \bar{c}_v \right) \tag{6.15}$$

In order to simplify the calculation further, we will focus our attention only on the cost function $\tilde{c}$ with $V = \{v\}$, $Z = \{z\}$, $c_v = 60$, $N_v^{bz}(1) = 0.2$, $N_v^{bz}(2) = 1.7$ and $N_v^{bz}(3) = 0.7$. The Shapley value of $\tilde{c}$ can be computed in the following way. For each $j \in N = \{1, 2, 3\}$:

$$\phi_j(\tilde{c}) = \sum_{S \subseteq N\setminus\{j\}} \frac{s!(n-s-1)!}{n!} \sum_{z \in Z} \sum_{v \in V} \beta_v^{bz}(j, S) \bar{c}_v \tag{6.16}$$

where for each $j \in N$, for each $S \subseteq N\backslash\{j\}$

$$
\beta_v^{bz}(j, S) = \begin{cases} \lfloor N_v^{bz}(j)\rfloor \; if & \sum_{i\in S} N_v^{bz}(i) - \lfloor\sum_{i\in S} N_v^{bz}(i)\rfloor + N_v^{bz}(j) - \lfloor N_v^{bz}(j)\rfloor - 1, \\ & S \neq \varnothing, \; \sum_{i\in S} N_v^{bz}(i) \notin \mathbb{N} \qquad (6.17) \\ \lceil N_v^{bz}(j)\rceil \; otherwise, & \end{cases}
$$

In the example considered, the values assumed by $\beta_v^{bz}(j, S)$ are shown in Table 6.7. Hence, equation (6.16) yields the following vector as the Shapley value of the three-person game:

$$
\phi_1(\tilde{c}) = \left(\frac{2}{6}\lfloor 0.2\rfloor + \frac{1}{6}\lfloor 0.2\rfloor + \frac{1}{6}\lfloor 0.2\rfloor + \frac{2}{6}\lfloor 0.2\rfloor\right)60 = \left(\frac{2}{6}1 + \frac{1}{6}0 + \frac{1}{6}0 + \frac{2}{6}0\right)60 = 20
$$

$$
\phi_2(\tilde{c}) = \left(\frac{2}{6}\lfloor 1.7\rfloor + \frac{1}{6}\lfloor 1.7\rfloor + \frac{1}{6}\lfloor 1.7\rfloor + \frac{2}{6}\lfloor 1.7\rfloor\right)60 = \left(\frac{2}{6}2 + \frac{1}{6}1 + \frac{1}{6}2 + \frac{2}{6}2\right)60 = 110
$$

$$
\phi_3(\tilde{c}) = \left(\frac{2}{6}\lfloor 0.7\rfloor + \frac{1}{6}\lfloor 0.7\rfloor + \frac{1}{6}\lfloor 0.7\rfloor + \frac{2}{6}\lfloor 0.7\rfloor\right)60 = \left(\frac{2}{6}1 + \frac{1}{6}0 + \frac{1}{6}1 + \frac{2}{6}1\right)60 = 50
$$

Table 6.7   Values of β_v^{bz} (j, S), for each $j \in N = \{1, 2, 3\}$

S	$s!(n-s-1)/n!$	$\sum_{i\in S}N_v^{bz}(i)$	$\beta_v^{bz}(1, S)$	$\beta_v^{bz}(2, S)$	$\beta_v^{bz}(3, S)$
$\varnothing$	$^2/_6$	–	$\lfloor 0.2\rfloor$	$\lfloor 1.7\rfloor$	$\lfloor 0.7\rfloor$
$\{1\}$	$^1/_6$	0.2	–	$\lfloor 1.7\rfloor$	$\lfloor 0.7\rfloor$
$\{2\}$	$^1/_6$	1.7	$\lfloor 0.2\rfloor$	–	$\lceil 0.7\rceil$
$\{3\}$	$^1/_6$	0.7	$\lfloor 0.2\rfloor$	$\lceil 1.7\rceil$	–
$\{1, 2\}$	$^1/_6$	1.9	–	–	$\lfloor 0.7\rfloor$
$\{1, 3\}$	$^1/_6$	0.9	–	$\lceil 1.7\rceil$	–
$\{2, 3\}$	$^2/_6$	2.4	$\lfloor 0.2\rfloor$	–	–

6. CONCLUDING REMARKS

The European Commission (2000) suggests that inter-municipal coopera-tion can be very beneficial in achieving groupings of a sufficient size to provide a wms suitable to the high standards demanded at an affordable cost.

On the other hand, this suggestion does not seem to have had much impact on research topics. In fact, while several journals are dedicated to the physical management of municipal solid waste, relatively little attention has been paid to the creation, running and maintenance of an effective municipal solid wms (Wilson et al., 2001). The result of this lack is that it is still unclear how an economically affordable, environmentally effective and socially acceptable municipal solid waste management system can be developed.

We focused our attention on both economic efficiency and social acceptance. Using our model, municipalities can understand the value of savings provided by inter-municipal cooperation, in order to achieve a waste collection system suitable to the high EC standards. At the same time, by giving the cost that each single inter-municipal subgroup should pay to reach the same waste collection performances, the model provides the characteristic cost function of a cooperative game which is intended to study allocations (among the municipalities) of the overall cost supported by the largest grouping (Ferrari et al., 2001). We believe that economic efficiency, together with a fair allocation of the overall cost, could form the basis of a general acceptance by the community of an inter-municipal wms.

Comparison of the data yielded by our model and real data provided by the waste collection management seems to confirm that our model offers a good level of approximation in estimating waste collection costs. We also argue that the low level of effort demanded by our model for data mining was the key to achieving our purposes in such a dynamic system.

That low level of effort is also very important from the point of view of the cost allocation problem considered in the previous section. Nowadays, the three prominent sharing rules used in Italy are a proportional division, respectively, by the number of inhabitants, the amount of the waste collected and the area of each municipality. The reason for these widespread criteria could be the ease of obtaining the relevant data to implement these rules.

On the other hand, we proved that the allocations yielded by these rules in the cooperative cost game built on our simulation results, are not in the core of the game. Since allocations not in the core are not stable, this evidence shows that municipal managers usually skip over the considerations about the stability property at the moment of choosing a particular sharing rule.

On this view, we believe that our model, due to its low cost of application, could be a good compromise to foster the implementation of an allocation mechanism that is more equitable and provides more incentives to cooperate than those actually in use. We claim that one of these mechanisms could be the Shapley value.

NOTES

1. I thank Giulio Ferrari, Fioravante Patrone and two anonymous referees for valuable comments.

REFERENCES

Antonioli, B., R. Fazioli and M. Filippini (2000), 'Analisi dei rendimenti di scala per il servizio di igiene urbana in Italia', *Economia delle fonti di energia e dell'ambiente*, **2**, (2000).

Biagi, F., and A. Massarutto (2001), 'Efficienza e regolamentazione nei servizi pubblici locali: il caso dell'igiene urbana', *Working Paper, Department of Economic Science, University of Udine*, 05-01-eco.

Crocco, M. (2001), Personal communication of data by ASMT. Questionnaire provided by this work.

European Commission (2000), *Handbook on the Implementation of EC Environmental Legislation*, chapter 4: 'Waste Management'. http: //europa.eu.int/ comm/ environment/enlarg/handbook/handbook.htm

Everett, J.W., S. Maratha, R. Dorairaj and P. Riley (1998), 'Curbside collection of recyclables I: route time estimation model', *Resources, Conservation and Recycling*, **22**, 177–92.

Ferrari, G., S. Moretti and F. Patrone (2001), 'On some game theoretical issues arising from waste management', presented at the 12th International Conference on Game Theory, 16–20 July, Stony Brook, New York.

Fragnelli, V., I. García-Jurado and L. Méndez-Naya (2004), '*A Note on Bus Games*', *Economics Letters*, **82**, 99–106.

Gillies, D.B. (1953), 'Some theorems on N-person games', *Ph.D. thesis*, Princeton: Princeton University Press.

Kaulard, A. and A. Massarutto (1997), La Gestione Integrata dei Rifiuti Urbani – Analisi dei Costi Industriali, Milan: FrancoAngeli.

Schmeidler, D. (1969), 'The nucleolus of a characteristic function game'. *SIAM Journal of Applied Mathematics*, **17**, 1163–70.

Shapley, L.S. (1953), 'A value for n-person games', in H.W. Kuhn and A.W. Tucker (eds), Contributions to the Theory of Games. Annals of Mathematics Studies, **28(II)**, 307–17.

Shapley, L.S. (1971), 'Cores of convex games', *International Journal of Game Theory*, **1**, 11–26.

Tickner, G. and J. McDavid (1986), 'Effects of scale and market structure on the costs of residential solid waste collection in Canadian cities', *Public Finance Quarterly*, **14**, 371–91.

von Neumann, J. and O. Morgenstern (1944), *Theory of Games and Economic Behavior*, Princeton: Princeton University Press.

Wilson, E.J., F.R. McDougall and J. Willmore (2001), 'Euro-trash: searching Europe for a more sustainable approach to waste management', *Resources, Conservation and Recycling*, **31**, 327–46.

Young, H.P. (1995), *Equity: in theory and practice*, Princeton: Princeton University Press.

7. Co-insurance games and environmental pollution risk

Vito Fragnelli and Maria Erminia Marina

1. INTRODUCTION

In this chapter we consider a situation in which a large risk has to be insured and in particular the case of environmental pollution risks that depend on firms that in their production processes may have as a side-effect the release of polluting wastes that damage the environment.

Firms may interact with the environment in different ways; more precisely they can alter the basic environment, influence the possibility of using it if they damage public or private goods, compromise human health directly or indirectly, contaminate biological resources and ecosystems.

The consequences may be described as damage to persons and/or materials or interruption of various activities (industrial, agricultural or recreational).

We want to recall some environmental pollution risks according to a simple classification:

- *air pollution*, generated by emissions, harmful gases, exhaust fumes, stenches, waste disposal, chemical production;
- *water pollution*, when factories discharge effluents into rivers;
- *soil pollution*, deriving from rubbish, solid wastes, industrial wastes, for example from farms that use chemical manure or pesticides or from factories that dispose of their waste in the soil;
- *marine pollution*, where coastal firms get rid of waste and sewage into the sea or resulting from oil tanker accidents;
- *acoustic pollution*, due to high noise levels and vibrations with risk to workers and neighbouring inhabitants.

In order to limit the costs related to environmental risk a firm generally effects an insurance policy that covers both third-party liability for any damage that may be caused to persons or materials and depollution costs due to removal of pollutants (cf. Bazzano, 1994).

Table 7.1   Costs refunded after main accidents in OCSE countries,
1976–1988

Year	Place	Cost*	Cause (*pollutant*)
1976	Seveso (Italy)	103	Chemical plant (*dioxin*)
1978	Los Alfaques (Spain)	15	Tanker truck explosion (*propylene*)
1982	Livingstone (USA)	41	Derailment (*toxics*)
1984	Denver (USA)	20	Tank (*gasoline*)
1985	Kenora (Canada)	7	Spill (*PCB*)
1986	Basilea (Switzerland)	16	Fire with River Rhein pollution
1987	Herborn (Germany)	8	Tanker truck
1988	Floreffe (USA)	67	Tank explosion (*oil*)
1988	S. Basile (Canada)	39	Fire (*toxic wastes*)
1988	Piper Alpha (North Sea)	111	Explosion (*gas*)

Notes:
* In millions of euros. Naval transportation accidents are not included.

Source: 'Pollution', SCOR Notes (1989).

The losses from environmental pollution can be very heavy as shown in Table 7.1.

Moreover we want just to mention that Lloyd's alone were charged about 15 billion euros (cf. 'Il sole 24 ore', 27 September 2001), to refund damages related to asbestos alone over a period of about twenty years (but some trials are still continuing). So it is not possible for a single insurance company to assume this risk on its own; as a consequence it is insured by a pool of companies. Finally we want to stress that environmental accidents have a low probability of happening, but, as shown above, may require a high refund, so that they are a natural candidate for a co-insurance approach. For example in Italy there is a pool of 61 insurance companies that is uniquely responsible for all such kinds of risk, where each company assumes a percentage of risk as in Table 7A.1 in the Appendix.

In this chapter we study the general problem of the co-insurance of large risks.

More precisely we suppose that n companies have to insure a given risk together. Two important intertwined practical questions then arise: Which premium should they charge? How should they split the risk and the premium in order to make the n companies as competitive as possible and obtain a fair division? These questions can be tackled using a cooperative game-theoretical model.

We want to remark that the first examples of applications of game theory to insurance were given by Borch (1962a, 1962b) and Lemaire (1977, 1991) and more recently by Suijs et al. (1999); we refer to Suijs (2000) for a survey on these topics.

The organization of the chapter is as follows: In Section 2 we give a formal description of the co-insurance problem introducing suitable notations and hypotheses, and state some preliminary results. Section 3 deals with a class of co-insurance games, paying particular attention to the property of balancedness and analyzing some classical game-theoretical solutions. Section 4 is devoted to the case of optimal decomposition of the risk in constant quotas. In Section 5 we summarize our results, applying them to a case study using data from the Italian situation. Section 6 contains some concluding remarks.

2. HYPOTHESES AND NOTATIONS

As stated in the introduction to this chapter, we consider a problem in which a risk is evaluated as too heavy for a single insurance company, but it can be insured by n companies that share the risk and the premium.

We consider a fixed and suitable probability space; we denote the set of companies by $N=\{1, ..., n\}$ and we suppose that every company $i \in N$, expresses her valuation of a random variable X as the value $H_i(X)$, where H_i is a functional from a class $\mathcal{L}$ of random variables (the insurable risks) into the set of real numbers, **R**; this means that, given a risk X, $H_i(X)$ provides a measure of X (expected claims and security considerations). In order to determine the commercial premium to be charged, each company has to take into account its evaluation of the risk and the usual economic factors (commissions and expenses).

As in Deprez and Gerber (1985) (see also Gerber, 1980 and Goovaerts et al., 1984), we add the hypotheses that a loading for a degenerate risk is not justified (**a**) and that if a risk is increased by an additive constant, this constant has to be added to the evaluation of the risk (translation invariance **b**), so for each $i \in N$ we ask that:

Hypothesis 1

(a) $H_i(w)=w, \forall\ w \in \mathbf{R}$;
(b) $H_i(w+X)=w+H_i(X), \forall\ w \in \mathbf{R}, \forall\ X \in \mathcal{L}$.

Many classical principles satisfy this hypothesis, for example:

- the *net premium principle* $H(X)=E(X)$, where $E(X)$ is the expectation of X;

- the *variance principle* $H(X)=E(X)+aV(X)$, where $V(X)$ is the variance of X and $a>0$;
- the *standard deviation principle* $H(X)=E(X)+\beta\sqrt{V(X)}$, where $\beta>0$;
- the *zero utility principle* $H(X)=\bar{H}$, where $\bar{H}$ satisfies $E[u(z+\bar{H}-X)]=u(z)$ and u is the utility function of the insurance company which has an initial surplus z; in particular for exponential utility $u(x)=1/a$ $(1-e^{-ax})$, with $a>0$ we have $\bar{H}=1/a \ln E(e^{aX})$.
- the *ε-percentile principle* $H(X)=\min\{x|F(x)\geq 1-\varepsilon\}$, where F is the distribution function of X.

Now we suppose that the n companies have to insure a given risk R and receive a premium π. Each company can decide to co-insure the risk or not, that is, it has to be considered a decision-maker; as a consequence in order to define 'fair' allocations of the pair (π, R) we introduce the following notations, referring to all subsets (coalitions) S of the companies involved. For any non-empty subset of companies $S\subseteq N$ we denote by $\mathcal{D}(S)$ the set of feasible divisions of the premium π, that is:

$$\mathcal{D}(S)=\{(d_i)_{i\in S}\in\mathbf{R}^{|S|} \text{ s.t. } \Sigma_{i\in S}d_i=\pi\}$$

and by $\mathcal{A}(S)$ the set of the feasible decompositions of the risk R, i.e.:

$$\mathcal{A}(S)=\{(X_i)_{i\in S}\in\mathcal{L}^{|S|}, \text{ s.t. } \Sigma_{i\in S}X_i=R\}$$

and we suppose that $\mathcal{A}(S)$ is non-empty. According to the allocation $(d_i, X_i)_{i\in S}\in\mathcal{D}(S)\times\mathcal{A}(S)$, for each $i\in S$ the company i receives the amount d_i and pays the random variable X_i. Now we suppose that for each subset $S\subseteq N$ it is possible to compute an optimal decomposition of the risk, that is, we introduce the hypothesis:

Hypothesis 2 $\forall S\subseteq N$ there exists $\min\{\Sigma_{i\in S}H_i(X_i)|(X_i)_{i\in S}\in\mathcal{A}(S)\}=P(S)$.

$P(S)$ can be seen as the evaluation that the companies in S (as a whole) give of the risk R.

Example 1 $\forall i\in N$ the variance principle holds, that is:

$$H_i(Y)=E(Y)+a_i Var(Y) \qquad \forall Y\in\mathcal{L}, 0<a_1\leq ... \leq a_n$$

It is possible to prove (Deprez and Gerber, 1985) that $P(N)=\Sigma_{i\in N}H_i(q_iR)$; moreover as in Fragnelli and Marina (2003) we have:

$$P(S) = \Sigma_{i \in S} H_i(q_i/q(S) R) \qquad \forall S \in N$$

where $1/a(S) = \Sigma_{i \in S} 1/a_i$, $q_i = a(N)/a_i$ and $q(S) = \Sigma_{i \in S} q_i$ and we can also write:

$$P(S) = E(R) + a(S) \, Var(R) \qquad \forall S \subseteq N$$

Now we consider the allocations of (π, R) that assign to each company a risk and an amount high enough to cover this risk. Formally for any subset of companies $S \subseteq N$ we define the set of individually rational allocations:

$$\mathcal{B}(S) = \{(d_i, X_i)_{i \in S} \in \mathcal{D}(S) \times \mathcal{A}(S) \mid d_i - H_i(X_i) \geq 0, \ \forall i \in S\}$$

Remark 1 $\mathcal{B}(S) \neq \varnothing \Leftrightarrow P(S) \leq \pi$, that is, if the premium is larger than the evaluation (of the set of companies in S) of the optimal decomposition of the risk, individually rational allocations do not exist and vice versa.

Remark 2 $\mathcal{B}(S) \neq \varnothing \Rightarrow \mathcal{B}(T) \neq \varnothing, \forall T \supset S$. In fact $P(T) \leq P(S)$ because $H_i(0) = 0, \forall i \in N$.

Remark 3 In order to avoid trivial situations we suppose that $\pi > P(N)$, that is, the n companies together may obtain a positive gain.

For any subset of companies $S \subseteq N$ such that $\mathcal{B}(S) \neq \varnothing$ we may define the set of allocations of (π, R) corresponding to optimal risk decompositions:

$$\mathcal{O}(S) = \{(d_i, X_i)_{i \in S} \in \mathcal{B}(S) \mid \Sigma_{i \in S} H_i(X_i) = P(S)\}$$

and the set of Pareto-optimal allocations of (π, R):

$$\mathcal{PO}(S) = \{(d_i, X_i)_{i \in S} \in \mathcal{B}(S) \mid \not\exists (d_i', X_i')_{i \in S} \in \mathcal{B}(S),$$
$$\text{s.t. } d_i' - H_i(X_i') > d_i' - H_i(X_i), \ \forall i \in S\}$$

We can state the following theorem similar to Proposition 3.5 of Suijs and Borm (1999):

Theorem 1 $\mathcal{O}(S) = \mathcal{PO}(S)$. The proof is close to that of Proposition 1 in Fragnelli and Marina (2003), with S in the role of N.

Remark 4 If $\mathcal{B}(S) \neq \varnothing$ then if we take $(X_i)_{i \in S} \in \mathcal{A}(S)$ s.t. $\Sigma_{i \in S} H_i(X_i) = P(S)$ and define $d_i = H_i(X_i) + 1/|S|(\pi - P(S))$, $\forall i \in S$ then $(d_i, X_i)_{i \in S} \in \mathcal{PO}(S)$.

Finally we define two subsets of the set of Pareto optimal allocations for the grand coalition N:

$$Q(N)=\{(d_i, X_i)_{i \in N} \in \mathcal{PO}(N) | \forall S \subset N \text{ s.t. } \mathcal{B}(S) \neq \varnothing, \nexists (d'_i, X'_i)_{i \in S} \in \mathcal{PO}(S)$$
$$\text{s.t. } d'_i - H_i(X'_i) > d_i - H_i(X_i), \forall i \in S\}$$
$$CO(N) = \{(d_i, X_i)_{i \in N} \in \mathcal{PO}(N) | \forall S \subseteq N \ \Sigma_{i \in S}(d_i - H_i(X_i)) \geq$$
$$\max\{0, \pi - P(S)\}\}$$

The allocations in the set $Q(N)$, restricted to the subsets $S \subset N$, are such that there do not exist Pareto-optimal allocations for the set S preferable to them (for those subsets S for which individually rational allocations exist), while the set $CO(N)$ contains those allocations for which the restriction to any subset $S \subseteq N$ is rational for that subset, that is, it guarantees that S cannot do better acting separately by itself. We have:

Theorem 2 $CO(N) = Q(N)$

Proof.

'$\subseteq$' Let $(d_i, X_i)_{i \in N} \in CO(N)$; if there exists a coalition S s.t. $\mathcal{B}(S) \neq \varnothing$ and there exists an allocation $(d'_i, X'_i)_{i \in S} \in \mathcal{PO}(S)$ s.t. $d'_i - H_i(X'_i) > d_i - H_i(X_i)$, $\forall i \in S$ then $\pi - P(S) = \Sigma_{i \in S}(d'_i - H_i(X'_i)) > \Sigma_{i \in S}(d_i - H_i(X_i))$. Contradiction.

'$\supseteq$' Let $(d_i, X_i)_{i \in N} \in Q(N)$; as $(d_i, X_i)_{i \in N} \in \mathcal{B}(N)$ then $\forall S \subseteq N$ $\Sigma_{i \in S}(d_i - H_i(X_i)) \geq 0$; suppose that there exists a coalition S with $\pi - P(S) > 0$ (so $\mathcal{B}(S) \neq \varnothing$) s.t. $\Sigma_{i \in S}(d_i - H_i(X_i)) < \pi - P(S)$. Let $(X'_i)_{i \in S} \in \mathcal{A}(S)$ s.t. $\Sigma_{i \in S} H_i(X'_i) = P(S)$. If we define, $\forall i \in S$, $d'_i = d_i - H_i(X_i) + H_i(X'_i) + 1/|S|(\pi - P(S) - \Sigma_{j \in S}(d_j - H_j(X_j))$ then $\Sigma_{i \in S} d'_i = \pi$ and $d'_i - H_i(X'_i) > d_i - H_i(X_i) \geq 0$, $\forall i \in S$. Contradiction. $\square$

The argumentation of the previous proof is similar to that of Theorem 2 in Lari and Marina (2000).

3. CO-INSURANCE GAMES

All we said in the previous sections can be reviewed in the light of game theory. We recall that a cooperative game in characteristic function form with transferable utility (TU-game) is a pair (N, v) where N is the set of players and v is a real valued function on 2^N, with $v(\varnothing) = 0$, where $v(S)$, $S \subseteq N$, is the worth of coalition S.

Given a game (N, v) the core is the set $Core(v) = \{(x_i)_{i \in N} \in \mathbf{R}^{|N|}$ s.t. $\Sigma_{i \in S} x_i \geq v(S), \forall S \subseteq N$ and $\Sigma_{i \in N} x_i = v(N)\}$. The first condition is called *coalition rationality* and expresses that given an allocation $x \in Core(v)$ each coalition S gets at least its worth; the second condition is called *efficiency* and says that the core allocations divide exactly the value of the grand coalition N. When a game has a non-empty core it is said to be *balanced*.

For our co-insurance problem we define a game whose characteristic function v is:

$$v(S) = \max \{0, \pi - P(S)\} \qquad \forall S \subseteq N$$

The following theorem states a connection between the allocations of the co-insurance problem and the allocations of the co-insurance game.

Theorem 3 $CO(N) \neq \emptyset \Leftrightarrow Core(v) \neq \emptyset$.

Proof.

'$\Rightarrow$' Let $(d_i, X_i)_{i \in N} \in CO(N)$; if we define $y_i = d_i - H_i(X_i)$ $\forall i \in N$ then $(y_i)_{i \in N} \in Core(v)$.

'$\Leftarrow$' Let $(y_i)_{i \in N} \in Core(v)$, $(X_i^*)_{i \in N} \in \mathcal{A}(N)$ s.t. $\Sigma_{i \in N} H_i(X_i^*) = P(N)$ and define $d_i^* = y_i + H_i(X_i^*)$ $\forall i \in N$; then $(d_i^*, X_i^*)_{i \in N} \in CO(N)$. $\square$

Before studying the properties of the game we can reorder the players in such a way that:

$$P(N) \leq P(N \setminus \{n\}) \leq \ldots \leq P(N \setminus \{1\}) \tag{7.1}$$

As a consequence we have $\Sigma_{j \in N} P(N \setminus \{j\}) - (n-1)P(N) \geq P(N \setminus \{i\})$, $\forall i \in N$.

In these general hypotheses we can state the following results:

Lemma 1 $\pi \leq P(N \setminus \{1\}) \Rightarrow$ the game is balanced.

Proof. If $P(N) < \pi \leq P(N \setminus \{1\})$ a core-allocation is given by $x = (\pi - P(N), 0, \ldots, 0)$. In fact x is efficient as $\Sigma_{i \in N} x_i = \pi - P(N) = v(N)$; x is coalitionally rational because if $S \supseteq \{1\}$ then $\Sigma_{i \in S} x_i = \pi - P(N) \geq \max \{0, \pi - P(S)\} = v(S)$ and if S does not contain $\{1\}$ then $S \subseteq N \setminus \{1\} \Rightarrow P(S) \geq P(N \setminus \{1\}) \Rightarrow \pi - P(S) \leq \pi - P(N \setminus \{1\}) \Rightarrow v(S) = 0 = \Sigma_{i \in S} x_i$. $\square$

Lemma 2 $\pi > \Sigma_{i \in N} P(N \setminus \{i\}) - (n-1) P(N) \Rightarrow$ the game is not balanced.

Proof. Note that by hypothesis it follows that $\pi > P(N \setminus \{i\})$ and then $v(N \setminus \{i\}) = \pi - P(N \setminus \{i\})$, $\forall i \in N$. For a balanced game we have that for each core allocation $(x_i)_{i \in N}$:

$$v(N) - x_i = \Sigma_{j \in N \setminus \{i\}} x_j \geq v(N \setminus \{i\}) \qquad \forall\, i \in N$$

and consequently:

$$(n-1)\, v(N) \geq \Sigma_{i \in N}\, v(N \setminus \{i\})$$

But we have:

$$\frac{1}{n-1} \Sigma_{i \in N}\, v(N \setminus \{i\}) > v(N) \Leftrightarrow \frac{n}{n-1}\, \pi - \frac{1}{n-1} \Sigma_{i \in N}\, P(N \setminus \{i\}) > \pi - P(N) \Leftrightarrow$$

$$\Leftrightarrow \frac{1}{n-1}\, \pi > \frac{1}{n-1} \Sigma_{i \in N}\, P(N \setminus \{i\}) - P(N)$$

that is equivalent to the hypothesis of the lemma, so the core is empty.☐

Finally we can state the following theorem:

Theorem 4 There exists $\hat{\pi}$ such that the game is balanced if and only if $\pi \leq \hat{\pi}$.

The proof is similar to that of Theorem 1 in Fragnelli et al. (2000). Now we introduce a hypothesis that allows us to determine the value of $\hat{\pi}$ defined in Theorem 4.

Hypothesis 3 We ask that the cost function P satisfies the (reduced concavity) hypothesis:

$$\text{for each } S \subset N \text{ s.t. } P(S) < \hat{\pi},$$
$$P(S) - P(S \cup \{i\}) \geq (P(N \setminus \{i\}) - P(N), \forall\, i \in N \setminus S$$

Theorem 5 Suppose that P satisfies Hypothesis 3, then $\hat{\pi} = \Sigma_{j \in N} P(N \setminus \{j\}) - (n-1)P(N)$.

Proof. In view of Lemma 2 and of Theorem 4 it is sufficient to prove that the game is balanced for $\pi = \Sigma_{j \in N} P(N \setminus \{j\}) - (n-1)P(N)$.

We will prove that the marginal solution $x = P(N \setminus \{1\}) - P(N), ..., P(N \setminus \{n\}) - P(N))$ is a core allocation. Note that $x_i \geq 0, \forall\, i \in N$. x is efficient in fact:

$$\Sigma_{i \in N} x_i = \Sigma_{i \in N} P(N \setminus \{i\}) - n\, P(N) = \pi - P(N) = v(N)$$

To prove that x is coalitionally rational we consider first the case of $v(S) = 0$ that is trivial as $x \geq 0$; in the case of $v(S) > 0$ we have:

$$\Sigma_{i \in S}\, x_i \geq v(S) \Leftrightarrow \Sigma_{i \in S}\, (P(N \backslash \{i\}) - P(N)) \geq \Sigma_{i \in N}\, P(N \backslash \{i\}) -$$
$$(n-1)P(N) - P(S) \Leftrightarrow$$
$$\Leftrightarrow \Sigma_{i \in N \backslash S}\, (P(N \backslash \{i\}) - P(N)) \leq P(S) - P(N)$$

Let $N \backslash S = \{t_1, ..., t_m\}$; the previous inequalities holds as a surrogate of the following relations:

$$P(N \backslash \{t_1\}) - P(N) \leq P(S) - P(S \cup \{t_1\})$$
$$P(N \backslash \{t_2\}) - P(N) \leq P(S \cup \{t_1\}) - P(S \cup \{t_1, t_2\})$$
$$...$$
$$P(N \backslash \{t_{m-1}\}) - P(N) \leq P(S \cup \{t_1, ..., t_{m-2}\}) - P(S \cup \{t_1, ..., t_{m-1}\})$$
$$P(N \backslash \{t_m\}) - P(N) = P(S \cup \{t_1, ..., t_{m-1}\}) - P(N) \qquad \square$$

Now we want to analyze the particular case in which P satisfies Hypothesis 3 and the premium is precisely $\hat{\pi} = \Sigma_{j \in N}\, P(N \backslash \{j\}) - (n-1)P(N)$, referring to classical game-theoretical solution concepts.

We claim that the core is the singleton whose only element is the marginal solution $x = (P(N \backslash \{1\}) - P(N), ..., P(N \backslash \{n\}) - P(N))$. Suppose that there exists a different core allocation y; by efficiency there exists a player j such that $y_j > x_j$; in this case

$$\Sigma_{i \in N \backslash \{j\}}\, y_i < \Sigma_{i \in N \backslash \{j\}}\, x_i = \Sigma_{i \in N \backslash \{j\}}\, P(N \backslash \{i\}) - (n-1)P(N) = \hat{\pi} - P(N \backslash \{j\}) =$$
$$= v(N \backslash \{j\})$$

so y is not coalitionally rational and does not belong to the core.

As a consequence x is also the nucleolus of the game. This solution concept corresponds to the unique allocation that minimizes the maximum excess of the coalitions, according to a lexicographic order and it lies in the core if it is non-empty (for more details see Schmeidler, 1969).

In 1981 Tijs introduced as a solution for a TU-game the τ-value, the first of a series of compromise values; it is defined as follows.

Let $M_i = v(N) - v(N \backslash \{i\})$, that is, the marginal contribution of player i and let $m_i = \max \{v(S) - \Sigma_{j \in S \backslash \{i\}}\, M_j | S \subseteq N, S \ni i\}$ if the game is quasi-balanced $(M_i \geq m_i, \forall\, i \in N$ and $\Sigma_{i \in N}\, m_i \leq v(N) \leq \Sigma_{i \in N} M_i)$ the τ-value is the unique convex combination of M and m s.t. $\Sigma_{i \in N} \tau_i = v(N)$. In our situation, for each player i we have:

$$M_i = v(N) - v(N \backslash \{i\}) = \hat{\pi} - P(N) - \hat{\pi} + P(N \backslash \{i\}) = x_i$$

As the game is balanced then it is also quasi-balanced and so $M_i \geq m_i$; on the other hand by definition of m_i we have:

$$m_i \geq v(N) - \Sigma_{j \in N \setminus \{i\}} M_j = M_i$$

and finally $m_i = M_i = \tau_i$.

Remark 5   If $\pi > \Sigma_{j \in N} P(N \setminus \{j\}) - (n-1) P(N)$ then not only is the game not balanced but neither is it quasi-balanced in fact:

$$v(N) = \pi - P(N) > \Sigma_{j \in N} P(N \setminus \{j\}) - P(N)) = \Sigma_{j \in N} M_j$$

Moreover we have also:

$$m_i \geq v(N) - \Sigma_{j \in N \setminus \{i\}} M_j > M_i$$

Referring to Example 1 we have that the cost function P satisfies the reduced concavity (Hypothesis 3) and the optimal decomposition consists of constant quotas. In the next section we study this situation.

4.   CONSTANT QUOTAS

In this section we suppose that there exist a convex function H and n real numbers $q_1 \geq ... \geq q_n > 0$, $\Sigma_{j \in N} q_j = 1$ s.t.:

$$H_i(Y) = q_i \, H\left(\frac{Y}{q_i}\right) \qquad \forall \, i \in N, \, \forall \, Y \in \mathcal{L}$$

(In Example 1 $H(Y) = E(Y) + a(N) \, Var(Y)$).

We show in the following that the above hypothesis is sufficient to guarantee that an optimal decomposition can be obtained by sharing the risk according to constant quotas, represented by the numbers $q_1, ..., q_n$ and that the cost function P satisfies the reduced concavity hypothesis.

In fact if the function H verifies Hypothesis 1 and is strictly convex (that is, $H(sY + tZ) < sH(Y) + tH(Z)$ for $s + t = 1$, $s \in]0, 1[$, $\forall \, Y, Z \in \mathcal{L}$, unless $Y - Z$ is a constant) and is Gâteaux differentiable, we have (cf. Deprez and Gerber, 1985 and Lari and Marina, 2000) that, for each $S \subseteq N$:

$$P(S) = q(S) \, H\left(\frac{R}{q(S)}\right) = \Sigma_{i \in S} \, H_i\left(\frac{q_i}{q(S)} R\right) \leq \Sigma_{i \in S} \, H_i(X_i) \qquad \forall (X_i)_{i \in S} \in \mathcal{A}(S)$$

where $q(S) = \Sigma_{i \in S} q_i$.

Remark 6   The equality holds only if there exist $(\gamma_i)_{i \in S} \in \mathbf{R}^{|S|}$ s.t. $\Sigma_{i \in S} \gamma_i) = 0$ and $X_i = \dfrac{q_i}{q(S)} R + \gamma_i, \, \forall \, i \in S$.

Now we have:

Proposition 1 The function P verifies Hypothesis 3.

Proof. We define the functions $g(z)=H(zR)$ and $h(z)=zg(1/z)$ for each $z>0$.

By the convexity of H we have that g is a convex function. Moreover let $0<z_1<z_2$ and let $\lambda \in]0, 1[$; we have

$$g\left(\frac{1}{\lambda z_1 + (1-\lambda)z_2}\right)=g\left(\frac{\lambda z_1}{\lambda z_1 + (1-\lambda)z_2}\frac{1}{z_1}+\frac{(1-\lambda)z_2}{\lambda z_1 + (1-\lambda)z_2}\frac{1}{z_1}\right)\leq$$

$$\leq\frac{\lambda z_1}{\lambda z_1 + (1-\lambda)z_2}g\left(\frac{1}{z_1}\right)+\frac{(1-\lambda)z_2}{\lambda z_1 + (1-\lambda)z_2}g\left(\frac{1}{z_2}\right)$$

and so

$$h(\lambda z_1 +(1-\lambda)z_2)=(\lambda z_1 +(1-\lambda)z_2)\, g\left(\frac{1}{\lambda z_1 + (1-\lambda)z_2}\right)\leq$$

$$\leq \lambda z_1 g\left(\frac{1}{z_1}\right)+(1-\lambda)z_2\, g\left(\frac{1}{z_2}\right)=\lambda h(z_1)+(1-\lambda)h(z_2)$$

So we have that h is a convex function and then P verifies Hypothesis 3.□

As a consequence of Theorem 5 also in this more general case if the value of the premium is exactly $\Sigma_{i\in N}\, P(N\backslash\{j\})-(n-1)P(N)$, the core is non-empty and the only core allocation is the marginal solution that assigns to each player exactly his marginal contribution; it corresponds to the co-insurance problem allocation $(q_i\, P(N)+ P(N\backslash\{i\})- P(N),\, q_i\, R)_{i\in N}$ that belongs to $CO(N)$.

Before concluding the chapter we want to analyze the widely used proportional (problem) allocation $(q_i\,\pi,\, q_i\, R)_{i\in N}$; more precisely we are interested in whether this allocation belongs to $CO(N)$. First we check that this solution belongs to $B(N)$; we have:

$$q_i\,\pi - H_i(q_i\, R)\geq 0 \Leftrightarrow q_i\,\pi \geq q_i\, H(R) \Leftrightarrow q_i\,\pi \geq q_i\, P(N) \Leftrightarrow \pi \geq P(N)$$

where the last inequality is true according to our hypothesis of non-trivial situation.

The previous result guarantees that $\Sigma_{i\in S}\,(q_i\,\pi - H_i(q_i\, R))\geq 0$, so if $\pi - P(S)\leq 0$ ∀ $S\neq N$ then trivially the proportional allocation belongs to $CO(N)$.

Otherwise at least $\pi - P(N\backslash\{n\})>0$ and for those $S\neq N$ such that $\pi - P(S)>0$ the condition is:

$$\Sigma_{i \in S} \, q_i(\pi - P(N)) \geq \pi - P(S) \Leftrightarrow q(S)(\pi - P(N)) \geq \pi - P(S) \Leftrightarrow$$

$$\Leftrightarrow \pi(1 - q(S)) \leq q(S)\left(H\left(\frac{R}{q(S)}\right) - H(R)\right) \Leftrightarrow \pi \leq \frac{H\left(\dfrac{R}{q(S)}\right) - H(R)}{\dfrac{1}{q(S)} - 1}$$

By the convexity of H the last condition holds for all $S \neq N$ s.t. $\pi - P(S) > 0$ if and only if it holds for $S = N \backslash \{n\}$, so for the proportional allocation we have:

$$(q_i \pi, q_i R)_{i \in N} \in CO(N) \Leftrightarrow \pi \leq \frac{1 - q_n}{q_n}\left(H\left(\frac{R}{q(N \backslash \{n\})}\right) - H(R)\right) = \tilde{\pi}$$

If the premium is exactly $\tilde{\pi}$ as above, reverting to the game we have:

$$v(N) = \tilde{\pi} - P(N) = \frac{1}{q_n} P(N \backslash \{n\}) - \frac{q(N \backslash \{n\})}{q_n} P(N) - P(N)$$

$$= \frac{1}{q_n} P(N \backslash \{n\}) - P(N))$$

In this case the game solution related to the previous proportional allocation is $(q_i/q_n \, (P(N \backslash \{n\}) - P(N)))_{i \in N}$; this means that player n gets exactly its marginal contribution, while each player $i \in N \backslash \{n\}$ gets the marginal contribution of player n times the ratio among q_i and q_n. Note that these amounts are non-increasing.

We can also investigate the relationship of the proportional solution to the marginal solution of the previous section, when the function P satisfies the hypothesis of convexity and the premium is $\pi = \Sigma_{j \in N} P(N \backslash \{j\}) - (n-1)P(N)$. In this case the proportional solution assigns to player i the amount $q_i(\Sigma_{j \in N} P(N \backslash \{j\}) - P(N))$, while the marginal solution assigns the amount $P(N \backslash \{i\}) - P(N)$. This means that the proportional solution divides each marginal contribution proportionally among all the players (who also receive a 'refund' of the risk assumed) while, as we said above, the marginal solution assigns to each player exactly his marginal contribution (besides the 'refund' of the risk assumed).

5. CASE STUDY

In this section we want to apply our results to the data of the Italian case (see Section 1). We lack suitable real data so we make some assumptions. We suppose that the 61 companies, as in Example 1, express their evaluation of a random variable X according to the variance principle. Next we suppose that $q_i, i \in N$ are the quotas of risk as in Table 7A.1 in the Appendix and a $(N) = 0.1$; finally we suppose that the distribution function of the risk R is $F(x) = 1 - e^{-\mu x}$, so we have $E(R) = 1/\mu$ and $Var(R) = 1/\mu^2$.

We make the assumption that $E(R)$ is 1.05 ($\mu = 1/1.05$ and $Var(R) = 1.1025$) and compute (in millions of euros).

$$P(N) = 1.160250$$
$$\hat{\pi} = 1.274612$$
$$\tilde{\pi} = 1.270816$$

and some allocations for the problem and for the game, as in Table 7A.2 in the Appendix.

These allocations clarify why if $\pi = \Sigma_{j \in N}, P(N \backslash \{j\}) - (n-1)P(N)$ the proportional allocation is not in the core of the game: It assigns too much to last players, compared with what is assigned to the first players. This means that the unique core allocation, that is, the marginal solution, is favourable to the first players, who are assuming larger quotas of risk. On the other hand, the proportional solution is more even so that in order to have a core allocation the premium must be lower so that the amounts assigned to the last player in the proportional allocation do not exceed those in the marginal one.

6. CONCLUDING REMARKS

In this chapter we have studied how to apply a co-insurance approach, one widely used one when large risks have to be managed, to a real situation, such as that of environmental risk; we were inspired by the Italian case, where a pool of 61 companies are involved in a co-insurance. We defined a suitable characteristic function for a TU-game and computed a value of the premium that leads to a balanced game, so any core allocation can be adopted by the companies for sharing the premium; next we investigated the value of the premium guaranteeing a balanced game when the companies agree on the proportional solution, as frequently happens in real-life situations.

NOTE

The authors gratefully acknowledge the valuable comments and helpful suggestions of two anonymous referees.

REFERENCES

Bazzano, C. (1994), *I rischi dell'azienda*, Milan: Pirola Editore.
Borch, K. (1962a), 'Equilibrium in a reinsurance market', *Econometrica*, **30**, 424–44.
Borch, K. (1962b), 'Application of game theory to some problems in automobile insurance', *Astin Bulletin*, **2**, 208–21.
Deprez, O. and H.U. Gerber (1985), 'On convex principle of premium calculation', *Insurance: Mathematics and Economics*, **4**, 179–89.
Fragnelli, V. and M.E. Marina (2003), 'A fair procedure in insurance', *Insurance, Mathematics and Economics*, **33**, 77–85.
Fragnelli, V., I. Garcìa-Jurado and L. Mèndez-Naya (2000), 'On shortest path games', *Mathematical Methods Operations Research*, **52**, 139–216.
Gerber, H.U. (1980), *An Introduction to Mathematical Risk Theory*, Philadelphia: The S.S. Huebner Foundation.
Goovaerts, M.J., F. De Vylder and J. Haezendonck (1984), *Insurance Premiums*, Amsterdam: North-Holland.
Lari, E. and M.E. Marina (2000), '*Coassicurazione e principi di calcolo del premio*', Preprint, Department of Economics and Quantitative Methods, University of Genoa.
Lemaire, J. (1977), 'Echange de risques entre assureurs et thèorie des jeux', *Astin Bulletin*, **9**, 155–79.
Lemaire, J. (1991), 'Cooperative game theory and its insurance applications', *Astin Bulletin*, **21**, 17–40.
Schmeidler, D. (1969), 'The nucleolus of a characteristic function game', *SIAM Journal of Applied Mathematics*, **17**, 1163–70.
Suijs, J. (2000), *Cooperative Decision Making under Risk*, Dordrecht: Kluwer Academic Publishers.
Suijs, J. and P.E.M. Borm (1999), 'Stochastic cooperative games: superadditivity, convexity, and certainty equivalents', *Games and Economic Behavior*, **27**, 331–45.
Suijs, J., P.E.M. Borm, A. De Waegenaere and S. Tijs (1999), 'Cooperative games with stochastic payoffs', *European Journal of Operational Research*, **113**, 193–205.
Tijs, S.H. (1981), 'Bounds for the core and the τ-value', in O. Moeschlin and D. Pallaschke (eds), *Game Theory and Mathematical Economies*, Amsterdam: North-Holland, pp. 123–32.

APPENDIX

Table 7A.1   Division plan for the Italian pool for environmental risk insurance

Company	Quota %
1 Allianz Subalpina	1.286
2 Le Assicurazioni di Roma	0.286
3 Assicurazioni Generali	5.263
4 Assimoco	0.429
5 Assitalia-Le Assicurazioni D'Italia	5.263
6 Augusta Assicurazioni	0.717
7 Aurora Assicurazioni	1.071
8 AXA Assicurazioni	2.460
9 Bayerische Ruck*	2.857
10 Bernese Ass. Ni-Comp. Italo-Svizzera	0.429
11 BNC Assicurazioni	0.286
12 Compagnia Assicuratrice UNIPOL	2.231
13 Compagnia Di Assicurazione di Milano	5.263
14 Il Duomo	0.574
15 ERC–Frankona AG*	5.714
16 F.A.T.A.	1.429
17 La Fondiaria Assicurazioni	5.263
18 GAN Italia	0.791
19 General Cologne RE*	2.714
20 Giuliana Assicurazioni	0.286
21 Italiana Assicurazioni	0.857
22 ITAS Assicurazioni	0.529
23 ITAS Soc. di Mutua Assicurazione	0.529
24 Levante Norditalia Assicurazioni	1.029
25 Liguria	0.429
26 Lloyd Adriatico	1.340
27 Lloyd Italico Assicurazioni	0.429
28 Maeci – Soc. Mutua di Ass.Ni e Riass.NI	0.286
29 Maeci Assicurazioni e Riassicurazioni	0.429
30 La Mannheim	0.429
31 Mediolanum Assicurazioni	0.429
32 Mete Assicurazioni	1.143
33 Munchener Ruck Italia*	3.286
34 La Nationale	0.429
35 Nationale Suisse	0.429
36 Navale Assicurazioni	0.963
37 New RE*	2.571
38 Nuova MAA Assicurazioni	0.429

Table 7A.1   (continued)

Company	Quota %
39 Nuova Tirrena	1.743
40 Padana Assicurazioni	2.143
41 La Piemontese Soc. Mutua di Ass.NI	0.429
42 La Piemontese Assicurazioni	0.429
43 Risparmio Assicurazioni	0.286
44 Riunione Adriatica di Sicurta'	5.263
45 Royal Sun Alliance	0.857
46 SAI	5.263
47 SARA Assicurazioni	0.429
48 SASA	0.429
49 SCOR Italia Riassicurazioni*	2.571
50 S.E.A.R.	0.286
51 SIAT-Societa' Italiana Ass.NI E Riass.NI	0.429
52 Societa' Cattolica di Assicurazione	1.186
53 Societa' Reale Mutua di Assicurazioni	1.429
54 Sorema*	2.571
55 Swiss Re – Italia	7.714
56 Ticino	0.306
57 Toro Assicurazioni	2.857
58 Uniass Assicurazioni	0.686
59 Universo Assicurazioni	0.429
60 Vittoria Assicurazioni	0.840
61 Winterthur Assicurazioni	0.857
Total	100.000

Note:
* Reinsurance company.

Table 7A.2 Some allocations for the problem and for the game (in euros)

Comp.(i)	%	q_i	PROBLEM			GAME		
			$q_i\tilde{\pi}$	$q_i\hat{\pi}$	marg	$q_i(\tilde{\pi}-P(N))$	$q_i(\hat{\pi}-P(N))$	marg
55	7.714	0.07714	98,031	98,324	98,717	8,529	8,822	9,216
15	5.714	0.05714	72,614	72,831	72,978	6,318	6,535	6,681
3	5.263	0.05263	66,883	67,083	67,189	5,819	6,019	6,125
5	5.263	0.05263	66,883	67,083	67,189	5,819	6,019	6,125
13	5.263	0.05263	66,883	67,083	67,189	5,819	6,019	6,125
17	5.263	0.05263	66,883	67,083	67,189	5,819	6,019	6,125
44	5.263	0.05263	66,883	67,083	67,189	5,819	6,019	6,125
46	5.263	0.05263	66,883	67,083	67,189	5,819	6,019	6,125
33	3.286	0.03286	41,759	41,884	41,872	3,633	3,758	3,746
9	2.857	0.02857	36,307	36,416	36,391	3,159	3,267	3,242
57	2.857	0.02857	36,307	36,416	36,391	3,159	3,267	3,242
19	2.714	0.02714	34,490	34,593	34,565	3,001	3,104	3,076
37	2.571	0.02571	32,673	32,770	32,739	2,843	2,940	2,909
49	2.571	0.02571	32,673	32,770	32,739	2,843	2,940	2,909
54	2.571	0.02571	32,673	32,770	32,739	2,843	2,940	2,909
8	2.460	0.02460	31,262	31,355	31,323	2,720	2,813	2,781
12	2.231	0.02231	28,352	28,437	28,401	2,467	2,551	2,516
40	2.143	0.02143	27,234	27,315	27,279	2,369	2,451	2,414
39	1.743	0.01743	22,150	22,216	22,179	1,927	1,993	1,956
16	1.429	0.01429	18,160	18,214	18,178	1,580	1,634	1,598
53	1.429	0.01429	18,160	18,214	18,178	1,580	1,634	1,598
26	1.340	0.01340	17,029	17,080	17,045	1,482	1,532	1,497
1	1.286	0.01286	16,343	16,392	16,357	1,422	1,471	1,436

Table 7A.2 (continued)

Comp.(i)	%	q_i	PROBLEM $q_i\tilde{\pi}$	$q_i\hat{\pi}$	marg	GAME $q_i(\tilde{\pi}-P(N))$	$q_i(\hat{\pi}-P(N))$	marg
52	1.186	0.01186	15,072	15,117	15,084	1,311	1,356	1,323
32	1.143	0.01143	14,525	14,569	14,536	1,264	1,307	1,275
7	1.071	0.01071	13,610	13,651	13,620	1,184	1,225	1,194
24	1.029	0.01029	13,077	13,116	13,085	1,138	1,177	1,146
36	0.963	0.00963	12,238	12,275	12,245	1,065	1,101	1,072
21	0.857	0.00857	10,891	10,923	10,896	948	980	953
45	0.857	0.00857	10,891	10,923	10,896	948	980	953
61	0.857	0.00857	10,891	10,923	10,896	948	980	953
60	0.840	0.00840	10,675	10,707	10,680	929	961	934
18	0.791	0.00791	10,052	10,082	10,057	875	905	879
6	0.717	0.00717	9,112	9,139	9,115	793	820	796
58	0.686	0.00686	8,718	8,744	8,721	758	785	762
14	0.574	0.00574	7,294	7,316	7,296	635	656	636
22	0.529	0.00529	6,723	6,743	6,724	585	605	586
23	0.529	0.00529	6,723	6,743	6,724	585	605	586
4	0.429	0.00429	5,452	5,468	5,452	474	491	475
10	0.429	0.00429	5,452	5,468	5,452	474	491	475
25	0.429	0.00429	5,452	5,468	5,452	474	491	475
27	0.429	0.00429	5,452	5,468	5,452	474	491	475
29	0.429	0.00429	5,452	5,468	5,452	474	491	475
30	0.429	0.00429	5,452	5,468	5,452	474	491	475
31	0.429	0.00429	5,452	5,468	5,452	474	491	475
34	0.429	0.00429	5,452	5,468	5,452	474	491	475

35	0.429	0.00429	5,452	5,468	5,452	474	491	475
38	0.429	0.00429	5,452	5,468	5,452	474	491	475
41	0.429	0.00429	5,452	5,468	5,452	474	491	475
42	0.429	0.00429	5,452	5,468	5,452	474	491	475
47	0.429	0.00429	5,452	5,468	5,452	474	491	475
48	0.429	0.00429	5,452	5,468	5,452	474	491	475
51	0.429	0.00429	5,452	5,468	5,452	474	491	475
59	0.429	0.00429	5,452	5,468	5,452	474	491	475
56	0.306	0.00306	3,889	3,900	3,889	338	350	338
2	0.286	0.00286	3,635	3,645	3,635	316	327	316
11	0.286	0.00286	3,635	3,645	3,635	316	327	316
20	0.286	0.00286	3,635	3,645	3,635	316	327	316
28	0.286	0.00286	3,635	3,645	3,635	316	327	316
43	0.286	0.00286	3,635	3,645	3,635	316	327	316
50	0.286	0.00286	3,635	3,645	3,635	316	327	316

Note:
For the problem marg $= q_i\,P(N) + P(N \setminus \{i\}) - P(N)$; for the game marg $= P(N \setminus \{i\}) - P(N)$

8. Environmental effects of consumption: an approach using DEA and cost sharing

Hans Keiding

1. INTRODUCTION

In economic models of production and exchange, consumption is usually considered as the ultimate goal of all economic activity; allocations are compared according to the utility they give consumers. Therefore it seems reasonable that consumption activities should also be considered the ultimate causes of pollution and environmental decay. Consumption does not usually cause any direct damage to the environment; what pollutes is the production carried out in order to make this consumption possible. Therefore, in order to disclose the impact on the environment of different consumption activities we face the task of assigning an environmental impact, which has arisen elsewhere in the economy, to the different consumption activities, in principle down to the consumption of each single commodity.

From a formal point of view, what we have here is a cost allocation problem (as considered, for example, by Young, 1994) with the additional feature that the 'cost' to be allocated (to consumption activities) is not a monetary cost but rather a vector of changes in environmental state, measured by the relevant indicators. Although a vector cost allocation problem is not qualitatively different from a standard cost allocation problem, some new features do arise, and since they have some relevance to the problem at hand, we shall consider them at some length in the text.

First of all, in the context of vector cost allocation it makes sense to consider compositions of cost functions; in the case of environmental impact one may consider the emissions (of relevant polluting gases) as a (multidimensional) 'cost' of consumption, whereas the final effect on the environment caused by the emissions may be considered as another vector cost function; their composition, then, gives us the effect of consumption on environment. In such a situation, where the composition of cost functions is a natural feature, it seems reasonable that the cost allocation rule should respect such compositions, at least for sufficiently well-behaved cost functions. It turns out that this composition compatibility is a crucial property of abstract cost allocation, since it entails other, more well-known properties of one-dimensional cost allocation rules such as additivity, and conversely is implied by this.

While the composition property takes us into the realm of additive cost allocation rules treated at length in the literature (as explained, for example, in the work by Friedman and Moulin, 1999), there are still many possible choices. However, the additional features of our application will narrow down the choice considerably. Indeed, since our ultimate task is that of assigning environmental impact to consumption, the allocation rule should satisfy the monotonicity property that if some particular consumption activity increases then its share in environmental cost should not decrease. Taking this property into consideration (together with a strong form of composition compatibility adapted to our situation), we can narrow down our choice of allocation rule to the family of random order allocation methods.

For the final stage, that of aggregating the different environmental costs of a given consumption activity into a single number or index of environmental impact, we rely on the Data Envelopment Analysis (DEA) methodology (cf. Charnes et al., 1978), which avoids the introduction of arbitrary weights for the evaluation of different aspects of the environment. In most applications of the DEA methodology, including those related to environmental efficiency (cf., for example, Taskin and Zaim, 2001), the comparisons are carried out between units for which it is at least in principle conceivable that they have access to the same underlying technology for producing outputs (good or bad) from inputs. In the application which we have in mind, namely the comparison of environmental effects of different consumption activities, this is no longer obviously the case. On the other hand, taking the market value of aggregate consumption of a given type as an indication of its importance to the consumers, measuring environmental effect per unit of market value may give an indication of the extent to which the particular consumption activity has detrimental side-effects. Therefore, our approach amounts to visualizing consumption as production of consumer satisfaction; the different consumption activities are individual technologies for producing satisfaction, and outcome is measured in money terms; the environmental 'bads' which are by-products of this production of consumer satisfaction may be treated as inputs in the aggregate consumption technology; the smaller their value, the better.

The chapter is organized as follows: in Section 2 we introduce the background model as a frame of reference for the subsequent discussion; this is a model of an economy where production and consumption give rise to externalities in the form of a change in certain variables describing the state of the environment. The problem to be considered is then to devise a system of accounting such that the change in environmental state is ascribed to the consumption activities in a suitable way. This problem, which is one of multidimensional cost allocation, is considered in general terms in Section 3. Adding in Section 4 certain features of the main application to the model, particularly the lack of reliable data on final environmental impacts leading to their replacement by emission data, we are led to a particular method of cost allocation, namely the so-called random order method. In Section 5 we describe the subsequent aggregation phase, where DEA is used to give an index of relative environmental impact. An example of such a computation using DEA on emission data for the Danish economy is given in Section 6, and finally Section 7 contains some concluding comments on the method and its future extensions.

2. A GENERAL MODEL OF EXTERNAL EFFECTS AND THE PROBLEM OF ASSIGNING EXTERNAL EFFECT TO INDIVIDUAL COMMODITIES

In the present section, which serves as a general background for the following sections, we introduce a formalized version of an economy with external effects (pollution) caused by the level of economic activity. In order to assign an environmental impact to a particular activity (in our model, to the consumption goods), two problems must be faced, namely (1) the allocation of each type of environmental effect on activities, and (2) aggregation of vectors of environmental effects to numbers or indices. These problems are then considered in the following sections.

We consider a society which engages in activities of production and consumption of commodities; the main point of our study is of course the environment effects of these activies, so that our basic model is one of an *economy with externalities*. To keep the model reasonably simple, we confine our attention to production externalities.

The economy is defined as follows: There is a set $L = \{1,...,l\}$ of commodities and a set $S = \{1,...,s\}$ of (undesirable) environmental effects; these effects are caused by the production activities and in their turn influence both production and consumption. We interpret the environmental effects literally as *deterioration of the environment* (reduction in the ozone layer, deterioration of water quality and so on); indeed, the distinction between environmental effects and *emissions* of polluting material is what creates the need for a 'cost allocation' approach.

It should be noticed at this point that for a more detailed analysis of an economy with externalities of the type considered here, we would need to distinguish between the state of the environment (as measured by the s indicators introduced above) at the beginning of each period, which would enter into the description of the production capabilities and utility functions in this period, and the state at the end of the period, changed by the activities carried out in the period. Since we have the more modest aim of devising a method for assigning environmental changes to consumption activities (rather than analysing the impact of the choices of the agents on the future path of the environmental indicators), our present approach will suffice.

The agents of the economy may be defined as follows: There is a finite set M of consumers, consumer i being described as (X_i, u_i, ω_i), where for each $i \in M$, $X_i \subset \mathbf{R}^{L \times S}$ is the set of feasible consumption plans, $u_i: X_i \to \mathbf{R}$ the utility function, $\omega_i \in \mathbf{R}^L$ the initial endowment. Furthermore, there is a finite set N of producers and for each $j \in N$, a production set $Y_j \subset \mathbf{R}^L \times \mathbf{R}^L \times S$, whereby a production plan $(y_j, \eta_j; \xi_j)$ is interpreted as the net production of commodity bundle y_j with an associated environmental effect of η_j given that the overall environmental change is ξ_j. Thus, production gives rise to externalities whereas consumption does not; however, consumption externalities may easily be introduced into the model.

An allocation z is a collection of consumption bundles $(x_i, \xi_i) \in X_i$ for $i \in M$ and of production plans $(y_j, \eta_j; \xi_j) \in Y_j$ for $j \in N$, which is aggregate feasible in the sense that

$$\Sigma_{i \in M} x_{ih} \leq \Sigma_{j \in N} y_{jh} + \Sigma_{i \in M} \omega_{ih}, \, h \in L,$$

(consumption of commodities does not exceed endowment plus net production), and

$$\xi_{ik} = \xi_{i'k} = \xi_{jk}, \, i, i' \in M, j \in N, k \in S, \xi_{ik} = \Sigma_{j \in N} \eta_{jk}$$

(the background environmental effect of type k is the same for all consumers and producers and is found by adding the outlets of all the producers). Thus, environmental effects are in the context of this model considered as public goods (or rather as public 'bads') which are created by individual producers but take the same value for all agents.

As is well known, the presence of externalities in the economy will prevent the market from working in a satisfactory way; indeed, the equilibria are not Pareto optimal, and there is a need for regulation. We shall not, however, consider this regulation problem but a much more humble problem of measuring the amount of externality caused by consumption. This can be done in several ways; in the context of the present model, what is aimed at is an assignment of the S-dimensional vector of environmental impacts to the consumption of each commodity, that is a function which to every allocation z with vector of environmental effects ξ gives an L-tuple of S-vectors $(\bar{\xi}_{ik})_{i \in L, k \in S}$ such that

$$\Sigma_{h \in L} \bar{\xi}_{hk} = \xi_k \text{ for each } k \in S.$$

At present, we shall confine ourselves to the search for a cost assignment method which satisfies some basic requirements. In the longer perspective, not to be touched upon at present, the assignment of environmental impacts to consumption goods may perhaps be carried out in such a way that it could be of use in decentralized decision-making.

3.   SHARING A VECTOR-VALUED COST

Following up on what was said above, in the present section we consider methods for allocating environmental impact of a given type to consumption of each commodity. The intuition behind such an allocation of environmental impact to each consumption activity, whereby the consumption as such may not give rise to any external effects although production does, or conversely, is that consumption is the ultimate activity responsible for the pollution which it has given rise to, albeit in an indirect way.

Thus, we consider a situation where there is a given functional relationship $C: \mathbf{R}_+^L \to \mathbf{R}^S$ which to each level of (consumption) activities $x = (x_1,..., x_l)$ assigns a vector $C(x)$, which may be interpreted as a vector-valued cost, or an environmental effect measured as several physical quantities. We are looking for a *sharing rule* which to each x_i assigns an S-dimensional vector interpreted as the *shares* (in environmental damage of each type) of the ith consumption activity. Thus, the sharing rule should distribute the total environmental impact among the different consumption activities which are considered as the ultimate causes of the pollution.

Since environmental effects are multiple, this is not a standard cost-sharing problem; it is however quite closely related to the cost allocation problem as treated extensively in the literature (Moulin and Shenker, 1992; Young, 1994; Sprumont, 1998; Friedman and Moulin, 1999). Below we introduce the vector valued cost allocation problem in some detail and describe its connection with the standard cost allocation problem.

In the following, a vector cost function is a non-decreasing map $C: \mathbf{R}_+^n \to \mathbf{R}_+^d$. A d-dimensional *vector cost allocation rule* is a map, which to each vector cost function $C: \mathbf{R}_+^n \to \mathbf{R}_+^d$ and each (input) array $q = (q_1,...,q_n)$ assigns numbers $x_{ij}(q; C)$, $i = 1,...,n, j = 1,...,d$, such that

$$\sum_{i=1}^{n} x_{ij}(q; C) = C_j(q).$$

We write the vector cost allocation rule as $x(.)$. A vector cost allocation rule is additive if

$$x_{ij}(q; C^1 + C^2) = x_{ij}(q; C^1) + x_{ij}(q; C^2)$$

for arbitrary functions $C^1, C^2: \mathbf{R}_+^n \rightarrow \mathbf{R}_+^d$. Under the assumption of additivity, we may write $C = C_1 + \cdots + C_n$, where C_i is the function whose ith coordinate is identical with that of C and with 0 in all other coordinates, and consequently the cost allocation rule splits into d one-dimensional (that is, ordinary) cost allocation rules. Thus, under additivity, there is nothing new to be obtained from considering vector cost allocation problems, since they are only a collection of the usual cost allocation rules. This is actually not too surprising, since our working with vector cost functions of the type described above presupposes that the d different 'costs' (or, as in our case, environmental damage effects) are produced in exact amounts from the inputs. We shall comment later on how the problem may be generalized to the case of not necessarily additive sharing rules.

In the context of vector cost functions, it makes sense to consider compositions of cost functions. Let $C: \mathbf{R}_+^n \rightarrow \mathbf{R}_+^m$, $D: \mathbf{R}_+^m \rightarrow \mathbf{R}_+^d$. be vector cost functions. We say that $x^{(.)}$ is consistent under left composition with vector cost functions in the class $\boldsymbol{C}$ if

$$x_{ij}^{(d)}(q; D \circ C) = \Sigma_{k=1}^{m} x_{ik}^{(m)}(q; C) \frac{x_{kj}^{(d)}(C(q); D)}{C_k(q)} \text{ for all } i, j, \quad (8.1)$$

holds for all C, when D is chosen from the class $\boldsymbol{C}$, and similarly, that $x^{(.)}$ is consistent under right composition with vector cost functions in the class $\boldsymbol{C}$ if (8.1) holds for arbitrary D and when C is taken from $\boldsymbol{C}$. Finally, $x^{(.)}$ is consistent under composition with cost functions in $\boldsymbol{C}$ if it is consistent under both left and right composition with functions in $\boldsymbol{C}$.

Thus, if a cost allocation rule satisfies composition consistency, then allocating directly from final costs to initial inputs or allocating final costs to intermediate costs which are then attributed to initial inputs will yield the same result. The assumption has some formal similarity with the assumption of distributivity discussed in Moulin and Shenker (1999) for cost sharing of a homogeneous good, but its interpretation here is different and it has therefore been given another name. In our main result below, the class $\boldsymbol{C}$ is taken to be the class $\boldsymbol{L}$ of (positive) linear mappings. In this case, composition consistency says that if there are some intermediate goods which are produced from original inputs in a linear way, then the cost shares of any original input may be found by multiplying cost shares for all intermediate inputs by the associated average cost of the original input and adding the resulting cost shares.

The summation in (8.1) gives some indication of a connection between our notion of composition consistency and the usual axiom of additivity of one-dimensional cost allocation rules. However, an additional property of the vector cost allocation rule is needed in order to establish the connection: We say that the vector cost allocation rule *reflects direct cost* if

$$x^{(1)}_i(q;+) = q_i, \ i=1,...,n, \text{ for each } q=(q_1,...,q_n) \in \mathbf{R}^n_+,$$

where $+$ is the 'cost' function taking $(q_1,...,q_n)$ to $\Sigma^n_{i=1} q_i$. The terminology is taken from cost accounting; indeed, if the aggregate cost of an array of goods is entirely composed of direct cost, so that aggregate cost is a sum of individual direct costs, then any meaningful cost allocation rule should indeed reflect this in the sense that the cost allocated to good i is its direct cost, no more no less.

Moreover, we need a rule for treating cost allocation when we concatenate two independent cost allocation problems to one. We say that that $x^{(\cdot)}$ satisfies *independence* if for any two cost functions $C^r: \mathbf{R}^{N_r}_+ \to \mathbf{R}^{D_r}_+, \ r=1, 2,$ with $N_1 \cap N_2 = \varnothing, \ D_1 \cap D_2 = \varnothing$, we have

$$x^{(d1+d2)}_{ij}((q^1, q^2); (C^1, C^2)) = x^{(dr)}_{ij}(q^r; C^r) \text{ if } i \in N_r, j \in D_r, r \in \{1, 2\},$$

and $x^{(d1+d2)}_{ij}((q^1, q^2); (C^1, C^2)) = 0$ otherwise. Thus, if independence holds, then the allocation in a given problem is not affected by the fact that another cost allocation problem is considered simultaneously, as long as neither the inputs nor the costs are in any way related.

Finally, we shall need the well-known *dummy property* for one-dimensional cost sharing rules, stating that if a cost function does not depend on some variable q_i, then the share of this variable is 0. For any cost function $C: \mathbf{R}^n_+ \to \mathbf{R}$, if $C(q'_i, q_{-i}) = C(q)$ for all $q \in \mathbf{R}^n_+$ and $q'_i \in \mathbf{R}$, then $x^{(1)}_i(q; C) = 0$, all q (here (q'_i, q_{-i}) is the vector q with the ith coordinate replaced by q'_i).

We now have the following result:

Theorem 1: *Assume that $x^{(\cdot)}$ is a vector cost allocation rule which is consistent under left composition with cost functions in $\mathbf{L}$, satisfies independence and reflects direct cost. Then the one-dimensional cost allocation rule $x^{(1)}$ satisfies additivity and the dummy property. Conversely, every one-dimensional cost allocation rule can be extended to a vector cost allocation rule which is consistent under left composition with maps in $\mathbf{L}$, satisfies independence and reflects direct cost.*

Proof: Let $C^1: \mathbf{R}_+^n \to \mathbf{R}_+$ and $C^2: \mathbf{R}_+^n \to \mathbf{R}_+$ be two cost functions, and consider the composition (to the left) of the vector cost function $C = (C^1, C^2): \mathbf{R}_+^n \to \mathbf{R}_+^2$ with the (linear) cost function $+: \mathbf{R}_+^2 \to \mathbf{R}_+$. Applying (8.1) we get that

$$x_i^{(1)}(q; C^1 + C^2) = x_i^{(1)}(q; + \circ (C^1, C^2)) = \sum_{k=1}^{2} x_{ik}^{(2)}(q; C) \frac{x_k^{(1)}(C(q); +)}{C_k(q)}$$

for each i. Now $C_k(q)$ for $k = 1, 2$ is the kth coordinate of $C = (C^1, C^2)$, so that $C_k(q) = C^k(q)$, and $x_{ik}^{(2)}(q; C)$, the assignment of the kth cost ($k = 1, 2$) to the ith product, equals $x^{(1)}(q; C^k)$ in our case. Therefore we have

$$x_i^{(1)}(q; C^1 + C^2) = \sum_{k=1}^{2} x_i^{(1)}(q; C) \frac{x_k^{(1)}(C(q); +)}{C^k(q)} \tag{8.2}$$

for each i. Since $x^{(\cdot)}$ reflects direct cost, the fractions in (8.2) are equal to 1, and we obtain

$$x_i^{(1)}(q; C^1 + C^2) = x_i^{(1)}(q; C^1) + x_i^{(1)}(q; C^2), \text{ for each } i,$$

so that $x_i^{(1)}$ is indeed an additive allocation rule.

Next, if $C: \mathbf{R}_+^n \to \mathbf{R}_+$ is a (one-dimensional) cost function which does not depend on the ith coordinate, then $C = + \circ (C_{-i}, 0)$, where $C_{-i}: \mathbf{R}_+^{n-1} \to \mathbf{R}_+$ is defined by

$$C_{-i}(q_1, ..., q_{i-1}, q_{i-1}, ..., q_n) = C(q_1, ..., q_{i-1}, 0, q_{i+1}, ..., q_n).$$

By independence, we have that $x_{i1}^{(2)}((q_{-i}, q_i); (C_{-i}, 0)) = 0$ and

$$x_{i2}^{(2)}((q_{-i}, q_i); (C_{-i}, 0)) = x_i^{(1)}(q_i; 0) = 0,$$

where the last equality follows from the definition of a cost allocation rule. Thus we have that $x_i^{(1)}$ has the dummy property.

Conversely, assume that x is a (one-dimensional) cost allocation rule which is additive. Define the vector cost allocation rule $x^{(\bullet)}$ by $x_i^{(1)} = x$ and

$$x_{ij}^{(m)}(q; C) = x_i(q; C_j), i = 1, ..., n, j = 1, ..., d,$$

for any vector cost function $C: \mathbf{R}_+^n \to \mathbf{R}_+^d$. It follows directly from the construction that $x^{(\bullet)}$ satisfies the independence property. We check that $x^{(\bullet)}$ reflects direct cost and satisfies composition consistency.

For the first of these properties, let $+$ be addition of n 'cost' components, $+(q_1, ..., q_n) = \sum_{i=1}^{n} q_i$. Then

$$+ (q_1,..., q_n) = \Sigma_{i=1}^{n} \mathrm{pr}_i (q_1,..., q_n),$$

where $\mathrm{pr}_i\colon \mathbf{R}_+^n \to \mathbf{R}_+$ is projection on the ith factor, so that

$$x_i^{(1)} (q; +) = x_i^{(i)}(q; \Sigma_{j=1}^{n} \mathrm{pr}_j) = \sum_{j=1}^{k} x_i^{(1)} (q; \mathrm{pr}_j) = q_i,$$

where we have used additivity together with the fact that $x_i^{(1)}(q; \mathrm{pr}_j) = q_i$ if $i = j$ and 0 otherwise by the dummy axiom. We conclude that $x^{(\bullet)}$ reflects direct cost.

Finally, let $C\colon \mathbf{R}_+^n \to \mathbf{R}_+^m$, $D\colon \mathbf{R}_+^m \to \mathbf{R}_+^d$ be maps with $D \in L$, and consider the composed map $D \circ C$. By independence, it suffices to treat the case $d = 1$. Since D belongs to L, we have that $D(q_1',..., q_m') = \Sigma_{k=1}^{m} b_k q_k'$ for some fixed $b_k \geq 0$, $k = 1,..., m$, so that

$$D \circ C (q_1,..., q_n) = \sum_{k=1}^{m} b_k C_k (q_1,..., q_n)$$

Using additivity, we therefore get that

$$x_i^{(1)} (q; D \circ C = \sum_{k=1}^{m} b_k x_{ik}^{(m)} (q; C) = \sum_{j=1}^{m} x_j^{(m)} (q; C),$$

and since $x_i^{(1)} (C(q); D) = b_k C_k(q)$ by linearity, we have that $b_k = x_k^{(1)}(C(q); D) / C_k(q)$, so that

$$x_i^{(1)} (q; D \circ C) = \sum_{j=1}^{m} x_j^{(m)} (q; C) \frac{x_k^{(1)}(C(q); D)}{C_k(q)},$$

showing that $x^{(\bullet)}$ satisfies consistency under left composition with maps in L.

The theorem shows us that the intuitively reasonable properties of consistency under left linear transformation, independence, and reflection of direct costs reduce the vector cost problem to the case of several cost allocation problems of the type usually considered (satisfying additivity and dummy, cf. Friedman and Moulin, 1999). However, the broader context of vector cost allocation may be useful, not only in the context of genuinely vector-valued cost, but also for deriving results in the simpler world of one-dimensional cost allocation.

4.   ENVIRONMENTAL IMPACT OF CONSUMPTION

Having considered in the previous section general methods for allocating vector valued cost among commodities or activities giving rise to this cost, we return now to our main case, that of constructing a measure of the environmental impact of consumption. As mentioned previously, environmental impact should be considered as the deterioration (of different types) of environmental conditions caused by the economic activities. However, these changes in the state of the environment are usually measured only in a partial and incomplete way; what is measured is the level of emission of various kinds. Indeed, the environmental impact of the economy in terms of emissions is already calculated in certain countries. In these calculations, which make use of the input-output tables for the national economy, emissions are assumed to be linear functions of activity.

Unfortunately, the connections between emissions and environmental changes are not very well documented, and they are presumably non-linear. Though desirable, it is as yet not possible to allocate environmental effects directly to consumption activities; instead, effort might be directed towards an allocation of environmental effects to emissions, which might then be followed up by allocating further back from emissions to consumption activities. There is a point in this two-step procedure – the assignment of environmental effects to emissions depends only on physics and is the same for every country, whereas the second step takes its origin in the national input-output relationships and as such must be country-specific.

For this two-step procedure to be viable, the cost allocation rule should be consistent with right composition with linear maps (assuming emission to be subject to constant returns to scale), which is seen to be a further restriction as compared with those considered in the previous section. The following lemma is straightforward.

Lemma 1: *Let $x^{(\bullet)}$ be a vector cost allocation rule which is consistent with compositions in L, satisfies independence, and reflects direct cost. Then each $x_{\bullet j}^{(m)}$ satisfies scale independence in the sense that*

$$x_{\bullet j}^{(m)} ((\lambda q_i, q_{-i}); C_{i,\lambda}) = x_{\bullet j}^{(m)} (q; C)$$

for each $i \in \{1,..., n\}$ and $\lambda > 0$, where $C_{i,\lambda}$ is the rescaled cost function defined by $C_{i,\lambda}(q) = C(\lambda^{-1} q_i, q_{-i})$.

Proof: Since the map $\tau_{i,\lambda}$ given by $\tau_{i,\lambda}(q_i, q_{-i}) = (\lambda q_i, q_{-i})$ is linear and $C = C_{i,\lambda}^{\circ} \tau_{i,\lambda}$ we have the result of the lemma.

In view of Lemma 1, the components of a vector cost allocation procedure to be used for determining the environmental 'cost' of consumption activities must satisfy scale invariance (in addition to the properties discussed in the previous section). This means that the components $x_{\bullet j}^{(m)}$ share some crucial properties of the so-*called random order* methods for cost allocation (cf. Friedman and Moulin, 1999, p. 293).

Actually, there is a further reason for choosing random order methods. Since data for environmental effects of emissions are as yet not sufficiently detailed for practical purposes, we shall have to concentrate on emissions for the numerical calculations. Since the problem of assessing environmental impact of consumption is anyway multidimensional and involves aggregation over emissions or environmental effects, it seems reasonable to demand that the cost allocation rule is *monotonic* (or respects dominance) in the sense that if $q \geq q'$ (in the application meaning that the emission vector q dominates the vector q', with the effect that the vector $C(q)$ of environmental effects dominates that of $C(q')$), then the effects are allocated to each emission in such a way that domination is retained.

The two conditions of scale invariance and monotonicity (together with a technical condition to be described) do indeed determine the method of cost allocation to be used.

Theorem 2: *Let $x^{(\bullet)}$ be a vector cost allocation method which is consistent under left composition with linear maps, satisfies independence, reflects direct cost, and further satisfies monotonicity and continuity at zero in the sense that $\lim_{q_i \to 0} x^{(m)}((q_i, q_{-i}); C) = x^{(m)}((0, q_{-i}); C)$ for each i. Then $x_{\bullet j}^{(m)}$ is a random order method for each j.*

Proof: Direct consequence of Lemma 1 and Theorem 1 in Friedman and Moulin (1999).

5.   AGGREGATION OF ENVIRONMENTAL INDICATORS BY DEA

In the context described above, the environmental effects of consumption activities may – at least in principle – be calculated, but so far in the form of vector cost assignments. If we want a one-dimensional measure of environmental impact of each consumption activity, we will have to aggregate over different effects, or rather, in view of the restrictions imposed by data, over different emissions.

The simplest way of aggregating environmental effects is by linear aggregation using fixed weights; this method has the additional advantage of being consistent with the cost allocation methods introduced above, since the linear aggregation amounts to a left composition of the vector cost function with a linear cost function. However, the choice of weights, which reflect the relative importance of the individual indicators, introduces a certain arbitrariness into the approach.

To avoid this arbitrariness, we propose to employ the techniques of Data

Envelopment Analysis (cf. Charnes et al., 1978). This means that we refrain from calculating an absolute index of environmental impact and replace this by an index of relative environmental impact. For each weight vector $w \in \mathbf{R}_+^L$ we may define the w-weighted effect of consumption activity h as the weighted sum (with weights w_k, $k \in S$) of environmental effects per unit value of the activity. For each activity, we then choose the weight vector w in such a way that when we compare its w-weighted effects with those of the other activities, its relative position is as good as possible. Writing the consumption activities as q_j for $j \in L$ and the environmental impacts as $C_k(q)$, $k \in S$, we define the index of relative environmental effect as

$$\rho^h = \max_w \frac{\min_{j \in L} \Sigma_{k \in S} w_k \dfrac{C_k}{q_j}}{\Sigma_{k \in S} w_k \dfrac{C_k}{q_h}}$$

where the maximum is taken over all weight vectors $w \in \mathbf{R}_+^S$ with $\Sigma_{k \in S} w_k = 1$.

The following result is well known in the context of productivity analysis by DEA and adapted to our current purpose.

Theorem 3: *Let ρ^h be the relative environmental impact index of commodity h, let $\bar{a} = (C_k/q_h)_{k \in S}$ be the column vector of environmental effects per unit value of consumption activity h, and let A be the matrix of environmental effects per unit value of the other consumption activities, $a_{kj} = C_k/q_j$, $k \in S$, $j \in L, j \neq h$. Then ρ^h is the solution of the LP problem*

$$\max \mu \text{ s.t}$$

$$\begin{pmatrix} a & -A \\ 0 & (1,\ldots,1) \end{pmatrix} \begin{pmatrix} \rho \\ \lambda \end{pmatrix} \leq \begin{pmatrix} 0 \\ \vdots \\ 0 \\ 1 \end{pmatrix} \tag{8.3}$$

where $\rho \geq 0$, $\lambda_j \geq 0$, $j \neq h$, are variables.

Proof: Let ρ^h be the solution of the problem in the statement of the theorem. Then, by duality, the linear program

$$\max \mu \text{ s.t}$$

$$(w_1,\ldots, w_L, \mu) \begin{pmatrix} a & -A \\ 0 & (1,\ldots,1) \end{pmatrix} \leq (1, 0,\ldots, 0)$$

has an optimal solution, and its optimal value μ^* equals ρ^h. From this we obtain that

$$\Sigma_{k \in S} w_k a_{kj} \geq \mu^* = \rho^h$$

for $j = 1, ..., n$, and there must be equality for some j, since otherwise the optimal value of μ could have been chosen to be larger than ρ^h, a contradiction. Also, we have that

$$\Sigma_{k \in S} w_k \bar{a}_k \leq 1,$$

and if the inequality was strict, the values of $w_1, ..., w_k$ could be increased so that the remaining inequalities could be satisfied for a larger value of μ, once again giving a contradiction. We have therefore that

$$\rho^h = \max_{w \in \mathbf{R}_+^s, w \neq 0} \frac{\min_{j \in L} \Sigma_{k \in S} w_k a_{kj}}{\Sigma_{k \in S} w_k \bar{a}_k}.$$

Since the quantity on the right-hand side does not change if the weight vector w is multiplied by a positive scalar, we may restrict the search for a maximum to the set $\Delta_S = \{w | \Sigma_{k \in S} w_k = 1\}$. Inserting the expressions for $\bar{a}_k$ and a_{kj}, we get the index of relative environmental impact.

6. AN EXAMPLE: AN EMISSION-BASED INDEX OF RELATIVE ENVIRONMENTAL EFFECT OF DANISH CONSUMPTION

In the approach to measuring the environmental effects of consumption via DEA, the consumption activities are viewed as desirable outputs of the economy, as end products in a technology which describes the interplay between economic activities and the environment; therefore inputs are the various environmental effects of the consumption activities. The analogy between ordinary production of goods from other goods, and the present case of producing economic 'goods' with the necessary side-effect of giving rise to environmental 'bads', is reasonable as far as the latter are quantities which should be as small as possible for any given level of output (consumption). On the other hand, it goes without saying that some of the implicit assumptions in an ordinary productivity analysis, namely that the technology behind the results actually achieved is the same for all units (in this case, consumption activities), cannot reasonably be upheld. On the other hand, this assumption is only needed in possible applications of the productivity analysis to the control of the individual units, not for the construction of productivity indices using DEA.

Below, we illustrate the method by some computation using Danish data from 1998 showing the emissions caused by main consumption activities.

The figures were computed using an input-output table for Denmark together with fixed coefficients for the emissions of each sector of production (in the widest sense, including imports) represented in the input-output table. They describe the direct and indirect environmental effects caused by consumption (both the immediate impact of the consumption acitivity and the emissions in the industries that produced the consumption goods or the inputs for these industries). Basically, the data of Table 8.1 represent a solution to the vector cost allocation problem considered in the previous sections. However, it is a very simple solution based on the assumption of linearity in production so that marginal and average cost become identical and the allocation problem becomes trivial. It would clearly have been preferable if data on emissions caused by the different consumption activities could have been constructed by a more sophisticated cost allocation method, but at the present this could not be done since data on society's production possibilities were only available in linear form.

For the first run, we use aggregated data showing the emissions in tons per millions of DKR economic activity. These aggregated data are shown in Table 8.1.

We have chosen aggregate data in order to get a result which is of limited size and as such easier to comprehend. The aggregation has the additional advantage of reducing the dependence on outliers; indeed, minor activities may dominate several or all of the individual consumption activities, something which is largely avoided when domination can only be carried out by larger, aggregate consumption activities.

The efficiency scores (and other information) are shown in Table 8.2. The table exhibits the relative efficiency index of the activities in Table 8.1 in the column headed 'Score'; thus, the index of 'Food' is 27 per cent, meaning that actual emissions from the production leading to this activity would have to be reduced to 27 per cent of its actual size, keeping the proportions of the emissions, if this activity were to be as little polluting as the best in the sample. The following columns in Table 8.2 show the implicit weights used for this activity; here only the emission of CO should be included if the system of weights is to be as favourable to this activity as possible (even so its emission should be drastically reduced). The last column shows the benchmarks, indicated as the activity index in the table: in the case of 'Food' it is a single consumption activity (namely activity 4 'Housing'); in other cases, the benchmark may be a weighted average of several activities, and the particular convex combination which is proportionally smaller in all emissions is indicated. For activities that are not dominated, the benchmark column shows the number of activities for which it acts as a benchmark and the corresponding percentages in parentheses. Thus, for activity 9 ('Leisure'),

Table 8.1 Emissions in tons per million Dkr, Denmark 1998

	CO_2	SO_2	NOx	CO	CH_4	N_2O	NMVOC	NH_3
Food	39.3190	0.064781	0.174453	0.117144	0.633230	0.071199	0.030654	0.333979
Beverages and tobacco	20.0370	0.035182	0.065033	0.051208	0.079953	0.008769	0.010056	0.039008
Clothing and shoes	12.2500	0.016105	0.042174	0.047304	0.009038	0.000762	0.008392	0.001700
Housing	9.73500	0.016691	0.036100	0.031859	0.004809	0.000431	0.007924	0.000553
Electricity and heating	603.0960	0.763201	1.262908	3.144886	0.469315	0.018633	0.275617	0.056594
Furniture, household services etc.	17.8420	0.022242	0.062647	0.069116	0.010570	0.000929	0.017812	0.001582
Medicines, health exp. etc.	15.0350	0.02063	0.049803	0.058844	0.013535	0.001198	0.010522	0.003421
Other transports and communication	146.8360	0.048009	0.941837	5.176978	0.059784	0.019821	0.919389	0.003063
Leisure and entertainment, travelling	25.0940	0.034509	0.084193	0.078246	0.037384	0.003851	0.032856	0.014656
Other goods and services	17.5100	0.025022	0.059771	0.056085	0.054481	0.005755	0.010708	0.024846
Marketed individual public consumption	13.7930	0.019791	0.045051	0.055153	0.011841	0.001049	0.010219	0.002879
Non-marketed individual public consumption	17.5020	0.024108	0.055207	0.041907	0.018131	0.001495	0.008032	0.004625
Collective public consumption	17.3510	0.021917	0.090382	0.069445	0.010655	0.001090	0.016447	0.002463
Investment	22.5740	0.040876	0.095967	0.081490	0.012670	0.001377	0.021794	0.002880

Source: Data computed by Statistics Denmark.

Table 8.2 Relative environmental effects (scores) and implicit weights of emissions for aggregate consumption activities

Consumption activity	Score (%)	CO_2	SO_2	NOx	CO	CH_4	N_2O	NMVOC	NH_3	Benchmarks	
1. Food	27.20	0.00	0.00	0.00	8.54	0.00	0.00	0.00	0.00	4(1.00)	
2. Beverages	78.80	0.00	0.00	0.00	0.00	0.00	0.00	99.44	0.00	4(1.00)	
3. Clothing	103.64	0.00	62.09	0.00	0.00	0.00	0.00	0.00	0.00	6	
4. Housing	286.08	0.00	0.00	0.00	0.00	0.00	0.00	0.00	8.32	12	
5. Electricity	2.88	0.00	0.00	0.00	0.00	0.00	0.00	3.63	0.00	4(1.00)	
6. Furniture	73.64	0.00	0.96	0.00	0.00	0.00	0.00	0.00	22.16	3(0.53)	4(0.47)
7. Medicine	79.34	0.00	39.32	3.80	0.00	0.00	0.00	0.00	0.00	3(0.56)	4(0.44)
8. Transport	34.24	0.00	20.17	0.00	0.00	0.00	0.00	0.00	10.31	3(0.43)	4(0.57)
9. Leisure	47.76	0.00	26.68	0.00	1.01	0.00	0.00	0.00	0.00	3(0.36)	4(0.64)
10. Other goods and services	74.00	0.00	0.00	0.00	0.00	0.00	0.00	93.39	0.00	4(1.00)	
11. Marketed individual public consumption	83.58	0.00	41.42	0.18	0.00	0.00	0.00	0.00	0.00	3(0.25)	4(0.75)
12. Non-marketed individual public consumption	98.66	0.00	0.00	0.00	0.00	0.00	0.00	24.50	0.00	4(1.00)	
13. Collective public consumption	74.20	0.00	42.75	0.00	0.00	5.92	0.00	0.00	0.00	3(0.73)	4(0.27)
14. Investments	43.12	0.04	0.00	0.00	0.00	0.00	0.00	0.00	0.00	4(1.00)	

the combination of 0.36 of 'Clothing' and 0.64 of 'Housing' will give the maximum proportional reduction of all emissions possible.

As was stated above, since the analogy with ordinary production should not be strained, the benchmarks are probably of minor importance in the context of relative environmental effects. However, a closer scrutiny of the results, in particular an identification of the undominated activities, may be useful for a refinement of the computation, adding restrictions on the weights employed as well as on the activities usable as potential benchmarks.

In the present computation, there are only two undominated activities, namely 'Clothing' and 'Housing'. The latter is far ahead of the rest, since the score (which in the table is the super-efficiency score, showing how much the emissions can be increased keeping the activity undominated) is very high indeed. Examining the data for 'Housing', one sees that the high score is due to a very low level of NH_3 emission. Similarly, the activity 'Clothing' is low in emission of SO_2. Adding restrictions on the weights which prevent assigning the weight to a single low (perhaps exceptionally low) emission could possibly give a more realistic picture.

An analysis of environmental effects using impact indices.   Although, as was stated above, there are as yet no data available to assess the actual environmental effects (as distinguished from the emissions of different types) of consumption activities, one can perform an analysis corresponding to that given above with two indices (see Table 8.3) which are currently computed as an indication of the effects on the environment. The two indices are both computed from the basic data in Table 8.1 using linear aggregation with fixed coefficients; the first, the GWP index (where GWP stands for Global Warming Potential) is constructed as:

$$GWP \text{ index} = CO_2 + 21 \, CH_4 + 310 \, N_2O$$

whereas the Acidification index is calculated as follows:

$$\text{Acidification index} = (10^6 / 64 \,)SO_2 + (10^6 / 46 \,)NOx + (10^6 / 17 \,)NH_3$$

(the weights being determined by physical considerations). Since the two indices are constructed as linear combinations of the emission series in Table 8.1, we have not really moved beyond the analysis of emission data, and it can be discussed whether the partial aggregation with fixed weights is justified; however, we have chosen to include this analysis (see Table 8.4) as a further illustration of the approach.

Incidentally, our use of the GWP and Acidification indices raises the

Table 8.3   Indices for GWP and Acidification for aggregate consumption activities

Consumption activity	GWP index	Acidification index
Food	74.688604	24450.48318
Beverages	24.434403	4258.067855
Clothing	12.676018	1268.466712
Housing	9.9969599	1078.304548
Electricity	618.727845	42708.59619
Furniture	18.351960	1802.481378
Medicines	15.690615	1606.143582
Transport	154.235974	21405.03449
Leisure	27.072874	3231.603381
Other goods and services	20.438151	3151.867727
Marketed individual public consumption	14.366821	1457.956881
Non-marketed individual public consumption	18.346201	1848.898497
Collective public consumption	17.912655	2452.161565
Investments	23.266940	2894.338395

Source: Data computed by Statistics Denmark.

Table 8.4   Relative environmental effects (scores) and implicit weights of environmental impacts for aggregate consumption activities

Consumption activity	Score (%)	GWP index	Acidification index	Benchmarks
Food	13.35	1	0	4 (1.00)
Beverages	40.80	1	0	4 (1.00)
Clothing	85.01	0	1	4 (1.00)
Housing	127.15	1	0	13
Electricity	2.52	0	1	4 (1.00)
Furniture	59.82	0	1	4 (1.00)
Medicines	67.14	0	1	4 (1.00)
Transport	6.46	1	0	4 (1.00)
Leisure	36.83	1	0	4 (1.00)
Other goods and services	48.78	1	0	4 (1.00)
Marketed individual public consumption	73.96	0	1	4 (1.00)
Non-marketed individual public consumption	58.32	0	1	4 (1.00)
Collective public consumption	55.66	1	0	4 (1.00)
Investments	42.85	1	0	4 (1.00)

question of whether the approach using DEA is at all necessary, since there are weights available from the considerations by the scientific specialists involved. However, even if this may be the case, so that global warming and acidification are both fully described by their respective indices, we are still left with a question of whether global warming or acidification is more important, something which cannot readily be answered by specialized scientists; moreover these are only two of several possible environmental problems which might be considered. In this context, it should also be mentioned that a weakness in the DEA method as presented above is that it does not detect an activity with a possibly disastrous enviromental effect of a particular type as long as it performs well with regard to all other effects; the method always chooses the system of weights most favourable to the activity to be evaluated, and this weight system would indeed assign a weight of zero to the disastrous effect. Fortunately, standard elaborations of the DEA methodology and software allow for setting lower bounds on the individual weights, thus avoiding situations of this kind.

The two series are shown in Table 8.3 and the results of the DEA analysis in Table 8.4. Not surprisingly, in view of what we have already seen, the activity 'Housing' is efficient and in this case involving only two indicators, it is the only efficient activity. This is also illustrated by the plot of the two series in Table 8.3 presented in Figure 8.1. The 'efficient' activities are situated close to the origin; far out in the diagram are the activities of energy consumption and transportation.

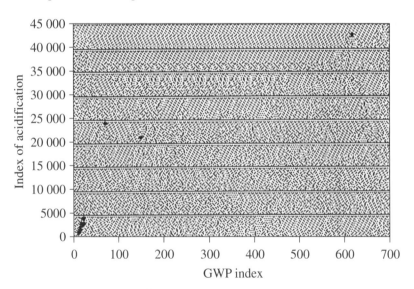

Figure 8.1   Environmental impact

Incidentally, the figure shows also that a comparison of different consumption activities based on their impact on the environment in many cases will give few surprises, since certain activities are obviously polluting while others are not. Therefore, the techniques developed in the previous sections may probably be more gainfully employed in comparing the consumption patterns of different segments of the population than comparing different types of consumption. This can be done as a next step, using data for the consumption patterns of these segments, and it seems to be a natural next step for the analysis.

7. CONCLUDING COMMENTS

In the previous sections we have considered a possible approach to the task of assigning environmental impact to consumption activities. This approach consisted of a multidimensional cost assignment followed by a construction of a relative index using the DEA methodology. As mentioned already, the approach is still in need of some refinement, and this in several respects.

First of all, the computations which can be carried out at present, using available data, are restricted to the relationships between consumption activities and emissions, and they are based on an assumption of constant returns to scale, which makes most of the considerations of cost allocation trivial. The interesting aspects of the approach will emerge when it is applied to non-linear relationships between consumption and environmental effects, and in this respect, the practical application is still to be done.

Secondly, in the theoretical aspects, the notion of a vector valued cost allocation problem is still somewhat restrictive, since what we would be dealing with in the general case is not vector cost functions but set-valued mappings which to every array $(q_1,..., q_n)$ of activities assigns a set $\Phi(q_1,..., q_n) \subset \mathbf{R}_+^S$ of environmental impacts (possibly with certain well-behaved properties, and satisfying $\Phi(q_1,..., q_n) + \mathbf{R}_+^S \subset \Phi(q_1,..., q_n)$ where the + on the left-hand side stands for Minkowski addition of sets). In other words, we should take into account the possible tradeoffs between different environmental indicators, even at a given level of economic activity. Clearly the methods of cost allocation treated in this chapter are not immediately applicable to this situation; on the other hand, extensions suggest themselves. We shall, however, not at present follow up on this topic for future research.

NOTE

This work is part of a research project undertaken jointly by the Institute of Local Government Studies, Statistics Denmark, and the University of Copenhagen. Financial support by the Danish Research Council is acknowledged. The author is grateful to two anonymous referees for valuable suggestions for improvements of an earlier version. Author's address: Institute of Economics, University of Copenhagen, Studiestraede 6, DK-1455 Copenhagen K, Denmark. Email: Hans.Keiding@econ.ku.dk

REFERENCES

Charnes, A., W. Cooper and E. Rhodes (1978), 'Measuring the efficiency of decision making units', *European Journal of Operational Research*, **2**, 429–44.

Friedman, E. and H. Moulin (1999), 'Three methods to share joint costs or surplus', *Journal of Economic Theory*, **87**, 275–312.

Moulin, H. and S. Shenker (1992), 'Serial cost sharing', *Econometrica*, **60**, 1009–37.

Moulin, H. and S. Shenker (1999), 'Distributive and additive costsharing of an homogeneous good', *Games and Economic Behavior*, **27**, 299–330.

Sprumont, Y. (1998), 'Ordinal cost sharing', *Journal of Economic Theory*, **81**, 126–62.

Taskin, F. and O. Zaim (2001), 'The role of international trade on environmental efficiency: a DEA approach', *Economic Modelling*, **18**, 1–17.

Young, H. P. (1994), 'Cost allocation', in R. J. Aumann and S. Hart (eds), *Handbook of Game Theory with Economic Applications*, volume 2, Amsterdam: Elsevier.

PART III

Environmental management and pollution control

9. Competition and cooperation in natural resources exploitation: an evolutionary game approach

Gian Italo Bischi, Fabio Lamantia and Lucia Sbragia

1. INTRODUCTION

Since the pioneering work of Gordon (1954), many bioeconomic models for the description of the commercial exploitation of common property renewable resources, such as fisheries, have stressed the problem known as 'the tragedy of the commons' (Hardin, 1968; see also Clark, 1990). This problem can be basically identified with a prisoner's dilemma (see for example, Mesterton-Gibbons, 1993) because the presence of firms playing their dominant strategy which maximizes their own profit (disregarding competitors' profits) leads to severe depletion of the resource, and consequently to low profits for all. On the other hand if firms cooperate to maximize total profits, then sustainable exploitation is more likely to obtain, which implies higher profits for all in the long run. However, unilateral defection, that is, the decision of an agent to harvest intensively while the other players harvest moderately in order to preserve resources, may lead to very high profits for the defector, and consequently to severe profit loss for the cooperators. This is the essence of the tragedy of the commons, often advanced in order to support the introduction of sanctions against defectors and/or restrictions to open access to common property resources.

Dynamic models based on Cournot oligopoly games have been proposed by Levhari and Mirman (1982) and, more recently, by Szidarovszky and Okuguchi (1998, 2000), to describe commercial fishing. In these models, strategic interaction among players is related not only to the selling price, determined by the total harvesting quantity through a given demand function, but also to a cost externality, since resource stock reductions, as a consequence of players' harvesting, lead to higher unitary fishing costs (see also Bischi and Kopel, 2002). In Szidarovszky and Okuguchi (1998) every player is assumed to decide his/her harvesting activity by solving a *profit maximization problem*, without any concern for the implications of this activity on the depletion of the natural resource. Instead, in Szidarovszky and Okuguchi (2000) it is assumed that the fishermen form a grand coalition (that is, a cooperative venture) and each player determines his/her harvesting activity such that the *joint profit of all players* is maximized. In both cases, the solution of the optimization problem leads to harvesting functions that depend on fish stocks, the dynamics of which is governed by a biological growth function with an extra mortality term representing harvesting activity.

A discrete time version of the oligopoly model proposed in Szidarovszky and Okuguchi (1998) is given in Bischi and Kopel (2002), where dynamics given perfect foresight (that is, fishermen are assumed to know the fish stock at the time when they solve their maximization problems) are compared with dynamics given limited knowledge of the fish stock and its estimate is obtained by adaptive expectations. In Bischi et al. (2004), discrete time versions of both models (one assuming non-cooperative oligopoly competition as in Szidarovszky and Okuguchi, 1998, and one with total cooperation, where all the players form a unique cooperative venture, so that they behave like a sole owner, as in Szidarovszky and Okuguchi, 2000) are considered with adaptive expectations.

In the model proposed in this chapter, the players (for example, fishermen) have access to a common property resource (for instance, a sea where a given fish stock is available) and sell the harvested resource in the same market. However, in contrast to the above cited literature, both competitors and cooperators are present. In fact, a fraction s of fishermen behaves as cooperators, and form a cooperative venture where each one decides the harvesting quota by maximizing the profit of the coalition, whereas the complementary fraction $(1 - s)$ of fishermen behave as competitors (or 'defectors' with respect to cooperative behaviour) each deciding harvesting quotas by maximizing his/her own profit (disregarding competitors' profits). Following the terminology typical of the prisoner's dilemma (see also Sethi and Somanathan, 1996) we call the latter group defectors, because they deviate from the socially optimal attitude of cooperating, and consequently they produce a negative externality on the rest of the community, in terms of potential severe depletion of the common property resource.

As in Szidarovszky and Okuguchi (1998, 2000) and Bischi and Kopel (2002), the harvesting of each group depends on strategic interactions related not only to the influence of total supply on the market prices, but also to the dependence of harvesting cost on the available fish stock, whose evolution is governed by biological laws as well as harvesting activities. Moreover, following Sethi and Somanathan (1996), we introduce the possibility that cooperators impose sanctions to punish defectors, and we propose an evolutionary mechanism to describe how the population share is updated over time, based on replicator dynamics, that is, on the principle, typical of evolutionary games, that the fraction of agents playing the strategy that earns higher payoffs increases in the next period.

As in Sethi and Somanathan (1996) we assume that, at any time period, the agents decide their harvesting by computing the Nash equilibrium of the game. However, differently from the model proposed in Sethi and Somanathan (1996), where the harvesting behaviour of cooperators and defectors is assumed to be described by general functions that satisfy some formal assumptions, we explicitly derive the profit maximization problem that cooperators and defectors are playing at any time period, founded on given demand and cost functions. This allows us to study, by analytical and numerical methods, the effects of some economic parameters, such as the market price (that is, the parameters that characterize the demand function) or the cost parameters (related to the technology adopted), on the long-run evolution of the resource stock and the population shares between the two groups. In particular, the proposed model allows us to detect which economic parameters may determine not only the extinction of the resource, but also the extinction of a given behaviour.

Another difference between the model studied in this chapter and the one proposed by Sethi and Somanathan, is in the time setting. In fact, the dynamic evolutionary model proposed by Sethi and Somanathan evolves in continuous time. This means that they assume that at every time instant a player can change his behaviour from cooperator to defector (or vice versa) according to the instantaneous profits. We consider this a strong assumption, because if a player decides upon a given behaviour, he will maintain that kind of behaviour for a given time period. In other words, we assume that he cannot change his mind just after his decision, as a minimum time lag is necessary to decide a change of behaviour, on the basis of observed profits. Such a time lag, which constitutes unitary time in our discrete time setting, may be assumed to be one week, or one month, according to the economic and social framework considered.

The chapter is organized as follows. In Section 2 we propose a static game where a population of profit maximizing agents decide the quantities to harvest on the basis of two different behaviours: a fraction of players form a coalition, each of them trying to maximize the overall profit, whereas the complementary fraction behave as 'selfish' profit maximizers. The reaction functions are obtained and the unique Nash equilibrium of the game is computed. In Section 3 a growth equation, governing the dynamics of the resource stock with harvesting, is introduced, the harvesting being decided by the two groups by choosing the Nash equilibrium quantities according to the game analyzed in Section 2. In this section the population share between the two kinds of agents is assumed to be a parameter, so the existence and stability of the steady states are studied as well as how these are influenced by population share. In Section 4 we introduce an evolutionary mechanism that, at each time period, describes how the population share is updated, based on replicator dynamics, and we study the problems of existence and stability of the equilibria. In particular a distinction is introduced between boundary equilibria, where all the players behave as cooperators or as defectors, and inner equilibria, where cooperators and defectors coexist in the long run. A short discussion of the results, a description of open problems and possible further developments are given in Section 5.

2.　THE STATIC GAME

Let us assume that a population of n agents harvests from a common property renewable resource stock, and sells the harvested resource at a price p determined by the total harvested quantity according to a given demand function. For example, we may imagine that the agents are fishermen who harvest fish from a sea where a given fish stock X is present. However, similar considerations may be applied to the harvesting of different renewable resources, such as forests or others. The agents decide the quantities to harvest on the basis of profit maximization problems. However, we assume that a fraction s of them, denoted as 'cooperators' form a coalition (a cooperative venture) and consequently each of them tries to maximize the overall profit of the coalition, whereas the remaining fraction $(1 - s)$ behave as 'selfish' profit maximizers, and are denoted as 'defectors' (with respect to the socially more desirable cooperative behaviour).

In this section we consider X and s as fixed parameters,[1] with $X>0$ and $0 \le s \le 1$. Let x_c^i be the quantity harvested by the cooperator i, $i = 1,..., ns$, and let x_d^i be the quantity harvested by defector i, $i = 1,..., n(1 - s)$. Then the total fish supplied and sold in the market is

$$H = \sum_{i=1}^{ns} x_c^i + \sum_{i=1}^{n(1-s)} x_d^i$$

We assume that the selling price p is determined by the linear demand function

$$p = a - bH \qquad (9.1)$$

where a and b are positive constants, and the cost function of player i for harvesting a quantity x when a fish stock X is present is given by

$$C(x, X) = \gamma \frac{x^2}{X} \tag{9.2}$$

This cost function can be derived from a Cobb-Douglas-type 'production function' with fishing effort (labour) and fish biomass (capital) as production inputs (see Clark, 1990; Szidarovszky and Okuguchi, 1998). It captures the fact that it is easier and less expensive to catch fish if the fish population is large.

Following Sethi and Somanathan (1996) we shall also consider an extra cost due to the presence of social norms that are intended to punish fishermen who behave as defectors, that is, self-interested profit maximizers without any concern for the social optimum. As in Sethi and Somanathan (1996) we assume that cooperators are entrusted to punish defectors by applying sanctions. This may be done directly by exerting a direct punishment, such as social disapproval damage or physical damage or destruction of equipment, as observed in less developed societies, or by alerting authorities so that they can impose sanctions according to the laws in force. Such punishment is costly for the defectors, the cost being $ns\xi$, where ξ is the amount of the sanction and ns represents the probability that a defector is notified by a cooperator. However, in general, this kind of punishment is also costly for the cooperators, the cost being proportional to the number of defectors. We shall represent by $n(1-s)\psi$ this extra cost for cooperators (of course $\xi > \psi$, and we shall often consider $\psi = 0$ in the following). All in all, the profit of i-th cooperator is

$$\pi_c^i = x_c^i(a - bH) - \gamma_c \frac{(x_c^i)^2}{X} - n(1-s)\psi \tag{9.3}$$

where γ_c is the fishing technology coefficient of cooperators and $n(1-s)\psi$ represents the cost that cooperators have to face in order to punish defectors, and the profit of i-th defector is

$$\pi_d^i = x_d^i(a - bH) - \gamma_d \frac{(x_d^i)^2}{X} - ns\xi \tag{9.4}$$

where γ_d is the fishing technology coefficient of defectors and $ns\xi$ represents the punishment that defectors have to bear for causing the negative externality in the community.

Each cooperator determines x_c^i by solving the optimization problem

$$\max_{x_c^i} \pi^V = \max_{x_c^i} \sum_{i=1}^{ns} \pi_c^i \tag{9.5}$$

where π^V, which is a concave function in the variables x_c^i, denotes the total profit of the cooperative venture. Assuming interior optimum, the first-order conditions give a system of linear equations in the unknowns x_c^i

$$\frac{\partial \pi^V}{\partial x_c^i} = a - 2b \sum_{k=1}^{ns} x_c^k - b \sum_{k=1}^{n(1-s)} x_d^k - \frac{2\gamma_c}{X} x_c^i = 0 \qquad (9.6)$$

Each defector determines x_d^i by solving the optimization problem

$$\max_{x_d^i} \pi_d^i \qquad (9.7)$$

Assuming, again, interior optimum, the first-order conditions give a system of linear equations in the unknowns x_d^i

$$\frac{\partial \pi_d^i}{\partial x_d^i} = a - b \sum_{k=1}^{ns} x_c^k - b \sum_{k=1}^{n(1-s)} x_d^k - bx_d^i - \frac{2\gamma_d}{X} x_d^i = 0 \qquad (9.8)$$

The equations (9.6) and (9.8) give a linear system of n equations with n unknowns. However, it is straightforward to see that any cooperator faces the same optimization problem, and analogously for the defectors. In fact, if we denote by $x_c^{TOT} = \sum_{k=1}^{sn} x_c^k$ the total harvest of the cooperators and by $x_d^{TOT} = \sum_{k=1}^{(1-s)n} x_d^k$ the total harvest of the defectors, from (9.6) we get

$$x_c^i = \frac{X}{2\gamma_c}(a - 2bx_c^{TOT} - bx_d^{TOT}) \qquad \forall i = 1,..., sn$$

and from (9.8) we get

$$x_d^i = \frac{X}{bX + 2\gamma_d}(a - b(x_c^{TOT} + x_d^{TOT})) \qquad \forall i = 1,..., (1-s)n$$

So, denoting the optimal harvesting decision of each cooperator by x_c, and the optimal harvesting decision of each defector by x_d, these quantities are obtained by solving the two linear equations

$$a - 2\left(bsn + \frac{\gamma_c}{X}\right)x_c - b(1-s)nx_d = 0$$

$$a - bsnx_c - \left[b(1 + (1-s)n) + \frac{2\gamma_d}{X}\right]x_d = 0$$

from which two linear *reaction functions* are obtained

$$x_c = h_c(x_d) = \frac{aX}{2(bsnX + \gamma_c)} - \frac{b(1-s)nX}{2(bsnX + \gamma_c)}x_d \qquad (9.9)$$

$$x_d = h_d(x_c) = \frac{aX}{b(1+(1-s)n)X + 2\gamma_d} - \frac{bsnX}{b(1+(1-s)n)X + 2\gamma_d}x_c$$

These reaction functions allow one to compute, respectively, the optimal harvesting decision of a 'representative cooperator', given the harvesting decision of a representative defector, and the optimal harvesting decision of a 'representative defector', given the harvesting decision of a representative cooperator. These two reaction functions always intersect at a unique point (x_d^*, x_c^*) whose coordinates are functions of fish stock X and the fraction of cooperators s, as well as of the cost parameters γ_c, γ_d and the market price parameters a and b, according to the expressions given in the Appendix in (9.29) and (9.30). The properties of the harvesting strategies x_d^* and x_c^*, of defectors and cooperators respectively, at the Nash equilibrium are given in the following Proposition

Proposition 1.   *A unique Nash Equilibrium* (x_d^*, x_c^*) *exists, with* $x_d^* > 0$ *and* $x_c^* > 0$, *located at the intersection of the reaction curves (9.9), such that:*

(i)   For each $s \in [0, 1]$ *both* $x_d^*(0, s)$ *and* $x_c^*(0, s)$ *vanish for* $X = 0$, *are positive for* $X > 0$ *and at* $X = 0$ *have slopes given by*

$$\frac{\partial x_d^*(X, s)}{\partial X}\bigg|_{X=0} = \frac{a}{2\gamma_d}; \quad \frac{\partial x_c^*(X, s)}{\partial X}\bigg|_{X=0} = \frac{a}{2\gamma_c}$$

(ii)   Both $x_d^*(0, s)$ *and* $x_c^*(0, s)$ *tend to saturate as* $X \rightarrow +\infty$, *at the values*

$$x_d^*(+\infty, s) = \frac{a}{b[(1 - s)n + 2]} \quad \text{and } x_c^*(+\infty, s) = \frac{a}{bsn[(1 - s)n + 2]}$$

respectively;

(iii)   The gap between x_d^* *and* x_c^*, *for large values of the fish stock, increases with increasing prices and with the number ns of cooperators, being*

$$x_d^*(+\infty, s) - x_c^*(+\infty, s) = \frac{a}{b[(1 - s)n + 2]}\left(1 - \frac{1}{sn}\right);$$

(iv)   The total harvesting at the Nash equilibrium, given by

$$H^*(X, s) = n\left[sx_c^*(X, s) + (1 - s)x_d^*(X, s)\right] \tag{9.10}$$

is an increasing and concave function with respect to X, *such that,* $H^*(0, s) = 0$,

$$\frac{\partial H^*(X, s)}{\partial X}\bigg|_{X=0} = \frac{na}{2}\left(\frac{s}{\gamma_c} + \frac{1 - s}{\gamma_d}\right)$$

and for $X \rightarrow +\infty$ *it saturates at the value*

$$H^*(+\infty, s) = \frac{a}{b}\left(1 - \frac{1}{2 + (1 - s)n}\right)$$

A proof of this proposition is outlined in the Appendix.

Typical graphs of x_d^* and x_c^*, as functions of X, are shown in Figure 9.1a, and a typical graph of H^* is shown in Figure 9.1b. The properties of the harvesting function H^* are similar to the ones assumed by Sethi and Somanathan (1996), but in our case the harvesting function is micro-

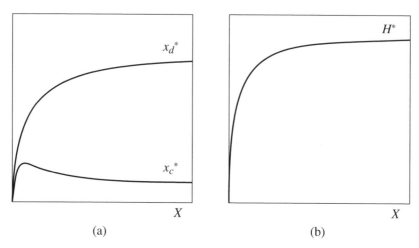

Notes:
(a) Harvesting of defectors x_d^*, and cooperators, x_c^*. (b) Total harvesting H^*

Figure 9.1   Typical graphs of harvesting quantities at the Nash equilibrium depending on the available resource stock X

founded, that is, it is derived from an explicit underlying optimization problem. This implies that the effects of the economic and biological parameters can be explicitly studied. First of all we notice that, for $sn \geq 2$ (that is, if at least two cooperators exist) then $x_c^* < x_d^*$ for large values of fish stock, whereas for small values of X the comparison between x_d^* and x_c^* depends on the respective cost parameters. It is also worth noticing that both x_d^* and x_c^* increase if the selling price increases, that is, a increases and/or b decreases in the demand function (9.1).

Notice also that $H^* < a/b$ for each $X > 0$, so that prices are always positive. Moreover, if s decreases, that is, the number of defectors increase, then $H^*(+\infty, s)$ increases, that is, as expected, in the presence of an abundant resource the total harvest is greater if the number of defectors increases. In the limiting case $s=0$ (all defectors) we have $H^*(+\infty, 0)=a/b(1-1/2+n)$, and in the opposite limiting case $s=1$ (all cooperators, equivalent to the case of a sole owner) we get $H^*(+\infty, 1)=a/2b$, the monopolist optimum.

These results given in Proposition 1 allow us to compute, at the Nash equilibrium, the profit of a representative defector and that of a representative cooperator, given by

$$\pi_d^* = x_d^*(a-bH^*) - \gamma_d \frac{(x_d^*)^2}{X} - ns\xi \text{ and}$$

$$\pi_c^* = x_c^*(a-bH^*) - \gamma_c \frac{(x_c^*)^2}{X} - n(1-s)\psi \qquad (9.11)$$

respectively. Plugging the expression of x_c^*, x_d^* and H^* into (9.11), π_d^* and x_c^*, can be rewritten as:

$$\pi_d^* =$$

$$\frac{a^2 X (bnsX + 2\gamma_c)^2(bX + \gamma_d)}{[bX(bn(-n(1-s)-2))sX - 2bX(n(1-s)+1)\gamma_c - 4(bnsX + \gamma_c)\gamma_d]^2}$$

$$-ns\xi \qquad (9.12)$$

and

$$\pi_c^* =$$

$$\frac{a^2 X (bnsX + \gamma_c)(bX + 2\gamma_d)^2}{[bX(bn(-n(1-s)-2))sX - 2bX(n(1-s)+1)\gamma_c - 4(bnsX + \gamma_c)\gamma_d]^2}$$

$$-(1-s)n\psi \qquad (9.13)$$

respectively. These expressions show that, at the Nash equilibrium, the profits of defectors (cooperators) are positive provided that the applied sanctions (the costs to apply sanctions) are not too heavy. For example, under the assumptions $\psi=0$ and $\xi>0$, which we shall often consider in the following, we have π_c^* always positive and π_d^* positive or negative according to the sanctions applied and to the number of cooperators.

3.   THE ONE-DIMENSIONAL DYNAMICS WITH FIXED s

We now regard X as a dynamic variable and s as a parameter, that is, we consider the time evolution of the resource stock $X(t)$, that depends on its natural growth function and on the harvesting activity, and we assume a fixed division of fishermen population between cooperators and defectors.

Let $X(t)$ denote the fish stock at time period t. We consider the following discrete time equation to describe the time evolution of the fish stock

$$X(t+1) = F(X(t)) = X(t)(1 + \alpha - \beta X(t)) - H^*(X(t), s) \qquad (9.14)$$

that is, we assume that in the absence of any harvesting the stock of the fish population in period t is determined by the discrete time logistic equation,[2] with α and β *biological parameters* that characterize the fish population we are considering and the environment where it lives: α is the *intrinsic growth rate* and α/β the *carrying capacity*, that is, the positive equilibrium value of the unharvested resource population, since for $H^* = 0$ and $X = \alpha/\beta$ (9.14) gives $X(t+1) = X(t)$. We also assume that the fish stock is harvested according to the Nash equilibrium of the static game described in the previous section. Under these assumptions, and by imposing in (9.14) the equilibrium condition $X(t+1) = X(t)$, we get that the steady states of the model with harvesting are the non-negative solutions of the equation

$$X(\alpha - \beta X) = H^*(X; s, \gamma_c, \gamma_d, a, b, n) \qquad (9.15)$$

So, for any given value of s, the equilibria are located at the non-negative intersections between a parabola and the concave function (9.10) (see Figure 9.2) and the following Proposition holds (the three situations denoted by (a), (b) and (c) in Proposition 2 are represented, respectively, by the curves a, b and c of Figure 9.2).

Proposition 2. *The point $X_0 = 0$ (extinction of the resource) is an equilibrium point for each set of parameters. Concerning the existence of positive equilibria, we can distinguish the following three different situations:*

(a) A unique positive equilibrium exists, say X_1, with $0 < X_1 < \alpha/\beta$. A sufficient condition for this is

$$\frac{na}{2}\left(\frac{s}{\gamma_c} + \frac{1-s}{\gamma_d}\right) < \alpha \qquad (9.16)$$

(b) Two positive equilibria exist, say X_2 and X_1, such that $0 < X_2 < \alpha/2\beta < X_1 < \alpha/\beta$. A sufficient condition for this is

$$\frac{na}{2}\left(\frac{s}{\gamma_c} + \frac{1-s}{\gamma_d}\right) > \alpha \text{ and } \frac{a}{b}\left(1 - \frac{1}{2 + (1-s)n}\right) < \frac{\alpha^2}{4\beta} \qquad (9.17)$$

(c) No positive equilibria exist. A necessary condition for this is

$$\frac{na}{2}\left(\frac{s}{\gamma_c} + \frac{1-s}{\gamma_d}\right) > \alpha \text{ and } \frac{a}{b}\left(1 - \frac{1}{2 + (1-s)n}\right) > \frac{\alpha^2}{4\beta} \qquad (9.18)$$

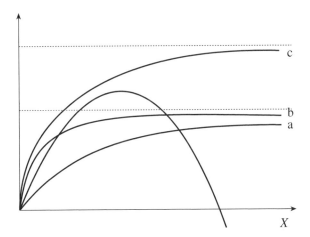

Notes:
The curves denoted by a, b, c can be obtained, respectively, by decreasing values of s or increasing values of a or decreasing values of b.

Figure 9.2 *Qualitative graphical representation of equation (9.16) with fixed values of the parameters α and β and three different functions H^**

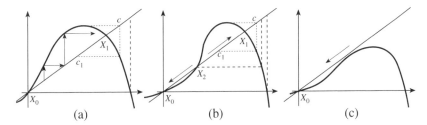

Notes:
(a) One positive equilibrium; (b) Two positive equilibria, (c) No positive equilibria.

Figure 9.3 *Qualitative representation of the function F, that governs the one-dimensional dynamics of the resource stock X according to (9.15), in the three different cases represented in Figure 9.2*

A proof of this proposition is outlined in the Appendix.

Proposition 2 only concerns existence of equilibria. We now give conditions for their stability and local bifurcations that cause stability switches as well as creation or destruction of positive equilibria. We start from the case of a unique positive equilibrium. If (9.16) holds, then $DF(0)>1$, so the fixed point $X_0=0$ is unstable (see Figure 9.3a). This means that if (9.16) is satisfied, that is, the number of fishermen is not too high, prices are not too high nor cost parameters too small, then even if the resource stock is reduced to an arbitrary small positive value by some exogenous shock, the endogenous dynamics of the system is such that it spontaneously evolves to viable levels of the resource stock, close to X_1. The unique positive equilibrium X_1 may be stable, that is, $|DF(X_1)|<1$, or unstable, with $DF(X_1)< -1$. In the latter case, which occurs with high values of the parameter α, a more complex bounded attractor, which may be periodic or chaotic, may exist around X_1. The bounded attracting set is confined inside the trapping set $I=[c_1, c]$ where c is the maximum value of the function F and $c_1 = F(c)$. In any case, the basin of the bounded attractor is bounded by the unstable fixed point $X_0=0$ and its rank-1 pre-image X_{0-1}, that is,

$$B=(0, X_{0-1})$$

where X_{0-1} is the positive solution of the equation

$$1+\alpha-\beta X=\frac{H^*(X)}{X} \tag{9.19}$$

It is straightforward to see that under the assumption (9.16) the equation (9.19) has a unique positive solution X_{0-1} such that $X_1<X_{0-1}<(1+\alpha)/\beta$. An initial condition with $X(0)>X_{0-1}$ is mapped by the iterated function F to a negative value, so we consider as *unfeasible* such kinds of trajectory.[3]

It is worth noticing that the equilibrium value X_1 is influenced by the value of s. In fact, if s is increased, then the asymptote of H^* moves downwards, and this implies that X_1 increases with s, that is, $X_1(s)$ is an increasing function. The intuition behind this is clear: more cooperators imply a higher resource stock at the long-run equilibrium due to a more conservative (or sustainable) resource exploitation.

If the aggregate parameter at the left-hand side of (9.16) is increased, that is, the number of fishermen and/or prices become higher compared with intrinsic growth of the fish species in the environment considered, and/or the fishing costs are lowered by using more sophisticated technologies, for

$$na\left(\frac{s}{\gamma_c}+\frac{1-s}{\gamma_d}\right)=2\alpha \tag{9.20}$$

we have $DF(0)=1$ and if $na/(s/\gamma_c+(1-s)/\gamma_d)$ is further increased (or α decreased) then a transcritical (or stability exchange) bifurcation occurs after which the equilibrium $X_0=0$ becomes stable, that is, $-1<DF(0)<1$, and a second fixed point X_2 enters the positive orthant, thus giving the situation (b). The new positive equilibrium X_2 is unstable, being $DF(X_2)>1$, and it belongs to the boundary which separates the basin of the stable equilibrium $X_0=0$ from the basin of the positive attractor. So, in this situation X_2 constitutes a threshold population level such that if the current population $X(t)$ falls below X_2 then the resource stock will spontaneously evolve towards extinction. It is worth noticing that if s increases, so that the asymptote of H^* moves downwards, then threshold value X_2 moves to the left, that is, it is a decreasing function of s. This means that more cooperators imply not only a higher resource stock at the long-run equilibrium X_1, but also an enlargement of its basin of attraction.

As usual with non-invertible maps, all the rank-1 pre-images of X_2 belong to basin boundaries, so the basin of the positive attractor is now given by

$$B=(X_2, X_{2-1}), \qquad (9.21)$$

X_{2-1} being the greater solution of the equation $F(X)=X_2$. The set of positive initial conditions which asymptotically converge to $X_0=0$, and give rise to extinction in the long run, is formed by the union of two disjoint intervals

$$BP\,(0)=(0, X_2)\cup(X_{2-1}, X_{0-1}) \qquad (9.22)$$

whereas the initial condition $X(0)>X_{0-1}$ generates unfeasible trajectories.

When two positive equilibria exist, the dynamic scenario is the one described above, and represented in Figure 9.3b. With given values of the biological parameters α and β, so that the parabola in Figure 9.2 is fixed, if the other parameters are varied with the consequence that the asymptote of H^* moves upwards, the two positive equilibria become closer and closer, so that the basin of X_0 enlarges and, therefore, the basin of the viable equilibrium X_1 shrinks. This can be obtained, for example, by increasing prices (that is, increasing a/b) or with decreasing values of s, that is, by increasing the number of defectors. We are particularly interested in the latter effect: decreasing values of s imply less robustness of the viable equilibrium with respect to exogenous shocks. Of course, a study of the effects of the parameter β may also be interesting, as a higher value of β may be interpreted as the effect of a damaged environment, due to pollution or other factors.

Finally, the situation (c), where the extinction equilibrium $X_0=0$ is the unique steady state, may be obtained as the final effect of increasing $H^*(+\infty, s)$. The transition from a dynamic scenario characterized by two positive steady states to one with no positive steady states occurs via a fold (or tangent) bifurcation, due to a progressive decrease of X_1, increase of X_2 (so that the basin B becomes smaller and smaller) until they merge with $DF(X_1) = DF(X_2) = 1$, and then disappear. It is trivial to prove that when X_0 is the unique equilibrium, then for every initial condition the system evolves towards extinction (see Figure 9.3c). Once more, we remark that a sequence of bifurcations such as that described above may occur for increasing prices, decreasing costs or decreasing values of s, that is, by increasing the number of defectors.

4. THE TWO-DIMENSIONAL MODEL WITH EVOLUTIONARY DYNAMICS OF s

We now relax the assumption of a fixed population share between cooperators and defectors, and we introduce an evolutionary mechanism that, at each time period, describes how the population share is updated. In the spirit of evolutionary games, we assume that the fraction of agents playing a strategy that, with respect to the other strategies, earns higher payoffs, increases in the next period. In our case, the payoffs associated with the two available strategies of cooperation and defection are the profits $\pi_c^*(t)$ and $\pi_d^*(t)$ respectively, that, according to (9.13) and (9.12), depend on the current population share $s(t)$ as well as on the current resource stock $X(t)$. Since, as argued in the previous section, the dynamics of $X(t)$ are influenced by $s(t)$, this will give rise to a two-dimensional non-linear dynamical system with dynamic variables $X(t)$ and $s(t)$, the study of which may give us information on the long-run evolution of the system. For example, we may ask not only if the resource stock will survive or become extinct in the long run, but we may also ask if some behaviour (cooperation or defection) will survive or become extinct as the system evolves. Since, under the reasonable assumption $\gamma_c = \gamma_d$ (that means that the two groups adopt the same technology) the strategy chosen by defectors is dominant if no sanctions are applied, the assumption $\xi > \psi \geq 0$ will be crucial in order to obtain stable equilibria with a non-vanishing fraction s of cooperators.

4.1 Replicator Dynamics

The simplest (and more frequently used) model proposed in the literature which gives an evolutionary pressure in favour of groups obtaining the highest payoffs is that of *replicator dynamics* (Taylor and Jonker, 1978; see also Vega-Redondo, 1996, chapter 3; Hofbauer and Sigmund, 1998, chapter 7; Weibull, 1995, chapter 3). The discrete time replicator dynamics for the fraction of cooperators can be written as

$$s(t+1) = s(t)\frac{\pi_c^*(t)}{\bar{\pi}} \tag{9.23}$$

where

$$\bar{\pi}(t) = s\pi_c^*(t) + (1-s)\pi_d^*(t) \tag{9.24}$$

represents the average profit observed at time t. So, (9.23) states that $s(t+1)$ will be greater than $s(t)$ if $\pi_c^*(t) > \bar{\pi}(t)$ whereas $s(t)$ will decrease if $\pi_c^*(t) < \bar{\pi}(t)$. As $\pi_c^*(t) > \bar{\pi}(t)$ if and only if $\pi_c^*(t) > \pi_d^*(t)$, it follows that the population share related to the better performing strategy at time period t increases in the next period.

Both $\pi_c^*(t)$ and $\bar{\pi}(t)$ depend on $s(t)$, as well as $X(t)$ so the difference equations (9.14) and (9.23) define a two-dimensional discrete dynamical system. Starting from a given initial biomass $X(0)$ and a given initial population share $s(0)$, the recurrences (9.14) and (9.23) allow one to obtain $X(t)$ and $s(t)$ for each $t \geq 0$, from which the corresponding values of $x_c^*(t)$, $x_d^*(t)$, $\pi_c^*(t)$, $\pi_d^*(t)$, $H^*(t)$ can be obtained.

It is interesting to study whether the dynamic variables $X(t)$ and $s(t)$ converge to a given steady state in the long run, that is, as $t \to +\infty$, or if they exhibit some more complex time pattern.

4.2 Qualitative Study of the Two-Dimensional Dynamical System

The time evolution of the discrete time two-dimensional dynamical system in the dynamic variables X and s is obtained by the iteration of a map of the plane $T: (X(t), s(t)) \to (X(t+1), s(t+1))$ defined by

$$X(t+1) = X(t)(1 + \alpha - \beta X(t)) - H^*(X(t), s(t)) \tag{9.25}$$

$$s(t+1) = s(t)\frac{\pi_c^*(X(t), s(t))}{s\pi_c^*(X(t), s(t)) + (1-s)\pi_d^*(X(t), s(t))}$$

where $H^*(X, s)$ is given by (9.10), with x_c^* and x_d^* defined in (9.30) and (9.29) respectively, and $\pi_c^*(t)$, $\pi_d^*(t)$ are given in (9.13) and (9.12) respectively.

It is straightforward to see that if $\pi_c^*(t) > 0$ and $\pi_d^*(t) > 0$ then $s(t) \in (0, 1)$ implies $s(t+1) \in (0, 1)$ as well. However, negative profits may arise if the parameters ξ and/or ψ are positive. As the influence of these parameters is always related to the difference $\xi - \psi$, without loss of generality we shall assume $\psi = 0$, and whenever $\pi_d^*(t) < 0$ we shall assume $s(t+1) = 1$ (instead of the meaningless $s(t+1) > 1$, as obtained by simply applying (9.25)).

4.3 Two Benchmark Cases

It is important to notice that if $s(t)=0$ then $s(t+1)=0$ for each $t \geq 0$, and if $s(t)=1$ then $s(t+1)=1$ for each $t \geq 0$, that is, the two boundary lines $s=0$ and $s=1$ are trapping lines, on which the dynamics are governed by one-dimensional unimodal maps, given by the restrictions of the two-dimensional map (9.25) to them. These two cases correspond to particular benchmark cases, where we have all cooperators and all defectors respectively, that is, the cases considered in Szidarovszky and Okuguchi (1998) and Szidarovszky and Okuguchi (2000) respectively (see also Bischi et al., 2003). The properties of these one-dimensional dynamical systems can easily be obtained on the basis of the results of Section 3. For example, the dynamics along the invariant edge $s=0$, where all players are defectors, is governed by the one-dimensional map (9.14) with

$$H^*(X, 0) = nx_d^*(X, 0) = \frac{naX}{b(n+1)X + 2\gamma_d}$$

So the steady states are $X=0$ and the solutions (if any) of the equation

$$b\beta(n+1)X^2 + (2\beta\gamma_d - \alpha b(n+1))X + na - \alpha\gamma_d = 0 \qquad (9.26)$$

The analysis is the same as in Szidarovszky and Okuguchi (1998) or in Bischi et al. (2003).

On the other invariant edge $s=1$, where all players are cooperators, the dynamics are governed by (9.14) with

$$H^*(X, 1) = nx_c^*(X, 1) = \frac{naX}{2(bnX + \gamma_c)}$$

So the fixed points are $X=0$ and the solutions (if any) of the equation

$$2b\beta nX^2 + 2(\beta\gamma_c - \alpha bn)X + na - 2\alpha\gamma_c = 0 \qquad (9.27)$$

The analysis is the same as in Szidarovszky and Okuguchi (2000) or in Bischi et al. (2003).

4.4 Steady States

As usual, the starting point for the qualitative analysis of a non-linear dynamical system is the localization of the steady states and the study of their local stability. The steady states of the two-dimensional dynamical system (9.25) are the fixed points of the map T, solutions of the system $T(X, s) = (X, s)$. It is straightforward to see that two *corner equilibria* always exist, given by $E_0 = (0, 0)$ and $E_1 = (0, 1)$, characterized by extinction of the resource. Other boundary equilibria may exist along the invariant lines $s = 0$ and $s = 1$, given by the solutions, if any, of (9.26) and (9.27) respectively. If two equilibria with positive fish stocks exist both on the invariant edge $s = 0$ and on invariant edge $s = 1$, say $X_2(0)$, $X_1(0)$ and $X_2(1)$, $X_1(1)$, respectively, then, on the basis of the arguments of Section 3, the following relation must hold: $X_2(1) < X_2(0) < X_1(0) < X_1(1)$. A necessary condition for the existence of two positive equilibria along $s = 0$ is that two positive equilibria exist along $s = 1$. However, it may happen that two positive equilibria exist along $s = 1$ and no positive equilibria exist along $s = 0$. Of course, sufficient conditions for the existence of two positive boundary equilibria along the invariant edges are obtained from (9.17) with $s = 0$ and $s = 1$ respectively.

Instead, if (9.16) is satisfied for $s = 1$, that is, $na < 2\alpha\gamma_c$, then a unique equilibrium exists along the edge with only cooperators, and the same holds on the other invariant edge if $na < 2\alpha\gamma_d$. These two conditions are equivalent under the reasonable assumption $\gamma_c = \gamma_d$. However, even when a unique equilibrium exists, the inequality $X_1(0) < X_1(1)$ holds, that is, the long-run equilibrium under sustainable fishing is characterized by higher values of resource stock in the limiting case of all cooperators than in the opposite limiting case of all defectors.

The stability of these equilibria with respect to the one-dimensional dynamics trapped inside the invariant edges can easily be deduced from the discussion on the one-dimensional dynamics given in Section 3 applied to the particular benchmark cases $s = 0$ and $s = 1$. However, we are now mainly interested in the stability with respect to perturbations transverse to the invariant edges, that is, what happens if a few defectors appear starting from a situation with all cooperators, or what happens if a few cooperators appear starting from a situation with all defectors. Are such small mutations eliminated by the evolutionary dynamics, so that the original benchmark case is restored (case of transverse stability) or do they grow up thus causing an irreversible departure from the original benchmark case?

An answer to these questions requires the study of the local stability of the boundary equilibria, that is, the localization, in the complex plane, of the eigenvalues of the Jacobian matrix of (9.25) computed at the boundary steady states. This is not difficult in principle, as eigenvalues are always real because the Jacobian matrix of (9.25) is a triangular matrix along the invariant edges. This implies that we can only have nodes or saddle equilibria on the boundaries. However, the expressions of the eigenvalues are quite involved, and the stability conditions obtained are not easy to interpret.

So, in the following we prefer to follow a numerical and graphical method in order to obtain a global view of the dynamic properties of the dynamical system (9.25).[4]

First of all, we consider the question of the existence of inner equilibria, that is, steady states characterized by the coexistence of cooperators and defectors. These are obtained solving the non-linear system

$$X(\alpha - \beta X) = H^*(X, s)$$
$$\pi_c^*(X, s) = \pi_d^*(X, s) \qquad (9.28)$$

with $0 < s < 1$. The set of points on the plane (X, s) that satisfy the first equation represent the locus of points that give a one-period stationary resource stock, that is, $X(t + 1) = X(t)$.[5] For each s in the range [0, 1] the X coordinates of these points can be computed by solving the equation (9.15), already analyzed in Section 3. So, this set of points may be formed by two branches, say $X_1(s)$ and $X_2(s)$, with $X_2(s) < X_1(s)$ for each s. Moreover, from the results of Section 3, $X_2(s)$ is a decreasing function and $X_1(s)$ is increasing, so the branch $X_1(s)$ has a positive slope and the branch $X_2(s)$ has a negative slope in the plane (X, s) (see Figures 9.4(a) and 9.5(a)). The

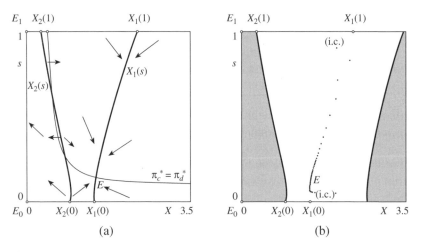

(a)   (b)

Notes:
(a) Obtained with the set of parameters $n = 10$, $\alpha = 3$, $\beta = 1$, $a = 1.05$, $b = 0.3$, $\gamma_c = \gamma_d = 1$ $\psi = 0$, $\xi = 0.01$. The arrows give a qualitative indication of the directions of one-step advancement of the discrete dynamical system (9.26). (b) For the same parameters as those used in (a) the basins of attraction are represented: the white region represents the basin of the inner equilibrium E, the grey region is the set of points that generate trajectories leading to extinction (that is, $X \leq 0$). Two trajectories, starting from initial conditions (2, 2, 0.9) and (2, 0.05), are also represented by sequences of black dots.

Figure 9.4   Numerical graphical representation of the equation (9.29)

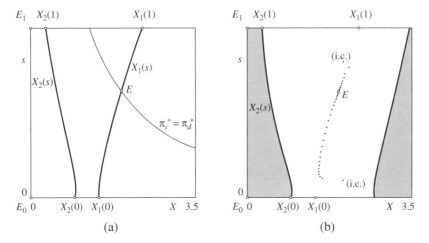

Figure 9.5   Numerical graphical representation of equation (9.29), with
        $\xi = 0.05$

intersection of the branch $X_1(s)$ $(X_2(s))$ with the invariant edge $s = 1$ gives
the boundary equilibrium of X coordinate $X_1(1)$ $(X_2(1))$, and the same
holds for the intersections (if any) with the other invariant edge $s = 0$.
However, it may happen that the two branches intersect at $s = 1$ but have no
intersections with $s = 0$, because they may merge for $s > 0$ (see Figure
9.6(a)). If the condition (9.16) is satisfied for all $s \in [0, 1]$, then the locus of
points such that $X(t+1) = X(t)$ is only formed by the branch $X_1(s)$. The
knowledge of these curves gives us the following information: starting from
a given point (X, s), a one-step iteration of (9.25) generates a new point $(X',
s') = T$, rank-1 image of (X, s) by T, with $X' > X$ if (X, s) is in the strip
between the curves $X_2(s)$ and $X_1(s)$ (or between the axis $X = 0$ and the curve
$X_1(s)$ if only the branch $X_1(s)$ exists) and with $X' < X$ if (X, s) is on the left
of the curves $X_2(s)$ (provided it exists) or on the right of the curve $X_1(s)$.

A similar reasoning can be applied to the set of points that satisfy the
second equation (9.28), which represents the locus of points that give a one-
period stationary population share, that is, $s(t+1) = s(t)$. A qualitative
study of this curve is more difficult, due to the complicated expressions of
$\pi_c^*(X, s)$ and $\pi_d^*(X, s)$. However, the numerical solution of the equation
$\pi_c^*(X, s) = \pi_d^*(X, s)$ for different sets of parameters gives rise to decreasing
curves in the plane (X, s), as shown in Figures 9.4(a), 9.5(a) and 9.6(a).
The points above the curve $\pi_c^*(X, s) = \pi_d^*(X, s)$ are points where
$\pi_c^*(X, s) < \pi_d^*(X, s)$, hence the rank-1 images $(X', s') = T(X, s)$ of points $(X,
s)$ above the curve have $s' < s$. Of course, the points below the curve are
characterized by $\pi_c^*(X, s) > \pi_d^*(X, s)$, hence $(X', s') = T(X, s)$ are such that

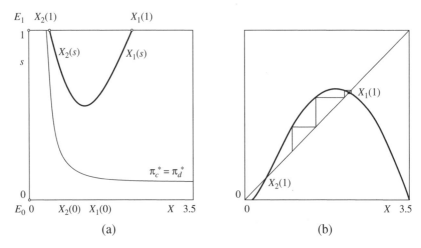

Notes:
(a) Parameters as for Figure 9.4a, except for $\alpha = 1.2$. (b) (b) For the same parameters as those used in (a) the function $F(X)$ that governs the one dimensional dynamics along the invariant edge $s = 1$ is represented, with a trajectory starting from $X = 1$ and converging to the equilibrium $X_1(1)$.

Figure 9.6 Numerical graphical representation of equation (9.29), with $\alpha = 1.2$

$s' > s$. These arguments allow us to obtain a global qualitative picture of the dynamic behaviour of the dynamical system (9.25), as shown by the arrows represented in Figure 9.4a.

Any intersection between the curve $\pi_c^*(X, s) = \pi_d^*(X, s)$ and one of the curves $X_i(s)$, $i = 1, 2$, represents a steady state of the dynamical system. All the steady states along the branch $X_2(s)$ cannot be stable, because all the points on that branch behave as repelling points along the X direction. Instead, steady states located along the branch $X_1(s)$ are candidates to be stable equilibria.

We try to explain this point by some numerical experiments. In Figure 9.4(a), obtained with the set of parameters $n = 10$, $\alpha = 3$, $\beta = 1$, $a = 1.05$, $b = 0.3$, $\gamma_c = \gamma_d = 1$, $\psi = 0$, $\xi = 0.01$, the two equilibria on $X_2(s)$ are unstable, whereas the equilibrium point $E = (1.48, 0.15)$, located on $X_1(s)$ is stable. In Figure 9.4b, the numerically computed basin of attraction of the stable equilibrium E is represented by the white region, whereas the grey region represent the initial conditions leading to extinction of the resource. Two typical trajectories are also represented as sequences of black dots. From this picture the role of the curve $X_2(s)$ is quite evident: as in the one-dimensional model studied in Section 3, the locus points $X_2(s)$ constitute the boundary that separates the basin of attraction of the stable positive equilibrium from the basin of the trajectories leading to the extinction of the resource.

In the situation shown in Figure 9.4, the long-run evolution of the system leads to an equilibrium situation characterized by a small fraction of cooperators (only 15 per cent of the fishermen population). The number of cooperators at the stable equilibrium can be increased by varying some parameters, for example by increasing ξ, that is, imposing heavier sanctions, or by decreasing a/b, that is, lowering prices. Both these variations cause an upward movement of the curve $\pi_c^*(X, s) = \pi_d^*(X, s)$. For example, Figure 9.5 has been obtained by increasing the parameter ξ from 0.01 to 0.05. The consequence is that the new stable equilibrium is $E = (1.91, 0.62)$, that is, 62 per cent of fishermen are cooperators and, consequently, a higher resource stock is present at equilibrium. If, starting from this situation, the parameter ξ is further increased, or a/b is decreased, the equilibrium E moves upwards along the curve $X_1(s)$ until it merges with the boundary equilibrium $X_1(1)$ through a transcritical (or stability exchange) bifurcation. After this, the boundary equilibrium $X_1(1)$ becomes the unique stable steady state, where only cooperators exist. This means that prices are so low that it is not convenient to be defectors, even if very few defectors are present, that is, even if a defector appears (a mutation in the population composition), it is eliminated by the evolutionary mechanism.

It is also interesting to see what happens when prices are very high, as in the situation shown in Figure 9.6(a), where the same parameters as in Figure 9.4 have been used, except for the parameter $a = 1.2$. In this case no positive boundary equilibria exist along the invariant boundary $s = 0$ with all defectors, and two positive equilibria, $X_2(1) < X_1(1)$ exist along the edge $s = 1$. In this situation all the initial conditions generate trajectories that approach the boundary $s = 0$ and then converge to the unique stable equilibrium $E_0 = (0, 0)$. This means that prices are so high that defectors prevail, but their harvesting is so high that the resource is exhausted. However, if we constrain the system to start with $s = 1$ (all cooperators) and sufficient initial resource stock, that is, $X(0) > X_2(1)$, then the system evolves towards the equilibrium $X_1(1)$, according to the one-dimensional dynamics shown in Figure 9.6(b). However, the equilibrium is not transversely stable. This implies that if just one defector appears, the endogenous evolutive dynamics will create more and more defectors, and the system will irreversibly evolve towards a situation with all defectors and extinction of the resource.

5. CONCLUSIONS

In this chapter we have presented a model that constitutes an attempt to put together two opposite approaches to commercial fishing: cooperation (that is, harvesting decisions obtained through the maximization of overall profit, that lead to more conservative resource harvesting) and the non-cooperative, or defective, attitude (that is, harvesting decisions obtained through the maximization of personal profit without any concern for social welfare). Oligopoly models based on one of these opposite attitudes, that is, all agents behaving as cooperators or all agents behaving as defectors, have recently been proposed by Szidarovszky and Okuguchi, 2000 and 1998 respectively (see also Bischi et al., 2004, for a comparison between the two cases). Instead, in the model proposed in this chapter we describe a common property resource exploitation with a population of agents switching between non-cooperative and cooperative behaviour according to an evolutive mechanism, known as replicator dynamics, based on the idea that the fraction of agents playing the strategy that earns higher payoffs will increase in the next period (as proposed in Sethi and Somanathan, 1996). As in the paper by Sethi and Somanathan, our model includes the possibility that cooperators impose sanctions to punish defectors. Indeed, without any sanction, the choice to be a defector is the dominant one (that is, the more profitable) and the evolutive process will consequently eliminate the cooperators. Instead, the presence of sanctions may eliminate defectors in the long run, or lead to a stable coexistence between cooperators and defectors.

The focus of our work is mainly methodological, as its primary goal is the set-up of the dynamic model: starting from a static oligopoly game, where each group chooses its harvesting according to the Nash equilibrium of the game, we realize that such an equilibrium depends on the available resource stock and the population share, and both these quantities evolve according to their dynamic equations. So, we first introduce the law of motion that governs the growth of the renewable resource and then we introduce the replicator dynamics that governs the time evolution of the population share between cooperators and defectors. This leads us to the study of a non-linear two-dimensional discrete time dynamical system. The results given in this chapter constitute only a first step towards a full understanding of the dynamic behaviours of the model, as we have given only a numerical and graphical characterization of the equilibria and their stability.

We can summarize our results as follows. First, the presence of many cooperators always leads to a relatively high level of the resource stock, and hence wealth in the long run, whereas many defectors can cause a severe depletion of the resource, and an enlargement of the basin of attraction of steady states

with extinction of the resource. Second, from the point of view of a regula-
tor, cooperative behaviour can be supported not only by increasing the level
of sanctions, or lowering prices, but it is also possible to reach steady states
characterized by the presence of only cooperators which are transversely
stable, that is, even if a defector enters the market this behaviour does not
spread through the population. Otherwise, low sanctions and/or high prices
could lead to steady states with only defectors, and the potential depletion
(even extinction) of the resource. In this case, even if the system starts from
an initial condition with only cooperators, non-cooperative behaviour will
prevail if just one agent decides to defect. Even if a qualitative analysis of the
model can be undertaken using the methods discussed in this chapter, a more
complete analysis of the effects of the parameters on the kinds of long-run
evolution, as well as on the transverse stability of corner equilibria, is under
development.

Further enhancements of this model could also relax the assumption of
perfect foresight about next-period fish stocks, replacing it by a weaker (and
more realistic) assumption on expectations formations (for example,
assuming that agents have adaptive expectations based on the available
resource stock). Another interesting improvement of the model might be
to assume sanctions that are not constant, but depend on some index of
performance (from an ecologic and economic point of view) of the fishery
system, so that the optimal kind of sanction is decided by methods of
dynamic programming.

APPENDIX

Proof of proposition 1. The existence and uniqueness of the intersection between
the reaction curves (9.9) trivially follows from the linearity of the reaction functions.
The positivity of both the coordinates of the intersection point can be deduced from
the fact that $h_d(0) < h_c^{-1}(0)$ and $h_c(0) < h_d^{-1}(0)$. In fact, the first inequality can be
written as $aX/b(1 + (1 - s)X + 2\gamma_d) < a/b(1 - s)n$, which is equivalent to $bX + 2\gamma_d > 0$,
the second inequality can be written as $X/2(bsnX + \gamma_c) < 1/bsn$, which is equivalent
to $bsnX + 2\gamma_c > 0$. The explicit computation of the intersection point gives

$$x_d^*(X, s) = aX \frac{bsnX + 2\gamma_c}{b^2sn(n(1 - s) + 2)X^2 + 2b(2ns\gamma_d + \gamma_c + \gamma_c n(1 - s))X + 4\gamma_c\gamma_d} \quad (9.29)$$

and

$$x_c^*(X, s) = \frac{Xa - b(1 - s)nx_d^*(X, s)}{2 \quad bsnX + \gamma_c} \quad (9.30)$$

from which the properties stated in (*i*) and (*ii*) are quite evident. Moreover, x_d^* is an
increasing and concave functions with respect to $X > 0$. The total harvesting at the
Nash Equilibrium, $H^*(X, s) = n[s\, x_c^*(X, s) + (1 - s)\, x_d^*(X, s)]$, is an increasing and
concave function with respect to X.[6]

For X→+∞ we get

$$H^*(+\infty, s) = na\left[\frac{1}{bn[(1-s)n+2]} + \frac{1-s}{b[(1-s)n+2]}\right] =$$

$$= \frac{a(1+n(1-s))}{b[(1-s)n+2]} = \frac{a}{b}\left(1 - \frac{1}{2+(1-s)n}\right)$$

Proof of proposition 2. Let us consider the function $Q(X) = X(\alpha - \beta X) - H^*(X)$, whose zeros are the equilibria of (9.14). Trivially it is $Q(0) = 0$, so $X_0 = 0$ is an equilibrium.

In order to prove (a) we notice that the condition (9.16) states that the slope at $X = 0$ of the function H^* is less than the slope at $X = 0$ of the parabola. This is equivalent to saying that $Q'(0) > 0$. Hence $Q(X) > 0$ in a right neighbourhood of $X = 0$, whereas $Q(\alpha/\beta) = -H^*(\alpha/\beta) < 0$. So, at least one equilibrium exists in the range $(0, \alpha/\beta)$. The uniqueness of the equilibrium follows from the fact that $Q(X)$ is a unimodal function for $X > 0$. In fact, $Q'(X) = \alpha - 2\beta X - H^{*\prime}(X)$ vanishes in a unique point, because we have $Q'(0) = \alpha - H^{*\prime}(X) > 0$ from (9.16), $Q'(\alpha/2\beta) = -H^{*\prime}(\alpha/2\beta) < 0$ and $H'(X)$ is a positive, decreasing and convex function.[7]

To prove (b) we notice that the first inequality in (9.17) states that at $X = 0$ the curve $H^*(X)$ has a slope greater than that of the parabola, and the second inequality states that the upper bound (that is, the horizontal asymptote) of H^* is lower than the vertex of the parabola. In fact, the first inequality implies $Q'(0) < 0$, hence $Q(X) < 0$ in a right neighbourhood of $X = 0$, whereas $Q(\alpha/2\beta) = \alpha^2/4\beta - H^*(\alpha/\beta) > 0$ (being $H^*(X) < \frac{a}{b}(1 - 1/2 + (1-s)n)$ for each $X \geq 0$) and $Q(\alpha/\beta) = -H^*(\alpha/\beta) < 0$ again. So, at least two positive zeros of $Q(X)$ exist inside the intervals $(0, \alpha/2\beta)$ and $(\alpha/2\beta, \alpha/\beta)$ respectively. However, more than two zeros of $Q(X)$ cannot exist, because $Q(X)$ cannot have more than two critical points due to the convexity of $H'(X)$.

Finally, the conditions (9.18), obtained by reversing the second inequality in (9.17), state that the slope of $H^*(X)$ at $X = 0$ is greater than that of the parabola, and the upper bound of H^* is above the vertex of the parabola, and this implies that no positive intersections can exist.

NOTES

We thank Laura Gardini for useful discussions and comments. The usual disclaimer applies. This work has been carried out under the auspices of the grant 'Le interazioni fra settore ittico e ambiente', financed by the Italian Ministry for Agriculture, and under the auspices of the national research project 'Dynamic Models in Economics and Finance: Evolution, Uncertainty and Forecasting', MIUR, Italy.

1. Since n is finite, admissible values of s should be discrete, that is, $s = k/n$ with $k = 0, 1, ..., n$. However, as usual in population dynamics and evolutionary games modelling, we abstract from this and allow s to be a real number in the interval $[0, 1]$, even if we shall consider ns and $n(1-s)$ integers that sum to n, by assuming some approximation of ns to the nearest integer.

2. A more general growth function $G(X) = XR(X)$, with $R(0) > 1$, $R(X) > 0$ for $0 < X < K$ and $R(X) < 0$ for $X > K$, $K > 0$ being the carrying capacity, may be considered. However, the choice $R(X) = 1 + \alpha - \beta X$, known as logistic growth, is one of the simplest and most commonly used for qualitative analysis purposes.

3. This may be interpreted as a resource extinction due to overcrowding effects, a definitely unrealistic situation in the context we are considering.

4. A more standard analytical study of the stability of the boundary equilibria, obtained with the help of software packages for symbolic algebraic manipulation, is in progress.
5. Of course, this does not mean that the dynamic system is in equilibrium, unless $s(t)$ is also stationary, that is, the second equation (9.28) is satisfied as well.
6. From (10) with (29) and (30) it is possible to prove (we tested the long expressions by a computer package) that $H'(X) > 0$ and $H''(X) < 0$. Details of these expressions are available from the authors.
7. From (10) with (29) and (30) it is possible to prove that $H^{*''}(X) < 0$ and $H^{*'''}(X) > 0$. Details of these expressions are available from the authors.

REFERENCES

Bischi, G.I. and M. Kopel (2002), 'The role of competition, expectations and harvesting costs in commercial fishing', in T. Puu and I. Sushko (eds), *Oligopoly Dynamics: Models & Tools*, Heidelberg: Springer Verlag, pp. 85–109.

Bischi, G.I., M. Kopel and F. Szidarovszky (2004), 'Competition and cooperation in multi-agent fisheries', forthcoming in *Annals of Operation Research*.

Clark, C.W. (1990), *Mathematical Bioeconomics*, 2nd edn, New York: Wiley John and Sons.

Gordon, H.S. (1954), 'The economic theory of a common property resource: the fishery', *Journal of Political Economy*, **62**, 124–42.

Hardin, G. (1968), 'The tragedy of the commons', *Science*, **162**, 1243–7.

Hofbauer, J. and K. Sigmund (1998), *Evolutionary Games and Population Dynamics*, Cambridge: Cambridge University Press.

Levhari, D. and L.J. Mirman (1982), 'The Great Fish War: An Example Using a Dynamic Cournot-Nash Solution', in L.J. Mirman and D.F. Spulber (eds), *Essays in the Economics of Renewable Resources*, Amsterdam: North-Holland, 243–58.

Mesterton-Gibbons, M. (1993), 'Game-theoretic resource modelling', *Natural Resource Modeling*, **7**, 93–147.

Sethi, R. and E. Somanathan (1996), 'The evolution of social norms in common property resource use', *The American Economic Review*, **86**, 766–88.

Szidarovszky, F. and K. Okuguchi (1998), 'An oligopoly model of commercial fishing', *Seoul Journal of Economics*, **11**, 321–30.

Szidarovszky, F. and K. Okuguchi (2000), 'A dynamic model of international fishing', *Seoul Journal of Economics*, **13**, 471–76.

Taylor, P. and L. Jonker (1978), 'Evolutionarily stable strategies and game dynamics', *Mathematical Biosciences*, **40**, 145–56.

Vega-Redondo, F. (1996), *Evolution, Games and Economic Behaviour*, Oxford: Oxford University Press.

Weibull, J.W. (1995), *Evolutionary Game Theory*, Cambridge, MA: The MIT Press.

10. Greenhouse gases, quota exchange and oligopolistic competition

Sjur Didrik Flåm and Odd Godal

1. THE BACKGROUND AND THE PROBLEM

Global warming now appears a menace – enhanced by anthropogenic emissions of greenhouse gases. Regulating these emissions has therefore gained notable priority in policy-making circles. Some regulation proceeds by voluntary quota transfers or trades. And quite naturally, since Montgomery (1972) first proved that such trade may foster cost-efficiency, market-based mechanisms have attracted much attention.[1]

In that setting agents are bestowed with emission permits and allowed to engage in subsequent exchange. Clearly, the permits – or licences to pollute – can be construed as production factors. As such they are likely to affect diverse forms of competition, including the imperfect ones. So, we state the following:

Problem: *Suppose here that emission quotas serve as inputs in oligopolistic competition. Then, how can quotas be shared in the 'emissions market'? And how can the agents reach an overall equilibrium in the product market?*

To come to grips with these questions we shall – for realism and applicability – presume coexistence of strategic and non-strategic behaviour. To wit, *on the production side* some agents – maybe all – are taken to be full-fledged Cournot oligopolists, perfectly foreseeing how own supply will affect market prices. Similarly, *on the factor side* – in the quota market – traders need not all come forward as price-takers. Admittedly, if somebody behaves strategically in merely one direction, then his split nature – resembling that of Dr Jekyll and Mr Hyde – stands to be criticized for lack of consistency or charm. Be that as it may. It is important for us to accommodate oligopolists (even cartels) surrounded by competitive fringes.

To analyze such a scenario we organize things as follows. Section 2 spells out the general setting. Section 3 addresses how emission rights are priced. As a vehicle it uses a so-called *production game* in which the marketed endowments are pooled.[2] Since trades and prices of emission rights are endogenous, the main object of Section 3 is to generate a *demand curve* for licences to pollute. That curve is crucial for the analysis in Section 4, dealing with the definition, existence and characterization of equilibrium. Section 5 provides a simple numerical simulation, focused on profit and welfare. It explores some implications of making quotas transferable. Section 6 contains some bibliographical remarks, and it concludes.

2. THE SETTING

A set I of firms compete in an oligopolistic market for a list P of products. Production entails polluting emissions of a collection G of 'greenhouse gases'. G, I and P are all fixed and finite. Individual $i \in I$ produces a quantity vector $q_i \in \mathbb{R}_+^P$ and brings it to a common market.[3] A *production profile* $\mathbf{q} = (q_i)$ yields *total supply* $Q := \Sigma_{i \in I} q_i$.

As stated, production generates *emissions* of the said gases (seen here as pollutants discharged into global commons). Agent i can – by employing appropriate abatement technology – choose to hold his emissions down to $x_i \in \mathbb{R}_+^G$. These must be fully matched – and justified – by a corresponding permit.

At the outset, agent i owns an emission endowment $\bar{e}_i \in \mathbb{R}_+^G$. Suppose permits are traded without friction under a price regime $p \in \mathbb{R}^G$. That regime is a function $p = P(\mathbf{q}, \mathbf{e})$ of the production and emission profiles $\mathbf{q} = (q_i)$ and $\mathbf{e} := (e_i)$, the vector $e_i \in [0, \bar{e}_i]$ being what agent i chooses to make available in the emission market. Section 3 spells out how $P(\cdot, \cdot)$ is defined.

Agent i shows no humility in worshipping profit. So, he vigorously seeks to maximize

$$\Pi_i(\mathbf{q}, \mathbf{e}, x_i) + p \cdot (e_i - x_i) \tag{10.1}$$

with respect to his three decision variables: the quantity q_i produced, the emission e_i supplied (sold) in the emission market, and the permit x_i bought there. These transactions, amounting to net sale $e_i - x_i$, bring him additional revenues $p \cdot (e_i - x_i) := \Sigma p_g \{e_{ig} - x_{ig}\}$ in the emission market. While e_i must belong to the 'interval' $[0, \bar{e}_i]$, the more flexible choice $x_i \in [0, \Sigma_{i \in I} \bar{e}_i]$ is subject only to the coupling constraint, $\Sigma_{i \in I} x_i = \Sigma_{i \in I} e_i$.

The payoff function $\Pi_i(\mathbf{q}, \mathbf{e}, x_i)$, not including revenues from emission trade, is jointly concave in (q_i, e_i, x_i) and strictly concave in x_i.[4] The argument $\mathbf{e}$ in this function accounts for 'tragedies of the commons' if any. For convenience we posit $\Pi_i(\mathbf{q}, \mathbf{e}, x_i) = -\infty$ whenever (q_i, e_i, x_i) is inadmissible. This device saves us explicit and repeated mention of evident constraints, be they capacity limits or non-negativity restrictions.

To close the model we must say how the emission price p comes about. It will emerge here as a *shadow price* that supports equilibrium – in the form of a *core solution* – of a cooperative *production game*. This sort of pricing is described next.

3.   PRICING OF EMISSIONS

Let $\mathbf{q}=(q_i)$ and $\mathbf{e}=(e_i)$ be fixed here. So, temporarily we simplify notation by writing shortly $\Pi_i(x_i)$ for $\Pi_i(\mathbf{q}, \mathbf{e}, x_i)$.

Agent i, instead of achieving profit $\Pi_i(x_i)$ alone, may join a *coalition* $S \subseteq I$, thereby making an emission permit $e_i \leq \bar{e}_i$ available for joint use. As a result, S has *aggregate emission* $e_S := \Sigma_{i \in S} e_i$. If this coalition really forms, its most efficient, total profit would equal

$$\Pi_S(e_s) := \max_x \left\{ \sum_{i \in S} \Pi_i(x_i): \sum_{i \in S} x_i = e_S \right\}, \tag{10.2}$$

where $\mathbf{x} := (x_i)$ denotes the allocation. As in Shapley and Shubik (1969) construction (10.2) defines a *cooperative game* with player set I and *characteristic function* $S \mapsto \Pi_S(e_S)$.[5] For games of this sort efficiency and stability conditions are well cared for by so-called *core* solutions. Specifically, a payoff *allocation* $(co_i) \in \mathbb{R}^I$, where i receives the monetary amount co_i, belongs to the *core* iff it entails

  Pareto efficiency: $\Sigma_{i \in I} co_i = \Pi_I(e_I)$
  and social stability: $\Sigma_{i \in S} co_i \geq \Pi_S(e_S)$ for all coalitions $S \subset I$. (10.3)

Social stability means that no singleton or set $S \subset I$ of agents could improve their outcome by leaving the society and making exchanges between themselves instead. Obviously, stability could be guaranteed by paying everybody so handsomely that $\Sigma_{i \in S} co_i \geq \Pi_S(e_S)$, $S \subseteq I$. Therefore, insisting on overall efficiency is what makes the cooperative game challenging. Nonetheless, as pointed out next, since each $\Pi_i(x_i)$ is concave, core solutions not only exist; they are explicitly computable as well. To see this, define

$$L_I(p, \mathbf{x}) := \sum_{i \in I} [\Pi_i(x_i) + p \cdot (e_i - x_i)]$$

as the standard Lagrangian associated with problem (10.2) for the *grand coalition* $S = I$. Any vector $p \in \mathbb{R}^G$ that satisfies $\Pi_I(e_I) \geq \max_x L_I(p, \mathbf{x})$ will be declared a *shadow price* p. This item, being a Lagrange multiplier (vector), is a familiar object, obtainable via ordinary duality theory (Rockafellar, 1970):

Proposition 0. (Shadow prices yield core solutions; Evstigneev and Flåm (2001))

- (Existence of shadow prices) *Suppose the aggregate emission* $e_I :=$ $\Sigma_{i \in I} e_i$ *belongs to the interior of the set* $\{\Sigma_{i \in I} x_i : \Sigma_{i \in I} \Pi_i(x_i) > -\infty\}$. *Then there exists at least one shadow price regime.*
- (Explicit core solutions) *Any shadow price p generates a payoff allocation*

$$co_i := \max_{x_i} \{\Pi_i(x_i) - p \cdot x_i\} + p \cdot e_i \tag{10.4}$$

that belongs to the core (10.3).

- (Characterization of shadow prices) *p is a shadow price iff it is a supergradient of the reduced overall profit; that is, iff* $p \in \partial \Pi_I(e_I)$. *Conversely, when* $p \in \partial \Pi_I(e_I)$, *every optimal emission profile* $\mathbf{x} = (x_i)$, *satisfying* $\Sigma_{i \in I} x_i = e_I$ *and* $\Sigma_{i \in I} \Pi_i(x_i) = \Pi_I(e_I)$, *yields equal marginal profit across the players in that* $p \in \partial \Pi_i(x_i)$ *for all i.*
- (Uniqueness of choices and prices) *Since all* $\Pi_i(x_i)$ *are assumed strictly concave, an optimizing profile* (x_i) *must be unique. If some function* $\Pi_i(x_i)$ *is differentiable at a unique optimizing* x_i, *then p is unique and equals the derivative* $\Pi_i'(x_i)$. $\square$

In Proposition 0, and hereafter as well, the operator ∂ represents a generalized derivative (occasionally partial). If the function at hand (as right here) is concave (or convex), we deal with the commonplace notion as defined in convex analysis (Rockafellar, 1970).[6]

The core element (10.4) has an intuitive and well-known interpretation: When emission quotas are traded at price p, agent i takes home net value co_i (10.4). Typically, agents with relatively low marginal abatement cost would 'clean up' on behalf of others and be paid for doing so. The arrangement is decentralized and voluntary in that every individual i freely maximizes his modified objective $\Pi_i(x_i) + p \cdot (e_i - x_i)$.

It is time to step back now and recall that, in fact, $\Pi_i(x_i) = \Pi_i(\mathbf{q}, \mathbf{e}, x_i)$. Consequently, for $S = I$, the left-hand side of (10.2) is a function $\Pi_I(\mathbf{q}, \mathbf{e}, e_I)$. So, via the described exchange of permits, a reduced game will result in which player i obtains (reduced) profit

$$\pi_i(\mathbf{q}, \mathbf{e}) := \max_{x_i} \{\Pi_i(\mathbf{q}, \mathbf{e}, x_i) - p \cdot x_i\} + p \cdot e_i \tag{10.5}$$

where

$$p \text{ is a shadow price, belonging to } \frac{\partial \Pi_I(\mathbf{q}, \mathbf{e}, e_I)}{\partial e_I}, \tag{10.6}$$

and common to all players, as indicated by writing $p = P(\mathbf{q}, \mathbf{e})$. This completes the specification of (10.1). Note that, for fixed p, the right hand side of (10.5) is concave in (q_i, e_i). This property is most desirable for existence, computation and stability of the equilibria defined below. However, the same right-hand side is *convex* in p. Therefore, given $p = P(\mathbf{q}, \mathbf{e})$, the overall curvature properties of $\pi_i(\mathbf{q}, \mathbf{e})$ in (q_i, e_i) cannot easily be detected. This feature may entail problems with existence or properties of solutions.

4. THE GAME

After so much preparation we assemble now the modules considered so far and construe strategic interaction as a *two-stage game*:

At the first stage, all players – simultaneously, without communication or collaboration – choose their respective q_i and e_i subject to $e_i \le \bar{e}_i$.

At the second stage, with each pair (q_i, e_i) already committed, quotas are exchanged using a shadow price p as described in Section 3.

Expectations are presumed rational. That is, at the first stage, players can foresee the upcoming p. We observed that, when viewed at the first stage, the reduced profit (10.5) need not be concave in (q_i, e_i). This motivates the following

Definition 1. (Nash equilibrium) *The profiles $\mathbf{q} = (q_i)$, $\mathbf{e} = (e_i)$ together constitute a **Nash equilibrium** iff there exists a shadow price $p = P(\mathbf{q}, \mathbf{e}) \in \partial\Pi_I(\mathbf{q}, \mathbf{e}, e_I)/ \partial e_I$, such that each*

(q_i, e_i) *maximizes the reduced function $\pi_i(\mathbf{q}, \mathbf{e})$ subject to $p = P(\mathbf{q}, \mathbf{e})$.* (10.7)

Proposition 1. (Existence of Nash equilibrium) *Suppose each i obtains a reduced, finite-valued, jointly continuous profit $\pi_i(\mathbf{q}, \mathbf{e})$ iff $0 \le (q_i, e_i) \le (\bar{q}_i, \bar{e}_i)$ where $\bar{q}_i$ denotes i's production capacity. Suppose moreover, that each $\pi_i(\mathbf{q}, \mathbf{e})$ is quasi-concave in (q_i, e_i). Then there exists at least one Nash equilibrium.*

Proof. Agent i must make his first-stage choice (q_i, e_i) from the non-empty compact convex set $K_i := \{(q_i, e_i) \in \mathbb{R}_+^P \times \mathbb{R}_+^G : q_i \le \bar{q}_i, e_i \le \bar{e}_i\}$. As customary, let $B_i(\mathbf{q}, \mathbf{e})$ denote the best response (correspondence) of player i to the actions taken by his rivals. This correspondence B_i has non-empty convex values and closed graph. By Kakutani's theorem the product correspondence $B := (B_i)_{i \in I}$ from the product set $K_i := X_{i \in I} K_i$ into itself has a fixed point. Any such point is a Nash equilibrium.

Note that (10.7) presumes that each agent be a complete strategist in two directions: downstream (in the product market) as well as upstream (in the emission market). This excludes consideration of some interesting scenarios. Also, the quasi-concavity, required in Proposition 1, may be absent or hard to verify.

For these two reasons we proceed to introduce next a more relaxed equilibrium concept, invoking only first-order optimality conditions. At the same time we allow for diverse modes of strategical behaviour. To simplify somewhat, and to keep an eye on Cournot oligopolies, assume henceforth that profit $\Pi_i(\mathbf{q}, \mathbf{e}, x_i)$ is partly separable with respect to emission x_i. Specifically, for each i we posit that payoff comes in the 'separable' form

$$\Pi_i(\mathbf{q}, \mathbf{e}, x_i) := R_i(Q, e_I, q_i) - c_i(q_i, x_i).$$

where the first term on the right-hand side points to the *revenues* and the second term to the *costs*.

Behavioral assumptions: *Agent i behaves (not) strategically downstream, in the product market, iff he believes that – or acts as if – $\partial Q/\partial q_i = 1$ ($= 0$, respectively). For book-keeping put $\delta_i^+ := 1$ when i is a strategist there, and set $\delta_i^+ := 0$ otherwise. Similarly, i is (not) a strategist upstream, in the permit market, iff he does (not) account for the connection $(q_i, e_i) \to P(\mathbf{q}, \mathbf{e})$. Again, for book-keeping reasons, put $\delta_i^- := 1$ when he is a strategist there, and let $\delta_i^- := 0$ otherwise.*

Definition 2. (First-order equilibrium) *If instead of (10.7), it only holds with $p = P(\mathbf{q}, \mathbf{e}) \in \partial \Pi_i(\mathbf{q}, \mathbf{e}, e_I)/\partial e_I$, for each i that*

$$\left. \begin{array}{l} p \in \dfrac{\partial}{\partial x_i} \Pi_i(\mathbf{q}, \mathbf{e}, x_i) = - \dfrac{\partial}{\partial x_i} c_i(q_i, x_i), \\[3mm] 0 \in \dfrac{\partial}{\partial q_i} R_i(Q, e_I, q_i) + \delta_i^+ \dfrac{\partial}{\partial Q} R_i(Q, e_I, q_i) - \dfrac{\partial}{\partial q_i} c_i(q_i, x_i) + \delta_i^- \dfrac{\partial p}{\partial q_i}(e_i - x_i) \\[3mm] \text{and } \mu_i \in \dfrac{\partial}{\partial e_i} R_i(Q, e_I, q_i) + p + \delta_i^- \dfrac{\partial p}{\partial e_i}(e_i - x_i) \end{array} \right\} (10.8)$$

*with $\mu_i \in \mathbb{R}_+^G$ and $\mu_i \cdot (\bar{e}_i - e_i) = 0$ then we speak about a **first-order equilibrium**. In case all players are oligopolists in the product market and price takers in the permit market (that is, when, $\delta_i^+ = 1$, $\delta_i^- = 0$ for all i), we talk about a* **Cournot–Walras equilibrium**.

The three conditions in (10.8) say the following: *First*, there should be *one price* on emissions; *second*, an optimal choice q_i made by agent i must furnish him zero marginal profit; *third*, that same agent i imputes a non-negative value (vector) μ_i on marginal additions to his quota e_i.

It appears unlikely that some agent i acts non-strategically in the permit market ($\delta_i^- = 0$) and, at the same time, brings forward an interior amount e_i (that is, $0 \ll e_i \ll \bar{e}_i$). Indeed, existence of such an agent would imply that $p = 0$. It seems likely, though, that some well-endowed agents have $\delta_i^- = 1$ and $e_i \ll \bar{e}_i$.

We next address the asymmetric situation when everybody acts strategically in the product market (all $\delta_i^+ = 1$), but nobody does so in the other direction (each $\delta_i^- = 0$):

Theorem 1. (Existence of Cournot–Walras equilibrium) *Granted generalized differentiability, there exists a Cournot–Walras equilibrium.*

Proof. Define a fictitious game as follows. For any specified truncated profile $\mathbf{q}_{-i} := (q_j)_{j \neq i}$, in which player i does not figure, and for given aggregate emission x_{-i} from i's rivals, posit

$$C_{-i}(\mathbf{q}_{-i}, x_{-i}) := \min\left\{ \sum_{j \neq i} c_j(q_j, x_j) : \sum_{j \neq i} x_j = x_{-i} \right\}.$$

Let i take home payoff

$$r_i(\mathbf{q}, e_i + e_{-i}) := \max\{\Pi_i(\mathbf{q}, \mathbf{e}, x_i) - C_{-i}(\mathbf{q}_{-i}, x_{-i}) : x_i + x_{-i} = e_i + e_{-i}\}.$$

(The maximum on the right is taken with respect to x_i and x_{-i}.) Let now $\tilde{B}_i(\mathbf{q}, \mathbf{e},)$ denote the best response of player i in this game. Since $r_i(\mathbf{q}, e_i + e_{-i})$ is jointly continuous in all variables and concave in (q_i, e_i), that response has non-empty convex values and closed graph. As argued above, a game with such data admits at least one equilibrium. Applying the envelope theorem at equilibrium we see that all first-order conditions (10.8) are satisfied.

5. A NUMERICAL EXAMPLE OF COURNOT–WALRAS EQUILIBRIUM

Let here $P(Q) := \max(0, A - Q)$, $A > 0$, be the inverse demand function in a market featuring merely *one* product ($|P| = 1$). For simplicity we accommodate only two producers $i \in I = \{0,1\}$, each with $\delta_i^+ = 1, \delta_i^- = 0$, and each discharging the same greenhouse gas ($|G| = 1$). Emissions proportional to production and measured in those terms. The endowments are: $\bar{e}_0 = 0$ and $\bar{e}_1 > A$.[7] Firm 0 incurs cost $c_0(q_0, x_0) = c(q_0 - x_0)$ and $c_1 \equiv 0$.

Welfare, defined as the sum of consumers and producers surpluses, thus takes the form

$$W := [A - P(Q)]Q/2 + \sum_i [P(Q)q_i - c_i(q_i, x_i)].$$

When emission rights are non-transferable, firm i must maximize $\Pi_i(\mathbf{q}, \mathbf{e}, x_i) := P(Q)q_i - c_i(q_i, x_i)$ subject to $x_i = e_i \in [0, e_i]$ and $q_i \geq 0$. If both agents have strictly positive production, Cournot–Walras equilibrium is characterized by

$$q_0^* := \frac{A - 2c}{3}, q_1^* := \frac{A + c}{3}.$$

However, depending on c, the favoured firm 1 could find it profitable to produce $\tilde{q}_1 := A - c$ so as to drive its competitor out of the market. This happens when $\Pi_i(\tilde{q}_1, 0, \mathbf{e}, x_1) > \Pi_i(q_1^*, q_0^*, \mathbf{e}, x_i)$ and its occurrence hinges upon the credibility of firm 1 committing to $\tilde{q}_1$. Absent credibility, firm 0 could enter the market, predicting that his rival 1 would readjust. Credibility might depend on the particular product at hand.

Setting now $A = 10$ we propose to study equilibrium for various values of $c \in [0, +\infty)$. When permits are tradable, the well-endowed firm 1 can save the other firm's costs at some permit price in $p \in [0, c]$. The realized p will not change the aggregate profits considered below.

Transferable quotas. In this case, regardless of the value c, we have a classic duopoly without costs. Both agents produce $q_0^* = q_1^* = A/3 = 10/3$. This corresponds to the non-cooperative case with $c = 0$ (cf. Table 10.1). However, with non-transferable quotas the characteristics of equilibrium do depend on c.

Non-transferable quotas. When $c \in [0, 2)$ both agents operate in equilibrium. Thus, making quotas transferable leads to lower aggregate costs and increased outputs. The saved cost exceeds the lost revenues, stemming from lower product prices. Thus transferability also yields higher aggregate profits. Clearly, in this scenario consumers are better off and welfare increases.

When $c = 2$, first consider the case when 1 is able to make a credible commitment $\tilde{q}_1$. Then there is a discontinuity in firm 0's profit and in welfare. Firm 1 is now indifferent between producing $\tilde{q}_1$ (and thus driving his rival out) or producing q_1^*. The aggregate quantities are, however, very different. If 1 chooses $\tilde{q}_1 = 8$ (so that $P = c$), he earns 16 units. The equilibrium q_0^*, q_1^* is given by (2, 4), where firm 1 also earns 16 units (the other earns 4). Thus, there seems to be two equilibria.

When $c > 2$, only firm 1 operates. When $c \in (2, 10/3)$, aggregate profits (stemming from firm 1 only) are lower in the non-transferable case, and welfare is higher. This is because firm 1 is producing much to keep the

Table 10.1   Numerical results with non-transferable quotas

c	pf	Q	P	ps_0	ps_1	Σps	cs	W
0	0, 1	6.7	3.3	11.1	11.1	22.2	22.2	44.4
1	0, 1	6.3	3.7	7.1	13.4	20.6	20.1	40.6
2	0, 1	6.0	4.0	4.0	16.0	20.0	18.0	38.0
2	1	8.0	2.0	0.0	16.0	16.0	32.0	48.0
3	0, 1	5.7	4.3	1.8	18.8	20.6	16.1	36.6
3	1	7.0	3.0	0.0	21.0	21.0	24.5	45.5
3.33	0, 1	5.6	4.4	1.2	19.8	21.0	15.4	36.4
3.33	1	6.7	3.3	0.0	22.2	22.2	22.2	44.4
4	0, 1	5.3	4.7	0.4	21.8	22.2	14.2	36.4
4	1	6.0	4.0	0.0	24.0	24.0	18.0	42.0
5	0, 1	5.0	5.0	0.0	25.0	25.0	12.5	37.5
5	1	5.0	5.0	0.0	25.0	25.0	12.5	37.5

Note:
pf: producing firms, *ps*: producers' suplus; *cs*: consumers' surplus.

potential entrant out. When $c = 10/3$, the active firm produces the same aggregate quantity as in the transferable case, and aggregate profits and welfare are identical. When $c \in (10/3, 5]$, quite naturally, profits are higher without transferability at the expense of welfare.

If it is not credible for 1 to commit to $\tilde{q}_1$, both agents will operate in equilibrium for $c < 5$. Welfare is always higher when quotas are transferable, and aggregate profits lower whenever $c < 4$. For $c \in (4, 5)$ the reduction in costs (stemming from firm 0) when cooperating are smaller than losses due to reduced product prices, thus aggregate profits are higher without transferability.

For all $c > 5$, firm 1 always produces the classic monopoly quantity $q_1 = A/2$, yielding a price that is always lower than c, and firm 0 never operates. The numerical results are summarized in Table 10.1.

This numerical exercise, while lacking a fair amount of realism, was designed to emphasize some of the important features. Notably, the large firm becomes able to control its rival's costs via the permit market. However, when limit pricing is credible, and costs are small ($c < 2$), making quotas transferable enhances welfare and profits. When $c \in (2, 10/3)$ emissions trading would yield higher aggregate profits but lower welfare. Finally, for $c > 10/3$, emissions trading was good for welfare, but detrimental to aggregate profits. When limit pricing is not credible, making quotas transferable is always good for society, and sometimes also for profits ($c < 4$).

6. CONCLUDING REMARKS

Imperfections in markets for rights, such as emissions permits, were first studied by Hahn (1984). Along with others, he showed that efficiency depends on the initial quota distribution. Other studies include Misiolek and Elder (1989), von der Fehr (1993), Malueg (1990) and Sartzetakis (1997).

Our chapter differs from the existing literature in several ways. First, we place no restriction on the number or nature of agents acting strategically in either market. Second, we do not insist that firms behave similarly in both markets. Third, we explicitly construct the demand function in the permit market. This construction is typically left out of similar studies. Fourth, we relaxed the regularity assumptions on the functions at hand. Doing so may be important in realistic, mixed settings.[8] Uncertainty, particularly in demand and cost, can be made part of a similar, extended analysis.

Important issues, not considered here, include strategic (mis-)representation of the cost function (Hahn, 1984). Also a shortcoming of our setting is that it allows only 'one period' thereby ignoring possibilities for banking and borrowing of permits across periods (Rubin, 1996). No transaction costs affected the permit market (Stavins, 1995), and no rules constrained emissions trading (Bernstein et al., 1999; Ellerman and Wing, 2000).

Our numerical results – and experiments – are partial and based on simple model instances. We do not know the welfare implications in broad, more realistic scenarios, comprising more than two players. Thus, for the moment, it seems as though 'the devil is likely to be in the details' (Stavins, 1995).

NOTES

Good remarks from two referees helped to improve the first version of this chapter.

S.D. Flåm (corresponding author) thanks Røwdes stiftelse, Ruhrgas, and Norges Bank for generous support. O. Godal is grateful to the NFR, Stiftelsen Thomas Fearnley, Heddy og Nils Astrup and Professor Wilhelm Keilhau's Minnefond. Both authors are at the Department of Economics, Fossw. 6, University of Bergen 5007 Bergen, Norway; e-mail: {sjur.flaam,odd.godal}@econ.uib.no.

1. Examples include the trade of sulphur emissions in the USA. Such trade also inspired the design of the Kyoto Protocol.
2. See Evstigneev and Flåm (2001), Flåm and Jourani (2003) and references therein.
3. A word about notation is fitting here. When F is a finite non-empty set, let $\in \mathbb{R}^F$ denote the space of all real vectors $v = (v_f)_{f \in F}$. As customary, we write $v \in \mathbb{R}^F_+$ to express that $v_f \geq 0$ for all $f \in F$. And as usual, $v \leq v$ means $v - v \in \mathbb{R}^F_+$.
4. Thinking of a Cournot setting one may posit

$$\Pi_i(\mathbf{q}, \mathbf{e}, x_i) = P(Q) \cdot q_i - c_i(q_i, x_i)$$

where: ' · ' denotes the customary inner product, $P(Q)$ stands for *inverse demand*, and $c_i(q_i, x_i)$ records *cost of production and emission abatement*. We shall not rely on this specification, but use it in Section 5.

5. Somewhat heroically, we presume that no individual i is able to misrepresent his function Π_i to own advantage. Alternatively, we could posit that all functions Π_i are common knowledge.

6. p is declared a *super-gradient* of a function $\Phi: \mathbb{R}^G \rightarrow \mathbb{R} \cup \{-\infty\}$ at a point e, and we write $p \in \partial\Phi(e)$, iff $\Phi(e)$ is finite and

$$\Phi(e') \leq \Phi(e) + p \text{ A } (e' - e) \text{ for all } e' \in \mathbb{R}^G.$$

Absent concavity (or convexity) one may use any other suitable derivative; see texts on non-smooth analysis, for example Clarke et al. (1998). The advantage of this apparatus is fourfold: first, one may accommodate non-smooth data and non-differentiable reduced mappings; second, functions can embody constraints by assuming infinite values; third, the analysis become more compact; fourth and finally, many expressions become cleaner. If not conversant with generalized derivatives, one may pretend, when convenient, that each function be differentiable in the classical sense.

7. Thus, with an efficient permit market, there is no effect of emissions regulations. At a first glance, this may look unrealistic. However, it resembles the Kyoto Protocol after the USA refused to sign. Several studies indicate a modest or negligible effect from that agreement because Russia was allotted carbon permits that exceed her unconstrained, predicted emissions during the commitment period.

8. Examples include the market for greenhouse gas permits, coexisting with the European natural gas market (Hagem and Mæstad, 2002). Production and transportation of natural gas requires significant amounts of greenhouse gas permits. In the permit market, Russia can sell permits at constant (zero) costs. Russia naturally has market power on the supply side in the permit market. In the product market (natural gas) she shares market power with Norway and Algeria. The latter two countries are not, however, likely to influence permit prices.

REFERENCES

Bernstein, P., W.D. Montgomery, T.F. Rutherford and G. Yang (1999), 'Effects of restrictions on international permit trading: the MS-MRT model', *The Costs of the Kyoto Protocol: A Multi-model Evaluation, Special Issue of The Energy Journal*, 221–56.

Clarke, F.H., Yu. S. Ledyaev, R.J. Stern and P.R. Wolenski (1998), *Nonsmooth Analysis and Control Theory*, Berlin: Springer-Verlag.

Ellerman, A.D. and I.S. Wing (2000), 'Supplementarity: an invitation to mono-psony?' *Energy Journal*, **21(4)**, 29–59.

Evstigneev, I.V. and S.D. Flåm (2001), 'Sharing nonconvex cost,' *Journal of Global Optimization*, **20**, 257–71.

Fehr, N.-H.M. von der (1993), 'Tradable emission rights and strategic interactions', *Environmental and Resource Economics*, **3**, 129–51.

Flåm, S.D. and A. Jourani (2002), 'Strategic behavior and partial cost sharing', *Games and Economic Behavior*, **43**, 44–56.

Hagem, C. and O. Mæstad (2002), 'Market power in the market for greenhouse gas emission permits – the interplay with the fossil fuel markets', Working Paper 2002:8, Cicero, Oslo, Norway.

Hahn, R.W. (1984), 'Market power and transferable property rights', *Quarterly Journal of Economics*, **99(4)**, 753–64.

Malueg, D.A. (1990), 'Welfare consequences of emission credit trading programs', *Journal of Environmental Economics and Management*, **18**, 66–77.

Misiolek, W.S. and H.W. Elder (1989), 'Exclusionary manipulation of markets for pollution rights', *Journal of Environmental Economics and Management*, **16**, 156–66.

Montgomery, D.W. (1972), 'Markets in licenses and efficient pollution control programs', *Journal of Economic Theory*, **5**, 395–418.

Rockafellar, R.T. (1970), *Convex Analysis*, Princeton: Princeton University Press.

Rubin, J.D. (1996), 'A model of intertemporal emission trading, banking and borrowing', *Journal of Environmental Economics and Management*, **31**, 269–86.

Sartzetakis, E.S. (1997), 'Tradeable emission permits regulation in the presence of imperfectly competitive product markets: welfare implications', *Environmental and Resource Economics*, **9**, 65–81.

Shapley, L.S., and M. Shubik (1969), 'On market games', *Journal of Economic Theory*, **1**, 9–25.

Stavins, R.N. (1995), 'Transaction costs and tradeable permits', *Journal of Environmental Economics and Management*, **29**, 133–48.

11. A conjectural cooperative equilibrium for strategic form games

Sergio Currarini and Marco Marini[*]

1. INTRODUCTION

Intuitively a *cooperative equilibrium* is a collective decision adopted by a group of individuals that can be viewed as *stable* (that is, an equilibrium) against all feasible deviations by single individuals or by proper subgroups. While modelling the possibilities of cooperation may not pose the social scientist particular problems, at least once an appropriate economic or social situation is clearly outlined, the definition of stability may be a more demanding task for the modeller. This is because the outcome, and the profitability, of players' deviations depend heavily on the conjectures they make over the reaction of other players. As an example, a neighbourhood rule to keep a common garden clean possesses different stability properties depending on whether the conjectured reaction in the event of shirking is, in turn, that the garden would be kept clean anyway or, say, that the common garden would be abandoned as a result. Similarly, countries participating in an international environmental agreement will possess different incentives to comply with the prescribed pollution abatements depending upon whether defecting countries expect the other partners to be inactive or to retaliate.

The main focus of the present chapter are cooperative equilibria of games in strategic form. A cooperative equilibrium of a game in strategic form can be defined as a *strategy profile* such that no subgroup of players can 'make effective' – by means of alternative strategy profiles – higher utility levels for its members than those obtained at the equilibrium. As expressed in the example above, the content of the equilibrium concept depends very much on the utility levels that each coalition can potentially make effective and this, in turn, depends on conjectures as to the reactions induced by deviations. In this chapter we propose a cooperative equilibrium for games in strategic form, based on the assumption that players deviating from an arbitrary strategy profile have *non-zero conjectures* about the reaction of the remaining players. More precisely, the *conjectural cooperative equilibrium* we propose assumes that the remaining players are expected to react optimally and independently according to their best response map.

1.1   Related Literature

The problem of defining cooperative equilibrium concepts has been centred on the formulation of *conjectures* ever since the pioneering work of von Neumann and Morgenstern (1944). The concepts of α and β-core, formally studied by Aumann (1967), are based on their early proposal to represent the worth of a coalition as the aggregate payoff that it can guarantee its members in the game being played. Formally obtained as the minmax and maxmin payoff imputations for the coalition in the game played against its complement, the α and β characteristic functions express the behaviour of extremely risk-averse coalitions, acting *as if* they expected their rivals to minimize their payoff. Although fulfilling a rationality requirement in zero-sum games, α and β assumptions do not seem justifiable in most economic settings. Moreover, the low profitability of coalitional objections usually yields very large set of solutions (for example, a large core). Another important cooperative equilibrium proposed by Aumann (1959), denoted *Strong Nash Equilibrium*, extends the Nash Equilibrium assumption of 'zero conjectures' to every coalitional deviation. Accordingly, a Strong Nash Equilibrium is defined as a strategy profile to which no group of players can profitably object, given that remaining players are expected not to change their strategies. Strong Nash Equilibria are at the same time Pareto optima and Nash Equilibria; in addition they satisfy the Nash stability requirement for each possible coalition. As a consequence, the set of Strong Nash Equilibria is often empty, preventing the use of this otherwise appealing concept in most economic problems of strategic interaction.

Other approaches have looked at the choice of forming coalitions as a strategy in well-defined games of coalition formation (see Bloch, 1997 for a survey). Among others, the gamma and delta games in Hart and Kurz (1983) constitute a seminal contribution.[1] The gamma game, in particular, is related to this chapter's analysis, since it predicts that if the grand coalition N is objected to by a subcoalition S, the complementary set of players splits and act as a non-cooperative fringe. On the same behavioural assumption is based the concept of the γ core, introduced by Chander and Tulkens (1997) in their analysis of environmental agreements, where a characteristic function is obtained as the Nash Equilibrium between the forming coalition and all individual players in its complement. As in the present approach, based on deviations in the underlying strategic form game, the γ

core assumes that the forming coalition expects outside players to move along their (individual) reaction functions. In contrast to our approach, however, there the forming coalition forms before choosing its Nash Equilibrium strategy in the game against its rivals, while here deviating coalitions directly switch to new strategies in the underlying game, expecting their rivals to react in the same manner as followers in a Stackelberg game. In applying our concept to the analysis of the stability of environmental coalitions, we may interpret these differences as the description of different structures in the process of deviation. While the γ core seems to describe settings in which the formation of a deviating coalition is publicly observed before the choice of strategies, our approach best fits situations in which deviating coalitions can implement their new strategies before their formation is monitored, enjoying a positional advantage.

The *conjectural cooperative equilibrium* (CCE) we propose in this chapter, by assuming that remaining players are expected to react optimally according to their best response map, introduces a very natural rationality requirement into the equilibrium concept. Moreover, the coalitional incentives to object are considerably weakened with respect to the Strong Nash Equilibrium, thus ensuring the existence of a cooperative conjectural equilibrium in all symmetric games in which players' actions are strategic complements in the sense of Bulow et al. (1985), that is, in all supermodular games (see Topkis, 1998).

1.2 An Example of a Conjectural Cooperative Equilibrium

Before formally defining the conjectural cooperative equilibrium, it is easy to introduce the mechanics at work for the existence of such an equilibrium by means of the three by three bi-matrix game shown in Table 11.1. Suppose

Table 11.1 Three by three matrix game

	A	B	C
A	x, x	d, h	a, c
B	h, d	b, b	e, f
C	c, a	f, e	y, y

that (b, b) is an efficient outcome, that is, such as to maximize the sum of the players' payoff. To be a cooperative equilibrium, the outcome (b, b) has to be immune from either player switching her own strategy, given their expectation that the rival would react optimally to the switch. When players' actions are strategic substitutes (and the game submodular), each player's reaction map is downward sloping, implying that any move from (b, b) by one player would generate a predicted outcome on the asymmetric diagonal of the matrix. If, in the example, we let $a>b>c>h$, and $b>(a+c)/2$, then the efficient outcome (b, b) will not certainly be a conjectural cooperative equilibrium, for player 1 can profitably deviate from it (from B to A), conjecturing that her rival's best reply will go in the opposite direction (from B to C), and getting a payoff of $a>b$. The same will happen if $c>b>a>e$, in which case player 2 deviates by switching from B to C. In contrast, suppose that the game above is supermodular, with the associated increasing reaction maps. In this case, the conjectured outcomes in case of deviations from outcome (b, b) are only (x, x) and (y, y). As a result, if either player finds it profitable to switch either to A or to C (with $x>b$ and $y>b$, respectively) then the assumption that (b, b) is an efficient outcome is contradicted. We can conclude that (b, b) is a conjectural cooperative equilibrium of the symmetric game described above whenever supermodularity holds. Note that in our example, if $d>b$, the efficient outcome (b, b) is a conjectural cooperative equilibrium although it is neither a Strong Nash Equilibrium nor a Nash Equilibrium.[2] The above example, although providing a clear insight into how both supermodularity and symmetry work in favour of the existence of an equilibrium, contains two substantial simplifications: the presence of only two players, ruling out existence problems related to the formation of coalitions, and the restriction to three strategies, thus tending to make increasing best replies generate symmetric outcomes, from which, the fact that (B, B) is an equilibrium, directly follows. However, in the chapter we are able to show that the existence result holds for any number of players and strategies, provided a symmetry assumption on the effect of players' own strategies on the payoff of rivals is fulfilled.

The chapter is organized as follows. The next section introduces the conjectural cooperative equilibrium in the standard set-up of strategic form games. Section 3 presents the main result of the chapter: for a well-defined class of game – symmetric supermodular games – a conjectural cooperative equilibrium always exists. Section 4 discusses in detail the meaning of this result and presents a descriptive example of an environmental economy whose cooperative conjectural equilibrium exists depending on individuals' preferences. Section 5 concludes.

2.   SET-UP

We consider a **game in strategic form** $G=(N,(X_i, u_i)_{i\in N})$, in which $N=\{1,...,$ $i,..., n\}$ is the set of players, X_i is the set of strategies for player i, with generic element x_i, and $u_i: X_i \times ... \times X_n \to R_+$ is the payoff function of player i. We denote by $S\subset N$ any coalition of players, and by $\bar{S}$ its complement with respect to N. For each coalition S we denote by $x_s \in X_s \equiv \Pi_{i \in S} X_i$ a profile of strategies for the players in S, and use the notation $X = X_N$ and $x = x_N$. A **Pareto Optimum (PO)** for G is a strategy profile such that there exists no alternative profile which is preferred by all players and strictly preferred by at least one player. The Pareto Optimum x^e is **efficient** if it maximizes the sum of the payoffs of all players in N. In the example discussed in the introduction to this chapter, letting outcomes be ordered as follows: $a > b > c > d > e > h > x > y$, assuming that $b > (a + c)/2$, the profiles (a, c), (c, a) and (b, b) are all Pareto Optima, while the efficient profile is (b, b).

A **Nash Equilibrium (NE)** for G is defined as a strategy profile $\bar{x} \in X_N$ such that no player has an incentive to change his own strategy, that is, such that there exists no $i \in N$ and $x_i \in X_i$ such that:

$$u_i(x_i, \bar{x}_{N/i}) > u_i(\bar{x}).$$

Nash equilibria are stable with respect to individual deviations, given that the effect of such deviations is evaluated by keeping the strategies of the other players fixed at the equilibrium level.

In trying to formulate equilibrium concepts that allow coalitions of players to coordinate the choice of their strategies, a natural extension of the Nash equilibrium is given by the concept of **Strong Nash Equilibrium (SNE)**, a strategy profile that no coalition of players can improve upon given that the effect of deviations is, again, evaluated keeping the strategies of other players fixed at the equilibrium levels. So, $\hat{x} \in X_N$ is a SNE for G if there exists no $S \subset N$ and $x_s \in X_S$ such that

$$u_i(x_s, \hat{x}_s) \geq u_i(\hat{x}) \quad \forall i \in s$$
$$u_h(x_s, \hat{x}_s) > u_h(\hat{x}); \text{ for some } h \in S$$

Obviously, all SNE of G are both Nash Equilibria and Pareto Optima. As a result, SNE fails to exist in many economic problems, and in particular, whenever Nash Equilibria fail to be optimal. Although the lack of existence of SNE can be interpreted as a poor specification of the game-theoretic model, it precludes the use of this otherwise appealing concept of a cooperative equilibrium in many important applications.

In this chapter we propose a concept of cooperative equilibrium for G based on the introduction of non-zero conjectures in the evaluation of the profitability of coalitional deviations. The concept we propose captures the idea that players outside a deviating coalition are expected to react by making optimal choices (contingent on the strategy profile played in the deviation) as independent and non-cooperative players. In order to describe the conjectured optimizing reactions of players outside a deviating coalition S, let us define first the restricted game $G(x_s)$ obtained from G by considering the restricted set of players $\bar{S}$ and parameterizing payoffs by letting each j in $\bar{S}$ obtain the payoff $u_j(x_{\bar{s}}, x_s)$ out of the profile $x_{\bar{s}}$, for each $x_{\bar{s}} \in X_{\bar{s}}$. We denote by $R_{\bar{s}} : X_s \rightarrow X_{\bar{s}}$ the map associating the set $R_{\bar{s}}(x_s)$ of Nash Equilibria of the restricted game $G(x_s)$ to each joint strategy x_s of coalition S. The set $R_{\bar{s}}(x_s)$ describes the conjecture of coalition S about the possible reactions of players in $\bar{S}$ to the choice of the joint strategy x_s.

Definition 1: *A **Conjectural Cooperative Equilibrium** (**CCE**) is a strategy profile $\tilde{x}$ such that there exists no coalition S with strategy profiles $x_s \in X_s$ and $x_{\bar{s}} \in R_{\bar{s}}(x_s)$ such that:*

$$u_i(x_s, x_{\bar{s}}) \geq u_i(\tilde{x}) \qquad \forall i \in S;$$

$$u_h(x_s, x_{\bar{s}}) > u_h(\tilde{x}) \text{ for some } h \in S.$$

So defined, a CCE satisfies very restrictive stability requirements. According to this definition, any coalition S can look for improvements upon any proposed strategy profile by selecting among its feasible joint profiles $x_s \in X_s$ and, for each possible x_s it may choose, by selecting among all the Nash responses of players in $\bar{S}$ (formally, the set $R_{\bar{s}}$) the most profitable strategy $x_{\bar{s}}$. Definition is indeed well defined both when the set $R_{\bar{s}}(x_s)$ may be empty for some (possibly all) $x_s \in X_s$, and when the set $R_{\bar{s}}(x_s)$ is multivalued for some (possibly all) $x_s \in X_s$. In this sense, it applies to all games in strategic form. This generality comes at the price of the arguably unreasonable assumption that a deviating coalition faces no constraint in selecting among the possibly non-unique reactions of outside players. A more realistic approach would assume that a deviating coalition could form expectations about which equilibrium reaction would be played by outside players, and that these expectations should be based on some sort of rationality requirement about the behaviour of such outside players. We remark, however, that the present approach generates a smaller set of equilibria than would result from any arbitrary selection from the set of Nash responses of outside players. Our result that there exists a CCE in all supermodular games, contained in Theorem 1 in Section 3.3, therefore extends to any equilibrium concept associated with the choice of such a selection. In addition, lemmas 7 to 10 show that the present definition generates the same set of equilibria that would result from the selection of the Pareto-dominant element of the set $R_{\bar{s}}(x_s)$. Since the existence of such elements is not generally ensured, but always holds in the class of symmetric supermodular games for which our result is obtained (see Section 3.1 for definitions), we have chosen to present definition 1 in its present and more general form.

3. EXISTENCE OF A CONJECTURAL COOPERATIVE EQUILIBRIUM IN SUPERMODULAR GAMES

This section contains our main result, showing that if a strategic form game G is supermodular, and satisfies some symmetry requirements, then it admits a conjectural cooperative equilibrium.

3.1 Supermodularity

We start by defining the concept of a supermodular function and by recording some results in the theory of supermodularity that will be used in the analysis of the next section. For a partially ordered set $A \subset R^n$ and any pair of elements x, y of A we define the join element $(x \wedge y)$ and the meet element $(x \vee y)$ as follows:

$$(x \wedge y) = (\min \{x_1, y_1\}, ..., \min \{x_n, y_n\});$$
$$(x \vee y) = (\max \{x_1, y_1\}, ..., \max \{x_n, y_n\}).$$

Definition 2:   *The set A is a sublattice of R^n if $(x \vee y) \in A$ and $(x \wedge y) \in A$ for all x, $y \in A$.*

Definition 3:   *The function $f{:}A \rightarrow R$ is supermodular if for all x, $y \in A$:*

$$f(x \vee y) + f(x \wedge y) \geq f(x) + f(y).$$

Definition 4:   *Let X, Y be partially ordered sets. The function $f{:}~X \times Y \rightarrow R$ has increasing differences in (x, y) on $X \times Y$ if the term $f(x, y'') - f(x, y')$ is increasing in x for all $y'' > y'$.*

Increasing differences describe a complementarity property of the function f, whose marginal increase with respect to y is increasing in x. If A is the Cartesian product of partially ordered sets, then the fact that f is supermodular on A implies that f has increasing difference in all pairs of sets among those whose product originates A (see Topkis, 1998 for a formal statement and proof of this fact).

Definition 5:   *The game in strategic form $G = (N, (X_i, u_i)_{i \in N})$ is supermodular if the set X of feasible joint strategies for N is a sublattice of R^n, if the payoff functions $u_i (x_i, x_{-i})$ are supermodular in x_i and have increasing differences in (x_i, x_{-i}) on $X_i \times X_{-i}$.*

We will extensively exploit two properties of supermodular games, related to the existence of a Nash Equilibrium and to the behaviour of the set of Nash Equilibria in response to changes in a fixed parameter on which these equilibria depend. We recall these properties below, and refer to Topkis (1998) for proofs.

Lemma 1: *Let $G = (N, (X_i, u_i)_{i \in N})$ be a supermodular game, with X non-empty and compact and u_i upper hemicontinuous in x_i for all i. Then the set of Nash Equilibria of G is non-empty and admits a greatest and least element.*

Lemma 2: *Let $G_t = (N, (X_i, u_i^t)_{i \in N})_{i \in T}$ be a set of supermodular games, parameterized by t, with T being a partially ordered set. Let the assumptions of Lemma 1 hold. Then the greatest and least elements of the set of Nash Equilibria of G are non decreasing in t on T.*

3.2 Assumptions and Preliminary Results

We impose the following lattice structure and continuity assumptions on our game in strategic form.

Assumption 1: *X_i is a compact sublattice of R, for all $i \in N$.*

Assumption 2: *u_i is continuous and supermodular in x_i on X_i for each $x_{-i} \in X_{-i}$, and exhibits increasing differences on $X_i \times X_{-i}$.*

Our requirement of continuity of u_i is unnecessarily strong for the establishment of existence and monotonicity of Nash Equilibria in the next lemmas. However, we will need such an assumption to ensure the existence of a strategy profile with certain properties in X as a step towards the proof of Theorem 1 (see Lemma 9). In addition to Assumptions 1 and 2, we impose two symmetry requirements on G.

Assumption 3 *(Symmetric Players):* *For all $x \in X$ and all pairwise permutations $p: N \to N$:*

$$u_{p(i)}(x_{p(1)}, ..., x_{p(n)}) = u_i(x_1, ..., x_n).$$

Assumption 4 *(Symmetric Externalities):* *One of the following two cases must hold:*

1. *Positive externalities: $u_i(x)$ increasing in $x_{N \setminus i}$ for all i and all $x \in X_N$;*

2. *Negative externalities: $u_i(x)$ decreasing in $x_{N \setminus i}$ for all i and all $x \in X_N$.*

Assumption 3 requires that players' payoffs are neutral to switches in the strategies adopted by other players, and that pairwise switches in strategies are mirrored by pairwise switches in payoffs. In other words, only strategies matter, and not who plays them. Assumption 4 requires that the effect of a change in other players' strategies on one's own payoff is monotonic, and its sign is the same for all players. Many well-known games (including Cournot, Bertrand and public good games) satisfy this symmetry assumption. The next results follow directly from an application to our game G of the properties of supermodular games listed in Lemmas 1 and 2.

Lemma 3:   *Let Assumptions 1 and 2 hold. For all $x_s \in X_s$, the set of Nash Equilibria $R_{\bar{s}}(x_s)$ is non-empty and has a greatest and a least element.*

Proof.   Application of Lemma 1. ■

Let $r_{\bar{s}}^g$ the $r_{\bar{s}}^l$ be selections of the map $R_{\bar{s}}$ obtained by considering its greatest and least element, respectively.

Lemma 4:   *Let Assumptions 1 and 2 hold. The maps $r_{\bar{s}}^g$ and $r_{\bar{s}}^l$ are non-decreasing in x_S.*

Proof.   Application of Lemma 2. ■

We finally make use of the symmetry assumptions 3 and 4 to show that the set $R_{\bar{s}}(x_s)$ is Pareto ranked.

Lemma 5:   *Let Assumptions 1 to 4 hold. If the payoff functions exhibit positive (negative) externalities, then for all x_S the element $r_{\bar{s}}^g(x_S)$ $\left(r_{\bar{s}}^l(x_s)\right)$ Pareto dominates all other elements in $R_{\bar{s}}$ on the set of players $\bar{S}$.*

Proof: Let $j \in \bar{S}$, $x_s \in R_s(x_S)$ and $x_{\bar{s}}' = r_{\bar{s}}^g(x_s)$ for some $x_s \in X_s$. Let externalities be positive. The following inequality follows:

$$u_i(x_S, x_{\bar{S}\backslash j}, x_j') \geq u_i(x_S, x_{\bar{S}\backslash j}', x_j) \geq u_j(x_S, x_{\bar{S}})$$

The first inequality is due to the Nash equilibrium property of $x_{\bar{s}}'$ for the restricted game $G(x_s)$. The second inequality is due to positive externalities. Since the argument applies to all j in $\bar{S}$ and for all $x_{\bar{s}} \in R_{\bar{s}}(x_s)$ the result follows. The proof for the case of negative externalities is similar and is omitted. ■

3.3   Results

This section contains our main result: all games satisfying Assumptions 1 to 4 admit a Conjectural Cooperative Equilibrium. The proof of Theorem 1 is constructive: we show that every efficient symmetric strategy profile in X_N satisfies the conditions for being a CCE. Before proving this fact in Theorem 1, we establish a few preliminary results. We first show that an efficiency symmetric strategy profile always exists under Assumptions 1 to 4.

Lemma 6:   *Let G satisfy Assumption 1 to 4. Then there exists an efficient strategy profile* $x^e \in X_N$ *such that* $x_i^e = x_j^e$ *for all* $i, j \in N$.

Proof.   Compactness of each X_i implies compactness of X. Continuity of each u_i implies continuity of the social payoff function $u_N = \Sigma_{i \in N} u_i$. Existence of an efficient profile follows directly from the Weierstrass theorem. To show that there exists a symmetric efficient profile, we need to exploit the supermodularity properties of payoff functions. Consider any arbitrary asymmetric profile x, with $x_i \neq x_j$ for some players i and j. By the symmetry assumption on payoff functions, we write

$$u_N(x) = u_N(x_i, x_j, x_{N\{i, j\}}) = u_N(x_j, x_i, x_{N\{i, j\}}) \tag{11.1}$$

where we have used the convention of writing the strategies of players i and j as first and second elements of x, respectively. Since the sum of supermodular functions is itself supermodular, Assumptions 1 and 2 imply:

$$2 \cdot u_N(x) \leq u_N(x_i, x_i, x_{N\{i \cup j\}}) + u_N(x_j, x_j, x_{N\{i \cup j\}}) \tag{11.2}$$

It follows that either

$$u_N(x) \leq u_N(x_i, x_i, x_{N\{i \cup j\}}) \tag{11.3}$$

or

$$u_N(x) \leq u_N(x_j, x_j, x_{N\{i \cup j\}}) \tag{11.4}$$

or both.

Suppose that (11.3) holds, and let $x' = (x_i, x_i, x_{N\{i \cup j\}})$. This is without loss of generality for the ongoing argument. If $x_k = x_i$ for all $k \in N\{i \cup j\}$ our proof is complete. If not, then let $x_k \neq x_i$. In this case, again by supermodularity of payoff functions, we write

$$2\, u(x') \leq u_N(x_i, x_i, x_i, x_{N\{i \cup j \cup k\}}) + u_N(x_i, x_k, x_k, x_{N\{i \cup j \cup k\}}) \tag{11.5}$$

Condition (11.5) implies, again, that either

$$u_N(x') \leq u_N(x_i, x_i, x_i, x_{N\{i \cup j \cup k\}}) \tag{11.6}$$

or

$$u_N(x') \leq u_N(x_i, x_k, x_k, x_{N\{i \cup j \cup k\}}) \tag{11.7}$$

or both. Suppose first that only (11.7) holds. Using the definition of x' we obtain

$$u_N(x_i, x_i, x_k, x_{N\{i \cup j \cup k\}}) \leq u_N(x_i, x_k, x_k, x_{N\{i \cup j \cup k\}}) \tag{11.8}$$

For this case, using again supermodularity, we write

$$2 \cdot u_N(x_i, x_k, x_i, x_k, x_{N\{i \cup j \cup k\}}) \leq u_N(x_i, x_k, x_i, x_k, x_{N\{i \cup j \cup k\}}) + $$
$$u_N(x_i, x_k, x_k, x_{N\{i \cup j \cup k\}}) \tag{11.9}$$

Using (11.8) and (11.9) we obtain that

$$u_N(x_i, x_k, x_k, x_{N\{i \cup j \cup k\}}) \leq (x_k, x_k, x_k, x_{N\{i \cup j \cup k\}}). \tag{11.10}$$

Conditions (11.8) and (11.10) directly imply

$$u_N(x') \leq u_N(x_k, x_k, x_k, x_{N\{i \cup j \cup k\}}). \tag{11.11}$$

We have therefore shown that either (11.6) or (11.9) must hold. By iteration of the same operation for each additional player in $N\{i \cup j \cup k\}$, we obtain the conclusion that there exists some symmetric profile x^s for which $u_N(x^s) \geq u_N(x)$. Since the starting profile x was arbitrary, and by the existence of an efficient profile proved in the first part of this proof, we conclude that a symmetric efficient profile x^s always exists under Assumptions 1 to 4. ∎

We now consider the possible joint strategies that an arbitrary coalition S can use in order to improve upon an efficient profile x^e. In particular, we focus on the 'best' strategies S can adopt, meaning by this the profiles $x^*(S) \in X_N$ satisfying the two following properties: (i) $x_{\bar{s}}^* \in R_{\bar{s}}(x_s^*)$; (ii) there exists no $x_s' \in X_s$ and $x_{\bar{s}}' \in R_{\bar{s}}(x_s')$ such that $u_i(x_s', x_{\bar{s}}') \geq u_i(x^*) \forall i \in s$ and $u_h(x_s', r_{\bar{s}}(x_s')) > u_h(x^*)$ for at least one $h \in S$. In words, $x^*(S)$ is a Pareto optimal profile for coalition S in the set $F(S)$ of all profiles that are consistent with the reaction map $R_{\bar{s}}$:

$$F(S) = \{x \in X_N : x_{\bar{s}} \in R_{\bar{s}}(x_s)\}.$$

Note that $F(S)$ is a compact set by the compactness of X_N and by the closedness of the Nash correspondence $R_{\bar{s}}(x_S)$.

Lemma 7:   *Let G satisfy Assumptions 1 to 4. Then for all $x' \in F(S)$ there exists some profile $x^*(S) \in X_N$ which is a best strategy for S in the sense of conditions (i) and (ii) above and such that $u_i(x^*(S)) \geq u_i(x')$ for all $i \in S$.*

Proof.   Let $x' \in F(S)$. If $x' = x^*(S)$ for some $x^*(S)$ then the lemma is proved for x'. If $x' \neq x^*(S)$ for all $x^*(S)$, then let the set

$$P_i(x') = \{x_N \in F(S): u_i(x) \geq u_i(x')\}$$

define the set of strategy profiles that are weakly preferred by player i to x'. The set $P_i(x')$ is non-empty by the fact that $x' \neq x^*(S)$ for all $x^*(S)$, and it is closed and bounded by continuity of u_i and by compactness of $F(S)$. Since this holds for all $i \in S$, it follows that the set $P_S(x') = \cap_{i \in S} P_i(x')$ is closed and bounded.[3] Moreover, it is non-empty because $x' \neq x^*(S)$. We can therefore conclude that the problem

$$\max_{i \in P_S(x)} \sum_{i \in S} \lambda_i u_i(x)$$

has a solution for all λ in the interior of the $\#S - 1$ dimensional unitary simplex. Call $x(\lambda)$ such a solution. Clearly, $x(\lambda)$ satisfies conditions (i) and (ii) defining the profile $x^*(S)$. Also, clearly $x(\lambda)$ Pareto dominates x' on the set of players S, which concludes the proof. ∎

By Lemma 7, we can restrict our analysis to the 'best' choices $x^*(S)$ of coalition S, since if S cannot profitably deviate by any such profiles, it cannot deviate by means of any profile in $F(S)$. We remark here that in the choice of a 'best' profile $x^*(S)$, coalition S is assumed able to select among all the possible (equilibrium) reactions of $\bar{S}$, as specified by $R_{\bar{S}}$, in order to maximize its joint payoff. This is in line with our definition of a CCE, in which this ability of S was implicitly assumed. The next lemma shows that under Assumptions 3 and 4 the best choice of S always selects strategies for $\bar{S}$ that are greater (least) elements of the set, depending on the sign of the externality being positive or negative, respectively.

Lemma 8:   *Let G satisfy positive (negative) externalities. Let $S \subset N$ and $x' \in F(S)$. Then $u_i(x'_s, r_{\bar{S}}^g(x'_s)) \geq u_i(x')$ (respectively, $u_i(x'_s, r_{\bar{S}}^l(x'_s)) \geq u_i(x')$) for all $i \in S$.*

Proof. We show only the case of positive externalities; the proof for negative externalities is symmetric and left to the reader. Since $r_{\bar{s}}^g(x_s') \geq x_{\bar{s}}$ for all $x_s \in R_{\bar{s}}(x_s')$, and since $x_{\bar{s}} \in R_{\bar{s}}(x_s')$, positive externalities imply that $u_i(x_s,$ $r_{\bar{s}}^g(x_s')) \geq u_i(x_s, x_{\bar{s}}')$ *for all* x_s. The implications of the lemmas 7 and 8 are better illustrated by referring to the sets $F^g(S) \subseteq F(S)$ and $F^l(S) \subseteq F(S)$, defined as follows:

$$F^g(S) = \{x \in F(S): x_{\bar{s}} = r_{\bar{s}}^g(x_s)\}$$
$$F^l(S) = \{x \in F(S): x_{\bar{s}} = r_{\bar{s}}^l(x_s)\}$$

Lemma 8 implies that, under positive externalities, the same strategy profile $x^*(S)$, maximizing (by lemma 7) the aggregate payoff of S over the set $F(S)$ for some vector of weights λ, also maximizes the same aggregate payoff over the set $F^g(S)$. The same conclusion can be drawn, with respect to the set $F^l(S)$, for the case of negative externalities. This result is important for two reasons. First, it endows the somewhat problematic assumption that S can select among Nash reactions of players in $\bar{S}$ which, as we said, is implicit in the definition of a CCE and of the set $F(S)$ above – with the more appealing interpretation that the Pareto dominant Nash equilibrium will be played by members of $\bar{S}$. This interpretation is supported by the result of Lemma 5, by which the greater and least elements of $R_{\bar{s}}(x_s')$ are the best choices for $\bar{S}$ under positive and negative externalities, respectively. Second, the result of Lemma 8 allows us to exploit the properties of the maps $r_{\bar{s}}^g(x_s)$ and $r_{\bar{s}}^l(x_s)$ in supermodular games. This is done in the next lemma, in which these properties are shown to imply that at $x^*(S)$ the strategies played by members of FS and of $\bar{S}$ are ordered according to the sign of the externality: under positive externalities, players in S play 'greater' strategies than those in $\bar{S}$, while the opposite is true under negative externalities.

Lemma 9: *Let* $i \in S$ *and* $j \in \bar{S}$ *and and denote by* $x \in X$ *and* $y \in X$ *the strategies of player* $i \in S$ *and player* $j \in \bar{S}$, *respectively, at* $x^*(S)$. *Then:*

(i) positive externalities imply $x \geq y$;

(ii) negative externalities imply $y \geq x$.

Proof. For simplicity of notation, let x^* denote the profile $x^*(S)$. Let U_i $(x, y) \equiv u_i(x_{S\backslash i}^*, x, x_{\bar{S}\backslash j}^*, y)$, and similarly let $U_j(x, y) = u_j(x_{S\backslash i}^*, x, x_{\bar{S}\backslash j}^*, y)$. We use supermodularity of u_i to write:

$$U_i(y, y) + U_i(x, x) \geq U_i(x, y) + U_i(y, x). \tag{11.12}$$

By the properties of x^*,

$$U_j(x, y) \geq U_i(x, x), \tag{11.13}$$

implying by symmetry that

$$U_i(y, x) \geq U_i(x, x) \tag{11.14}$$

Using (11.12) and (11.14) we obtain

$$U_i(y, y) \geq U_i(x, y) = u_i(x^*) \tag{11.15}$$

Now suppose that $y > x$ and assume that the game has positive externalities. By Lemma 4, the equilibrium best response map has a non-decreasing greatest element, so that

$$y > x \Rightarrow r_S^g(x_{S \setminus i}^*, y) \geq r_S^g(x_S^*) = x_S^*. \tag{11.16}$$

By positive externalities

$$u_i(x_{S \setminus i}^*, y, r_S^g(x_{S \setminus i}^*, y)) > u_i(x_{S \setminus i}^*, y, r_S^g(x_S^*)) = U_i(y, y) \tag{11.17}$$

Equations (11.15) and (11.17) imply

$$u_i(x_{S \setminus i}^*, y, r_S^g(x_{S \setminus i}^*, y)) > u_i(x^*) \tag{11.18}$$

Finally, since $y > x$, positive externalities also imply that for every player $k \in S \setminus i$

$$u_k(x_{S \setminus i}^*, y, r_S^g(x_{S \setminus i}^*, y)) > u_k(x^*) \tag{11.19}$$

Both (11.18) and (11.19) contradict the assumption that x^* is a Pareto Optimum. Suppose now that $y < x$ and assume that the game has negative externalities. Supermodularity of u_i and u_j imply:

$$y < x \Rightarrow r_S^l(x_{S \setminus i}^*, y) \geq r_S^l(x_S^*) = x_S^* \tag{11.20}$$

By negative externalities,

$$u_i(x_{S \setminus i}^*, y, r_S^l(x_{S \setminus i}^*, y)) > u_i(x_{S \setminus i}^*, y, r_S^l(x_S^*)) = U_i(y, y) \tag{11.21}$$

Again, equation (11.21) implies

$$u_i(x^*_{S\setminus i}, y, r^l_{\bar{S}}(x^*_{S\setminus i}, y)) > u_i(x^*) \tag{11.22}$$

And, by negative externalities,

$$u_k(x^*_{S\setminus i}, y, r^g_{\bar{S}}(x^*_{S\setminus i}, y)) > u_i(x^*) \tag{11.23}$$

for every $k \in S\setminus i$, a contradiction. ■

Since by lemma 7 we can restrict our attention to the profiles $x^*(S)$, we will use the above result as a characterizing of the strategies played in the only relevant profiles that may be used in any deviation from an efficiency profile x^e. The next result makes use of this characterization to prove that at any profile $x^*(S)$, the members of S cannot be better off than the members of $\bar{S}$. This result generalizes to the present setting of coalitional actions a well-known property of the subgame perfect equilibrium in two player symmetric supermodular games, in which the 'leader' is weakly worse off than the 'follower'.

Lemma 10:   *Let $i \in S$ and $j \in \bar{S}$ Then $u_j(x^*(S)) \geq u_i(x^*(S))$.*

Proof.   For simplicity, let x^* again denote the profile $x^*(S)$ The following inequalities hold:

$$u_j(x^*_S, x^*_{\bar{S}}) \geq u_j(x^*_S, x^*_{\bar{S}\setminus j}, x^*_i) \geq u_j(x^*_{S\setminus i}, x^*_j, x^*_{\bar{S}\setminus j}, x^*_i) \tag{11.24}$$

The first part is implied by the conditions defining the profile x^*; the second part follows from Lemma 9 and Assumption 4. By Assumption 3, we also have

$$u_j(x^*_{S\setminus i}, x^*_j, x^*_{\bar{S}\setminus j}, x^*_i) = u_i(x^*_S, x^*_{\bar{S}}) \tag{11.25}$$

Inequalities (11.24) and (11.25) imply

$$u_j(x^*) \geq u_i(x^*)$$

which is the result. ■

We are now ready to show that an efficient strategy profile x^e satisfies the requirements of a Conjectural Cooperative Equilibrium.

Theorem 1: *Let the game G satisfy Assumptions 1 to 4. Then, G admits a Conjectural Cooperative Equilibrium.*

Proof. Let x^e be a symmetric efficient strategy profile for G, that is, a symmetric strategy profile that maximizes the aggregate payoff of N. Let $u(x^e)$ denote the payoff of each agent at x^e. Suppose, by contradiction, that there exists a coalition $S \subset N$ such that for all $i \in S$:

$$u_i(x^*(S)) \geq u(x^e) \qquad (11.26)$$

with strict inequality for at least one $h \in S$. Note that by Lemma 10, it must be that

$$\frac{\sum_{i \in S} u_i(x^*(S))}{s} \leq \frac{\sum_{j \in S} u_j(x^*(S))}{n - s} \qquad (11.27)$$

otherwise there would exist $i \in S$ and $j \in \bar{S}$ for which

$$u_i(x^*(S)) \geq u_j(x^*(S))$$

By condition (11.27) we obtain the following implication:

$$\frac{\sum_{i \in S} u_i(x^*(S))}{s} > u(x^e) \Rightarrow \frac{\sum_{j \in S} u_j(x^*(S))}{n - s} > u(x^e) \qquad (11.28)$$

We conclude that if $u_i(x^*(S)) \geq u(x^e)$ for all $i \in S$, with strict inequality for at least one $h \in S$, then using (11.26) and (11.28), we obtain

$$s \frac{\sum_{i \in S} u_i(x^*(S))}{s} > (n - s) \frac{\sum_{j \in S} u_j(x^*(S))}{n - s} > su(x^e) + (n - s)u(x^e) \quad (11.29)$$

or,

$$\sum_{i \in N} u_i(x^*(S)) > n \cdot u(x^e) \qquad (11.30)$$

which contradicts the efficiency of x^e. ∎

4. ON THE EXISTENCE OF EQUILIBRIA IN SUBMODULAR GAMES

4.1 The Role of the Slope of the Reaction Map

Theorem 1 establishes sufficient conditions for the existence of a Conjectural Cooperative Equilibrium of the game G. The crucial condition, strategic complementarity in the sense of Bulow et al. (1985), generates non-decreasing best replies; in particular, the supermodularity of payoff functions implies that the Nash responses of players outside a deviating coalition are a non-decreasing function of the strategies of coalitional members. This feature ensures that each player outside S is better off than each coalitional member of S when deviating. Deviations by proper subcoalitions of players are therefore of little profit, while the grand coalition, not affected by this 'deviator's curse', produces a sufficiently big aggregate payoff for a stable cooperative outcome to exist. In this section we show how the same mechanics responsible for our existence result in the class of supermodular games, provides a useful insight for the analysis of games with strategic substitutes, as, for instance, environmental and public goods games. We will use as an illustration an environmental Cobb–Douglas economy to show that as long as best replies are not 'too' decreasing (thereby providing deviating coalitions with a not 'too' big positional advantage), stable cooperative outcomes exist.

4.2   An Illustration Using a Cobb-Douglas Environmental Economy

We consider an economy with a set of agents $N = \{1,...i,..., n\}$, in which $z \geq 0$ is the environmental quality enjoyed by agents, $x_i \geq 0$ is a private good, $p_i \geq 0$ is a polluting emission originating as a by-product of the production of x_i. We assume that for each i in N preferences are represented by the Cobb–Douglas utility function

$$u_i(z, x_i) = z^\alpha x^\beta$$

Technology is described by the production function

$$x_i = \gamma$$

and emissions accumulate according to the additive law

$$z(p) = A - \sum_{i \in N} P_i \qquad (11.31)$$

where A is a constant expressing the quality of a pollution-free environment. We will assume that γ, α and β are all positive and $\gamma \leq 1$. We associate with this economy the game G_e with players set N, strategy space $[0, p_i^0]$ for each i, with $\Sigma_{i \in N} p_i^0 < A$, and payoffs $U_i(p_1,..., p_n) = z^\alpha p_i^\delta$, where $\delta = \beta\gamma$. Using this (symmetric) set-up, we can express the maximal per-capita payoff of each coalition S in the event of a deviation from an arbitrary strategy profile in G_e as follows:

$$u_i(S) = s^{-\delta} A^{\alpha+\delta} \alpha^{2\alpha} (\alpha+\delta)^{-\alpha-\delta} (\alpha + \delta(n-s))^{-\alpha} \delta^{\delta} \qquad (11.32)$$

This simple set-up of an environmental economy can be used to illustrate how CCEa exist when best replies are not too decreasing or, in other terms, when there are not too many substitute strategies. This in turn requires that players' utilities do not decrease too much with other players' choice, a property mainly depending on the level of log-concavity of the term $z(p)^{\alpha}$. We prove this analytically for the case $\delta = 1$, while we rely on numerical simulation for the general case. Note that $z(p)^{\alpha}$ is log-concave (and the game is not log-supermodular) for $\alpha > 0$, and best replies are decreasing. The environmental game admits a unique Nash equilibrium $\bar{p}$ with $\bar{p}_i = (A/\alpha + n)$ for every $i \in N$, and a unique efficient profile p^e (by efficient we mean 'aggregate welfare maximizing'). Simple algebra yields the following expression:

$$u_i(S) = s^{-1} A \alpha^{\alpha+1} \alpha^{2\alpha} (\alpha+1)^{-\alpha-1} (\alpha+n-s)^{-\alpha}$$

The profitability of individual deviation from the efficient strategy profile p^e is evaluated as follows:

$$u_i(p^e) - u_i(S) = \alpha^{\alpha} (\alpha+n-1)^{-\alpha} n - 1 < 0 \Leftrightarrow \alpha < 1$$

It follows that when the function $z(p)^{\alpha}$ is strictly concave ($\alpha < 1$), then no CCE exists. However, when $\alpha = 1$ the CCE is unique, and equal to p^e. It is also easy to show that for $\alpha > 1$ ($z(.)^{\alpha}$ *convex*) the strategy profile p^e is still a CCE. We conclude that the existence of a CCE only requires a not too strong log-concavity of $z(.)^{\alpha}$. This ensures that the marginal utility of each consumer does not decrease too much with rivals' private consumption and hence, that a deviating coalition, by expanding its pollution (and private consumption) does not exploit too much its advantage against complementary players. When this is the case, although the environmental game is a natural 'strategic substitute' game, the CCE exists. It is interesting to relate the existence of a stable cooperative (and efficient) solution to the relative magnitude of the parameters α, β and γ, expressing the intensity of preferences for the environment and for private consumption, and the characteristics of technology. It turns out that in order for an agreement on emissions to be reached, agents must put enough weight on the environment in their preferences (high enough α), and emissions must not be too 'productive' according to the available technology. In other words, this conclusion rephrases the common intuition that a clean environment is sustainable only if agents care enough for ambient quality. As we have stated, analysis of the existence of a CCE for the general case (that is, removing the assumption $\delta = 1$) is not possible in analytical terms. In what follows we show by means of computations that the set of CCE of the game G_e can be characterized with respect to three possible configurations of the parameters α, β and γ of the economy: the case $\alpha = \beta\gamma$, in which the CCE is unique and assigning to each player the payoff $u_i(p^e)$ (for this case we provide an analytical proof); the case $\alpha > \beta\gamma$, in which the set of CCEa strictly includes the profile p^e; the case $\alpha < \beta\gamma$, in which the set of CCE is empty.

Proposition: *If $\alpha = \beta\gamma$ the unique CCE is the efficient profile p^e.*

Proof.   We first show that no profile $p \neq p^e$ can be a CCE. By (11.32) we obtain

$$u_i(p^e) - u_i(\{i\}) = \frac{\alpha^\alpha A^{\alpha+\delta}(\alpha+\delta)^{-\alpha-\delta}\,\delta^\delta\big[(\alpha+\delta(n-1))^\alpha - \alpha^\alpha n^\delta\big]}{n^\delta(\alpha+\delta(n-1))^\alpha}$$

from which

$$u_i(p^e) - u_i(\{i\}) = 0 \Leftrightarrow [(\alpha+\delta(n-1))^\alpha - \alpha^\alpha n^\delta] = 0$$

Using the fact that $\delta = \beta\gamma$ we get

$$\lfloor(\alpha+\delta(n-1))^\alpha - \alpha^\alpha n^\delta\rfloor = [(\alpha+\alpha(n-1)]^\alpha - (\alpha n)^\alpha = 0$$

from which

$$u_i(p^e) = u_i(\{i\}).$$

To show that p^e is a CCE, it suffices to show that $u_i(S) \leq u_i(p^e)$ for all coalitions S such that $s > 1$. Using (11.32) we obtain

$$u_i(p^e) - u_i(S) \geq 0 \Leftrightarrow [s^\delta(\alpha+\delta(n-s))^\alpha - \alpha^\alpha n^\delta] \geq 0$$

which, using again the fact that $\delta = \beta\gamma$ reduces to

$$u_i(p^e) - u_i(S) \geq 0 \Leftrightarrow [s(\alpha+\alpha(n-s))]^\alpha \geq (\alpha n)^\alpha.$$

The last condition can be rewritten as

$$u_i(p^e) - u_i(S) \geq 0 \Leftrightarrow s + (n-s)s + s^2 \geq n + s^2$$

which is always satisfied since $s > 1$.

Proposition 2:   *If $\alpha > \beta\gamma$ then p^e is a CCE.*

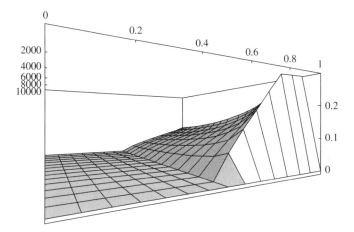

Figure 11.1 $f_i(\alpha, n)$ for the case $\delta=0.5$

Proof.   We proceed by numerical simulations. Our aim is to show that whenever $\alpha>\beta\gamma$ the difference $u_i(p^e) - u_i(S)$ is positive for every s. We first consider the case $s=1$. We plot the graph of

$$f_i(\alpha, n) \equiv \max\{(u_i(p^e) - u_i(\{i\})), 0\}$$

for the fixed value of $\delta=0.5$. The domains are taken to be $(1,10000)$ for n and $(0, 1)$ for α.

From Figure 11.1 it is evident that $u_i(p^e) > u_i(\{i\})$ whenever $\alpha>0.5=\delta$. Similar graphs are obtained for other values of δ in the range $(0, 1)$. We perform the same exercise for coalitions of size $s>1$. We plot the function

$$f_i(\alpha, s) \equiv \max\{(u_i(p^e) - u_i(\{S\})), 0\}$$

for fixed values of n and δ. The domains are taken to be $(\delta, 1)$ for α and $(1, n]$ for s. For the case $n=1000$ and $\delta=0.2$ we obtain the graph shown in Figure 11.2.

In Figure 11.2 the graph of $f_i(\alpha, s)$ lies above the zero plane for all values of $s \in (1, n]$ and of $\alpha \in (\delta, 1)$. Summing up, whenever $\alpha>\delta$ we found that $u_i(p^e) > u_i\{i\}$ for $s \geq 1$; we thus conclude that whenever $\alpha>\delta$ then p^e is a CCE.

Proposition 3:   *If $\alpha>\beta\gamma$ there exists no CCE.*

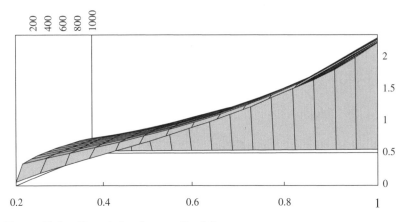

Figure 11.2   f(α, s) for the case δ=0.2

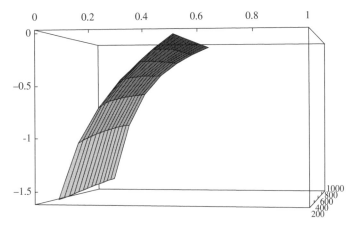

Figure 11.3 $f_i(\hat{α}, n)$ for the case δ = 0.5

Proof.   We again proceed by numerical simulations and evaluate the function

$$\hat{f}_i(α, n) \equiv \min\{(u_i(p^e) - u_i(\{i\})), 0\}$$

for an arbitrary player $i \in N$ and a fixed value of δ. The domains are taken to be (0, 1) for α and [1, 10000] for *n*. Figure 11.3 depicts the graph of $f_i(\hat{α}, n)$ for the case δ = 0.5.

It is evident from Figure 11.3 (and from numerical evaluations around the point α =0.5) that for any value of *n* in the selected range, $u_i(p^e) < u_i(\{i\})$ for

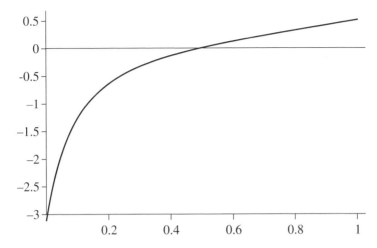

Figure 11.4 $u_i(p^e) - u_i\{i\}$ *for the case* $\delta = 0.5$ *and* $n = 10\,000$

the whole range values $\alpha < \delta$. We thus conclude that for such values there is no CCE.

The above results can be usefully summarized by plotting the value of the difference $\lfloor u_i(p^e) - u_i\{i\} \rfloor$ as a function of the parameter α for fixed values of δ, n and for $s = 1$.

5.   CONCLUDING REMARKS

In this chapter we have proposed a new cooperative equilibrium concept for games in strategic forms, based on the assumption that deviators expect other players to react optimally and independently according to their best response map. We have employed the properties of reaction maps in supermodular games to show that equilibria exist in this class of games under some additional symmetry axioms. We have also discussed the existence of equilibria in submodular games, and in particular in the case of a specific Cobb–Douglas environmental economy. In particular, we have shown how the degree of submodularity of the associated game, and the existence of an equilibrium, are closely related to the intensity of preferences for environmental quality and for private consumption. This example formalizes the intuitive insight that if agents care 'enough' about the environmental quality, then an efficient agreement on pollution emissions and on cost sharing can be achieved.

NOTES

*Correspondence address: Marco Marini, Istituto di Scienze Economiche, Università degli Studi di Urbino, Via Saffi, 42-60129, Urbino, Italy. Tel.+39 -0722 -305557. Fax: +39-0722-305550. E-mail: marinim@econ.uniurb.it.
1. More precisely, Hart and Kurz (1983) present endogenous coalition formation games and look at the Strong Nash Equilibrium of these games. Other related papers (for example, Chander and Tulkens, 1998; Yi, 1997) look at the Nash Equilibrium taking as given the gamma and delta rule of coalition formation.
2. Similarly, in a two by two Prisoner's Dilemma, although no Strong Nash Equilibria exist, the efficient strategy profile, which is not even a Nash Equilibrium, turns out to be a CCE.
3. We remind here that S is a finite set.

REFERENCES

Aumann, R. (1959), 'Acceptable points in general cooperative n-person games', *Annals of Mathematics Studies*, **40**, 287–324.

Aumann, R. (1967), 'A survey of games without side payments', in M. Shubik (ed.), *Essays in Mathematical Economics*, Princeton: Princeton University Press, pp. 3–27.

Bloch, F. (1997), 'Non cooperative models of coalition formation in games with spillovers', in C. Carraro and D. Siniscalco (eds), *New Directions in the Economic Theory of the Environment*, Cambridge: Cambridge University Press.

Bulow, J., J. Geanokoplos and P. Klemperer (1985), 'Multimarket oligopoly: strategic substitutes and complements', *Journal of Political Economy*, **93**, 488–511.

Chander, P. and H. Tulkens (1997), 'The core of an economy with multilateral externalities', *International Journal of Game Theory*, **26**, 379–401.

Hart, S. and M. Kurz (1983), 'Endogenous formation of coalitions', *Econometrica*, **51**, 1047–64.

Neumann, J. von and O. Morgenstern (1944), *Theory of Games and Economic Behaviour*, Princeton: Princeton University Press.

Topkis, D.M. (1998), *Supermodularity and Complementarities*, Princeton: Princeton University Press.

Yi, S.-S. (1997), 'Stable coalition structure with externalities', *Games and Economic Behaviour*, **20**, 201–37.

Index